Cannoneers in Gray

Larry J. Daniel

Cannoneers in Gray

The Field Artillery of the

Army of Tennessee, 1861–1865

The University of Alabama Press

Copyright © 1984 by
The University of Alabama Press
University, Alabama 35486

Manufactured in the United States of America

Library of Congress Cataloging in Publication Data

Daniel, Larry J., 1947–
  Cannoneers in gray.

  Includes bibliographical references and index.
  1. Confederate States of America. Army of Tennessee—
History. 2. United States—History—Civil War, 1861–1865
—Regimental histories. I. Title.
E579.4.D36 1984   973.7'468   83-17899
ISBN 0-8173-0203-4

For my wife Marilyn

Contents

Illustrations

Preface

In recent years, revisionists such as Thomas Connelly, James McDonough, Grady McWhiney, and Richard McMurry have provided valuable new insights concerning the historiography of the Confederate Army of Tennessee, its battles and leaders. The time seemed appropriate, therefore, to undertake a study of what one officer referred to as "the neglected branch of the Army [of Tennessee]": the artillery corps, or western "long arm." Its story is particularly instructive because, in many respects, that branch served as a microcosm of problems that transcended the entire army. Too, like the army as a whole, it lived under the shadow of its more accomplished counterpart in the Army of Northern Virginia.

The artillery branch of the Army of Tennessee labored under many obstacles. Its leadership was knowledgeable but lacked experience and creativity. Most of the army's commanding generals little understood or appreciated its supportive role. The battalion organization was slow in evolving and rarely used tactically. In sharp contrast to Robert E. Lee's artillery, practically no base of militia batteries existed upon which to build. Under the circumstances, the most significant factor in the western long arm's history is not that it ever equaled or surpassed the powerful Federal artillery, for it did not, but that it was able to accomplish as much as it did.

During the past five years, I have lived, in spirit, with the men of the "neglected branch." I long ago removed my rose-colored glasses and now see them as they were: fallible young men who were largely unacquainted with their chosen service. Something about their quality, however, is demonstrated by the fact that, though they were usually dominated by a superior Federal artillery, their reenlistment rate was the highest of any branch of the Army of Tennessee in the spring of 1864. This is their story.

A number of individuals have contributed generously of their time in helping me research and write this book. I am particularly indebted to Dr. Richard McMurry, of North Carolina State University, and L. Van Loan Naisawald, of Manassas, Virginia, both of whom read and offered critical advice on the manuscript. Several individuals called my attention to materials that might otherwise have been missed. These include George Reeves and Dennis Kelly, historians at Shiloh and Kennesaw Mountain national military parks, respectively; Riley Gunter and Rick Coehn, of Memphis; Mike Spradlin, of Gulfport, Mississippi; Grady Howell, of Jackson, Mississippi; Michael Hughes, of Fayetteville, Arkansas; and Jim Mundie, of Kenner, Louisiana. I extend my deep appreciation to all these people and to many others who offered encouragement and assistance.

Larry J. Daniel

Cannoneers in Gray

Chapter 1

"They Had Never Seen an Artilleryman"

During the spring and summer of 1861, Tennessee Governor Isham G. Harris pieced together the Provisional Army of Tennessee. Under the Army Bill of May 6, the state called for 55,000 volunteers, 25,000 to be armed and the remainder to be held in reserve. They were to be organized into twenty-one infantry regiments, one cavalry regiment, and ten artillery companies. This force, perhaps the best state army in the South, was to become the nucleus of the main Confederate army in the western theater: the Army of Tennessee.[1]

A vital, yet unheralded, dimension of this army was the Tennessee Artillery Corps. Formed in May 1861 as a part of the provisional army, it was discontinued a year later after its components had gradually been transferred into the Confederate service. By the fall of 1861, Harris had not only organized an impressive cadre of artillery companies but had also arranged for their ordnance supplies.[2]

It took time for the corps to come to fruition. Technically, thirteen companies of militia artillery in the state could be called upon, but they were merely a "paper" force. The only unit actually organized and drilling was an understrength German outfit in Memphis called the Steuben Artillery, and it had only one old, iron 6-pounder gun. These men were soon sent to man heavy artillery on the Mississippi River. On May 9, General Gideon Pillow, commanding the provisional army, wrote that, though 5,000 men were under arms, "we are without a single battery of field artillery."[3]

A number of artillery companies were mustered in throughout the summer of 1861. On July 2, Harris informed Confederate President Jefferson Davis that ten batteries were in the process of organization, but none were complete. A Nashville newspaper, though heartened at the response, commented that more "stout, able-bodied men" were required.[4]

The most serious weakness of the corps was not recruits but ordnance. Field artillery was practically nonexistent. The Nashville Armory possessed only four field pieces, including one unserviceable iron 6-pounder and a damaged bronze 12-pounder. By mid-June none of the batteries being organized had received a single cannon. Although Harris was able to obtain a number of heavy guns for river defense, he was unable to acquire field pieces. Until this was possible, several light artillery companies were assigned to man heavy artillery, and many personnel were issued old flintlock muskets and drilled as infantry.[5]

Left largely to fend for itself, the state government turned to its citizens for help. Contracts were awarded to various firms, and by the end of the summer dividends had been paid. T. M. Brennan & Company, of Nashville, furnished three six-gun batteries, complete with guns, carriages, and caissons. Ellis & Moore, of Nashville, and Thomas Webster & Company, of Chattanooga, each supplied a six-gun battery. Quinby & Robinson, a Memphis foundry, was under contract for thirty bronze field pieces as well as a large order of shot and shell. Four crews labored day and night, and the plant was soon turning out one gun a day.[6]

A handicap for state authorities in these efforts was the difficulty they experienced in obtaining drawings for gun carriages and caissons from the Confederate government, in Richmond. One of the state's emissaries there was instructed to "get tracings of details of gun carriages and caissons." In June, Captain M. H. Wright, ordnance officer in Nashville, ordered sixty-four tons of wrought-iron parts, such as axles and tire rims, cut to proper dimensions for fabrication of several hundred carriages and caissons. The parts were stored in the Nashville Armory and shipped to contractors as requested.[7] The convicts in the state penitentiary at Nashville were not exempt from the wartime activity. Some 400 of them produced a wide variety of items, including harness, artillery saddles, sponges, and rammers.[8]

As artillery companies were equipped, they were moved to camps of instruction for drill. A typical one was Captain Arthur M. Rutledge's battery from Nashville, which numbered 110 men. It was issued two iron 12-pounder howitzers and four iron 6-pounder guns, all cast by the T. M. Brennan foundry. Before leaving the city, the commissioned and noncommissioned officers posed for a photograph in Watkins Park. Their attire varied considerably. Some wore a solid gray uniform, including

pants decorated with a red stripe denoting artillery; others, a
solid dark coat and pants; still others, a combination of dark coat
and gray pants. Hats and caps were also nondescript, but the
crossed-cannon insignia of the artillery were affixed to most of
them.[9]

On August 7 a gunner in the battery wrote: "We have been
here [Knoxville] two weeks—have a pleasant camp, good water
and excellent drill ground. The horses are fast becoming accustomed to the firing of cannon, and the gunners have done
some target shooting which would have been creditable to more
experienced marksmen."[10]

A dearth of ordnance was not the only problem that confronted the fledgling artillery corps. Guidelines established by
the May 6 Army Bill required that all its field officers and battery commanders be nominated by the governor and confirmed
by the General Assembly. In searching for candidates, an effort
was made to obtain those who had received military training. In
this respect, state officials were largely successful. All three of
the field officers—Colonel Joseph P. McCown, Lieutenant Colonel Melton A. Haynes, and Major Alexander P. Stewart—were
West Point graduates who had served in the U.S. Artillery. Mc-
Cown and Haynes, forty-six and forty-seven years old, respectively, were veterans of the Seminole and Mexican wars. The
forty-year-old Stewart had performed garrison duty and taught

Officers and noncommissioned officers of Rutledge's Tennessee Battery at Watkins Park, Nashville, in May 1861. (Tennessee Historical Society)

mathematics at West Point, which earned him the sobriquet "Old Straight."[11]

Of the twenty-two captains who were eventually appointed, nine were college graduates, including three from West Point and three from the Virginia Military Institute. Three others were veterans of the U.S. Navy who were heavy-artillery experts.[12]

Unfortunately, the artillery was used as a stepping-stone, and the officer corps was soon decimated because of transfers to other branches. Colonel McCown and Major Stewart were promoted to brigadier generals of infantry in the fall of 1861. Captain William H. ("Red") Jackson quit the artillery in early 1862 to become colonel of the 7th Tennessee Cavalry. Captain Arthur M. Rutledge was promoted to major and assigned to staff duty. The artillery was thus stripped of its ablest leaders. As a result, only one (Smith P. Bankhead) of the twenty-five appointed officers of the Tennessee Artillery Corps would serve as a field officer in the Army of Tennessee.[13]

Another problem related to the governor's strategic policy. During the early months of the war, Harris committed his state forces to a defensive line along the Mississippi River, while neglecting the Tennessee border. The artillery corps reflected that policy. All three of the field officers were occupied with the construction of river defenses. By the end of the summer, more than half the state's organized batteries were engaged in heavy-artillery activities, primarily at Columbus, Kentucky, and New Madrid, Missouri. This left only a small and widely scattered contingent of mobile field artillery.[14]

Additional companies were organized throughout the fall of 1861. On September 8 a Nashville newspaper noted that "only a few hundred more men are required to fill up the Corps of Artillery of Tennessee. These are wanted immediately to be placed in the Camp of Light Artillery Instruction, near Nashville." Already the state was rushing into print Lieutenant Colonel Haynes's edition of *The Confederate Artillerist: Instructions in Artillery, Horse and Foot* to aid in training.[15]

All these troops were eventually transferred into the Confederate service, but not without much confusion and many delays. As late as January 1862, it had not been determined whether Harris at the state level or Davis at the Confederate level possessed the authority to appoint officers to the state artillery corps.[16] Harris ultimately created a state army of seventy-one infantry regiments, twenty-one cavalry regiments, and twenty-two batteries. The latter included thirteen companies of heavy artillery and nine field batteries. This nucleus formed the foundation of the Army of Tennessee's "long arm."[17]

•

Throughout the fall of 1861, thousands of volunteers across the western Confederacy flocked to recruiting stations. Most of them, of course, migrated to the infantry and cavalry; the artillery experienced difficulties. In February 1862 an officer from Bankhead's Tennessee Battery arrived in Memphis to sign up fifty men "for immediate active service" to fill vacancies. The company was "otherwise well equipped with horses, guns, etc." Despite frequent appeals, the response was negligible.[18]

The artillery was not an unpopular branch, but other factors were detrimental. Most of the men joined companies forming in their local communities, and in some instances the artillery was not even an option. It also required more technical skills than the infantry and lacked the romanticism in the popular mind of the cavalry. But the problem went still deeper. By the beginning of the war, an artillery tradition simply had not been established in the western Confederacy.

A number of crack militia batteries existed in the South when the war began, including the Chatham Artillery of Savannah, the Washington Artillery and Marion Artillery of Charleston, the Richmond Howitzers, Norfolk Light Artillery Blues, Portsmouth Light Artillery, and Delaware Kemper's Artillery of Alexandria. These outfits were concentrated in the East, however—in Virginia, South Carolina, and Georgia.[19]

The notable exception was the Louisiana Washington Artillery of New Orleans, which had been organized in 1838. This company served as a battery in Texas in 1845 and briefly as infantry during the Mexican War. It was reorganized in 1852, but by 1857 interest had waned to such a degree that only thirteen names remained on the roll. The pending war was to change all that. By 1861 the unit had been expanded to a battalion of four companies. In training and prestige it was the finest artillery outfit in the South. Unfortunately for the Army of Tennessee, it was soon whisked off to Virginia.[20]

The artillery corps of the Army of Northern Virginia was thus provided with a small but efficient base of militia upon which to build. If most of the men who formed these companies lacked battlefield experience, they at least enjoyed superiority in training, esprit de corps, and continuity of organizational existence. In comparison, the Army of Tennessee could rely upon only two such batteries: the Washington Artillery (Fifth Company) of New Orleans and the Washington Artillery of Augusta, Georgia.

When the Louisiana Washington Artillery was ordered to Virginia, it left behind twenty men to form the nucleus of a fifth company. Funds for uniforms and equipment were obtained from the state legislature, the New Orleans city council, and local merchants. Formal mustering in occurred at Lafayette Square in March 1862. The full complement of 155 consisted of 5 officers, 24 noncommissioned officers, 1 surgeon, 6 artificers, 1 bugler, 84 privates, and 34 drivers. Before leaving the city, these personnel posed for several photographs. They were dressed in dark-colored artillery jackets and pants, checkered shirts, black boots, and kepis decorated with the crossed-cannon insignia. On March 6 the company attended worship at the First Presbyterian Church. The next day, it boarded a train amidst the cheers of hundreds of spectators and was soon on its way to join the Confederate concentration at Corinth, Mississippi.[21]

The Washington Artillery of Augusta, Georgia, the "pride of old time Augusta," had been organized in 1854. The men drilled and paraded monthly in their dark blue uniforms. In 1860 the state presented the company with six field guns. They were later repossessed by the state, and the men exchanged their blue jackets for gray ones when they entered the Confederate service and were transferred to General Braxton Bragg at Pensacola. He foolishly attempted to convert the company to infantry, but relented when the men promptly requested a transfer to Virginia. Like their counterparts from New Orleans, the Augustans were soon boarding railroad cars for Corinth.[22]

Because of the lack of trained militia batteries, the foundation of the western artillery became the volunteer company. Such units as the Pettus (Mississippi) Flying Artillery, the Helena (Arkansas) Light Artillery, and Bankhead's Company of Tennessee Light Artillery were but a few of the many that were hastily organized. Who were the inexperienced but enthusiastic recruits who comprised these companies? Where did they come from? What drew them to the artillery?

Most of them were young. In Captain Charles Semple's Alabama Battery, which was representative, nearly 60 percent of the company was less than twenty-five. A fourth of the privates were nineteen or under, though the average age was twenty-two.

A sprinkling of men were seventeen. On the other end of the
scale was a patriarchal private who was sixty-one. Two of the
lieutenants were in their twenties. The specialized personnel—
the surgeon, blacksmith, artificer, harness maker, carpenter,
and farrier—tended to be older men in their forties.[23]

One of the youngest companies in the western artillery was
Stanford's Mississippi Battery. Seventy-seven percent of the personnel were under twenty-five. All four of the sergeants were
between twenty-one and twenty-three. Thirty-five percent of the
privates were eighteen and nineteen, though the average age
was twenty-two.[24]

A significant number hailed from cities. Bankhead's Tennessee Battery and the Pillow Flying Artillery were from
Memphis; Rutledge's Tennessee Battery and the Harding Light
Artillery from Nashville; and the Orleans Guard Artillery from
the Crescent City. Mobile furnished the batteries of Charles P.
Gage, D. D. Waters, and William H. Ketchum. Occupations reflected the city background. The Augusta Washington Artillery
counted among its ranks blacksmiths, molders, machinists, car-
penters, tailors, bookkeepers, printers, and butchers. The New
Orleans Washington Artillery (Fifth Company) included forty-
seven clerks, ten merchants, three planters, eleven students,
two doctors, five lawyers, one architect, three river pilots, eight
artisans, and thirty-one laborers.[25]

Western artillery officers, like the men they were to lead, were
a young lot drawn from all walks of civil life. Thomas Key, who
would command an Arkansas battery, was a thirty-three-year-
old Helena newspaper editor when hostilities began. Thomas L.
Massenburg would lead a Georgia battery throughout the war,
but in 1861 he was a twenty-five-year-old Macon druggist.
Robert Cobb would rise to the rank of major in the Army of
Tennessee, but before donning his uniform he was a twenty-
three-year-old Kentucky farmer.

Twenty-two-year-old R. F. Kolb had barely graduated from
college when he was commissioned as captain of an Alabama
battery in 1862. John W. Johnston would command a battalion,
but when the war began he was a twenty-three-year-old Virginia lawyer. James P. Douglas, who initially led a Texas battery
and later distinguished himself as a field officer, entered the
service as a twenty-five-year-old Tyler, Texas, school principal.[26]

Most western artillerymen were, of course, native-born
Southerners, but a scattering of foreigners was included. The
Orleans Guard Artillery was heavily infused with New Orleans

French, and Jackson's Tennessee Battery embraced a group of
Memphis Germans. Watson's Louisiana Battery was composed
almost entirely of Irishmen.[27]

Although most companies accepted virtually anyone, some
were looking for recruits of a certain type. The muster roll of
Lumsden's Alabama Battery read like a "Who's Who" of Tuscaloosa society. Captain Charles Lumsden, a graduate of the Virginia Military Institute, was commandant of cadets at the
University of Alabama. Also included were eight doctors, two
college professors, several prominent planters, and the superin-
tendent of education of Tuscaloosa County. Most of these men,
however, were quickly culled out by the Confederate government and detailed for duty elsewhere. When Captain Edward
Byrne recruited in Greenville, Mississippi, for his battery, he
accepted only "the better class of young men." Smith's Mississippi Battery was said to consist of "the best young men in
Clarke County."[28]

Captain Thomas Stanford, commanding a Mississippi battery, found himself in competition with an infantry unit for
recruits. As an inducement, he promised to make several men
noncommissioned officers, and he pledged to use his influence to
ensure the election of Dr. J. S. McCall as lieutenant. This did
occur, but several others were chagrined to learn that their
promised ranks were not forthcoming.[29]

A sense of curiosity drew some to the artillery. When a gun
crew recruited at Pontotoc, Mississippi, in the summer of 1861,
they found that their bronze field piece worked like a charm.
Eager men flocked around it like children around a new toy. A
recruit observed that "the idea of possessing such fine guns en-
thused the men very much. They had seen infantry and cavalry,
but never an artilleryman."[30]

•

Once companies were formally organized and accepted into the
Confederate service, they moved to their assigned destinations.
Captain Charles Swett's Warren (Mississippi) Light Artillery
was ordered to report to General William Hardee's command in
Arkansas. Lacking cannon or caissons, the company marched
through the streets of Vicksburg as infantry. When the troops
reached the dock to board the river steamer *Chasm* for the trip
north, a large crowd of relatives and well-wishers greeted them.
"As we moved off, the company who had assembled themselves

on the hurricane deck gave three cheers for the native city they were leaving never perhaps to return," wrote a seventeen-year-old private.[31]

On November 7, 1861, Stanford's Mississippi Battery was ordered to join the corps of General Leonidas Polk at Columbus, Kentucky. The troops marched to the depot of the Mississippi Central Railroad at Grenada, where they boarded flatcars. John E. Magee, a twenty-year-old private, described the parting scene: "At 3 o'clock the long whistle sounded the signal to start. The parting embrace and fervent kiss were given—tears stood in the eyes of many, and the waving handkerchiefs commenced as the train moved slowly off. Cheer after cheer was given, which died upon the air and soon Grenada was out of view."[32]

When Rutledge's Tennessee Battery was transferred from Nashville to Knoxville, the men found the trip to be quite enjoyable. "The treatment we received along the road was of the most pleasing kind," noted one of them. "Old men and old women, young men and blooming maidens, greeted us at every depot, and all along the road, throwing bouquets with inspiring mottoes attached, luscious apples in rows on sticks and strings and many other delicacies, into the cars as we passed."[33]

The "camps" to which units reported were frequently nothing more than open fields. Stanford's men spent the first few weeks at Columbus in plank-floored tents while they cleared an open area and began felling trees for more substantial quarters. Twenty-eight cabins were eventually constructed. Swett's company did not receive any tents until the end of October. Until then, the soldiers slept on the ground. The tent flies issued to Semple's battery were described as "simple square osnaburg cloths."[34]

The first few weeks in camp took much of the romance out of the war for many individuals. Stanford's company had been at Columbus barely three weeks before an epidemic of measles broke out. Two men died and several were furloughed, never to return.[35] Semple's company had not been mustered in five months before sickness struck. "I left one man sick with the [Catholic] sisters at Mobile," wrote Captain Henry Semple. "Churchill A. at home sick, Charlie Holt [had his] leg broke and another sick in Montgomery with rheumatism. . . . All others fit for duty except five or six who are ailing in camp."[36]

Bored with the drudgery of camp life, some personnel were lead astray by certain moral failings. "When bounty money was paid to the command, another new experience was had by many," observed a gunner in Lumsden's battery. "Released from restraints of home, church and public sentiment, it did not take long for many to learn to be quite expert gamblers." Captain Lumsden soon issued orders forbidding all gambling in camp, a rule that met "with the approval of the great majority of his men."[37] A somewhat more serious failing was the addiction of some men to alcohol. Unfortunately, even officers were not free of this vice. More than one battery commander in the Army of Tennessee was cashiered for drunkenness. Early in the war, Captain Lumsden fell victim to rumors that he was an alcoholic. The men in his company took quick steps to "sit down on the lie, to the great relief of friends and relatives at home."[38]

Few companies had their full complement of cannon, caissons, and horses when organized. The raw recruits consequently could not begin even the elementary instruction so badly needed to shape them into trained cannoneers. Captain Semple stated that his company "was drilled in squad drills until our guns arrived." When Stanford's battery left Grenada, it possessed only one gun and sixty-five horses. Not until several months later were three additional guns and four caissons delivered. A battery wagon and traveling forge arrived still later. Finally, in March 1862, when two more guns were received, the battery attained full six-gun strength.[39]

Obtaining horses was far easier than it was to be later in the war, but even at this early stage acquisition was often slow. By April 1862, Semple's battery had been issued guns but was still critically short of animals. In a newspaper advertisement entitled "Horses Wanted," Lieutenant E. J. Fitzgerald pleaded with the citizens of Montgomery "not to give but to sell them at a price the Government can afford to pay, which is a fair one." He dramatically concluded: "Our church bells even are being cast into field pieces, but they are useless without horses. Can any one prefer the luxury or comfort even of keeping horses, to the preservation of our homes and lives?"[40]

Once companies received some or all of their cannon and ordnance and most of their horses, specialized training began in earnest. This meant constant drill. The men in a gun crew soon learned to refer to one another by number. Cannoneer Number 2 placed a fixed round into the muzzle. This consisted of a pre-measured powder charge in a cloth cartridge bag that was attached to a projectile, which enabled the round to be handled as a unit. Number 1 then shoved the round down the bore by means of a rammer. During this process, Number 3 held his thumb on

the vent, a tiny hole on the top rear of the gun. After the round
was inserted, Number 3 placed a small wire pick in the vent to perforate the cartridge bag. Number 4 then inserted a friction primer into the vent. The primer was a device designed to send a flame down the vent to the powder. When an attached lanyard was jerked upon the appropriate command, the powder charge was ignited and the cannon discharged. Number 1 then sponged down the bore to extinquish any lingering sparks. Number 5 carried ammunition from 6 and 7 at the limber chest. The men at the limber prepared the fuze of the projectile, if any, according to the time in flight given in the battery fire commands. Despite the complicated process, a well-drilled and proficient crew could load and fire two rounds per minute.[41]

Supervision was provided by a noncommissioned officer, usually a sergeant. His key responsibility was sighting. Devices for this purpose were relatively crude and obtaining ranges was largely guesswork. A trail hand spike was used to move the cannon to the left or right. Elevation was achieved by moving the barrel up or down by means of an elevating screw. Because Civil War cannon lacked absorption mechanisms, they leaped back in recoil when discharged. They then needed to be rolled back into line and resighted. Aiming, rather than loading and firing, usually consumed the most time.

The drivers were also assigned specific duties. One was required for each of the three teams drawing the guns and caissons. To reduce the load on the animals, all other men in the battery were required to walk. In combat, the drivers would gallop their teams onto the field. While the guns were unlimbered and swung around, the horses were dashed back to whatever cover might be found. If one of them was disabled, it was quickly removed from the harness and the gun pulled by the surviving animals. The handling of frightened and bucking horses during the heat of battle called for real manhood.

Company officers provided the training. The problem was that few of them in the west enjoyed any prior military experience and were frequently as ignorant of tactics and maneuvers as their men. "Soon after we began to drill, it became evident to the company, that [Lieutenant Hugh R.] McSwine was not qualified to fill the position to which he was elected," lamented Sergeant W. H. Brown of Stanford's battery. "The company drill was a profound enigma to him. . . . He could not give commands for the most simple movements. With the company on the drill ground he was completely befogged. . . . [The troops] would indulge in noisy laughter at his expense." The majority of the men signed a petition calling for his resignation, but to no avail.[42] After the Battle of Shiloh, a gunner in the Louisiana Washington Artillery complained that his captain, I. W. Hodgson, gave "but few orders during the two days and those he did give were not to his credit."[43]

Drills were usually conducted daily. A cannoneer in Swett's Mississippi Battery wrote: "Drilled often and became accustomed to the various maneuvers of artillery drill." Still, training was often deficient. The men in Stanford's battery went through the motions, but, because of the critical shortage of ammunition, never received any target practice. When they went into action for the first time at Shiloh in April 1862, they had never fired their pieces![44]

•

A far more serious problem than recruiting, organizing, and training the batteries, was equipping them. The armories of the western Confederacy were all but depleted of artillery ordnance. In early 1861, Mississippi had only two 12-pounder howitzers and six 6-pounders. Not a caisson, battery wagon, or forge was available in the state. Louisiana authorities claimed they captured some field pieces at the Baton Rouge Arsenal, but these were issued to the Washington Artillery Battalion before it went to Virginia. Fiery Governor Joseph Brown was determined that none of the dozen Georgia field pieces would leave the state.[45]

Consequently, some companies even sought to procure obsolete guns. All four of those in Trigg's Arkansas Battery were survivors from the Mexican War. Bledsoe's Missouri Battery possessed an old bronze 9-pounder that had been captured from the Mexicans. It was a long gun of Spanish make, now covered with dents and scratches. It was bored out to the caliber of a 12-pounder howitzer, but the conversion caused a peculiar ringing sound when it was fired. The Helena Light Artillery acquired a 12-pounder howitzer that had adorned the campus of the Arkansas Military Institute.[46]

Early in the war, Chief of Ordnance Josiah Gorgas contracted with several establishments for the manufacture of cannon, carriages, and caissons. The primary supplier was the Tredegar Iron Works, of Richmond, whose proprietor was Joseph R. Anderson. It had long made cannon for the federal government. A few Tredegar field pieces were sent to the western theater in the

fall of 1861, but these were mostly heavy artillery for inland
river defenses. Contracts were also signed with two western
foundries: Noble Brothers & Company, of Rome, Georgia, and
Rice & Wright, of Florence, Alabama. Casting at the latter was
never initiated.[47]

In August 1861 Captain William Richardson Hunt, ordnance officer at the Memphis Arsenal, warned General Leonidas Polk, commanding Confederate forces in west Tennessee, that a more concerted effort must be made. He recommended that contracts be signed for fifty field batteries, each to consist of six guns and a like number of carriages and caissons, about sixty sets of harness, one battery wagon, one traveling forge, and 400 rounds per gun. The cost per battery was estimated at $15,500. To accomplish this, he recommended that agents be dispatched to Memphis, Nashville, Vicksburg, New Orleans, Montgomery, Mobile, and Huntsville.[48]

During the fall of 1861, the Confederate government belatedly bestirred itself to assist the west. Contracts were signed with a number of private firms, loan money was advanced, and drawings as well as molds were supplied. Dozens of field pieces were soon in the process of delivery:

Firm	Dates of Delivery	Guns Delivered
Quinby & Robinson, Memphis	Nov. '61–June '62	68
T. M. Brennan & Co., Nashville	Nov. '61–Feb. '62	64
Noble Bros. & Co., Rome, Ga.	April '61–Oct. '62	58
Leeds & Company, New Orleans	Oct. '61–March '62	49
Reading & Bro., Vicksburg	Dec. '61–April '62	44

By October 1, 1861, the Memphis Arsenal had outfitted and shipped fourteen complete field batteries. Most of these guns were made by Tredegar and the Memphis foundry of Quinby & Robinson. In November a six-gun battery made by the Noble Brothers foundry in Rome, Georgia, was received.[49]

Production never kept pace with demand. Units were always waiting to be issued guns. Byrne's Kentucky Battery was supplied by Quinby & Robinson; Gage's Alabama Battery, Robertson's Florida Battery, and the Louisiana Washington Artillery (Fifth Company) by Leeds & Company; Watson's Louisiana Battery and the Orleans Guard Artillery by the New Orleans shops of John Clark & Company; and other plants supplied various units.[50]

Local communities took deep pride in their newfound industry. Emma Crutcher, a Vicksburg resident, informed her soldier-brother that "Reading's foundry has an order for sixty brass cannon and 30,000 bombshells. . . . We saw cannon in all the various stages of completion and I was very much impressed. Several other parties of ladies were there." A Memphis newspaper reporter, comparing Tredegar field pieces with those cast locally at Quinby & Robinson, bragged: "For beauty and finish and general appearance the Richmond cannon cannot compare with those made here." The guns cast by Noble Brothers were tested with double charges of powder and found to be quite satisfactory. Those produced by John Clark & Company were judged to be "first rate specimens of ordnance."[51]

These positive expressions were not universal, however. The quality of some of these early products was so poor as to invoke the scorn of experts. "Many of the guns were defective and even dangerous," declared one ordnance officer. "One battery from the Memphis foundry [Street, Hungerford & Company] lost three guns in a month by bursting, one of them in the battle of Belmont, November 7." When General Lloyd Tilghman inspected a battery of two iron 6-pounders and two bronze 9-pounders made by the Clarksville, Tennessee, foundry of Whitfield, Bradley & Company he declared them to be worthless. The 9-pounders were "of very little account" and all the guns were mounted in a "wretched manner." He fumed about a "total ignorance of all mechanical principles evidenced in the construction of the carriages."[52]

Eighty percent of the field pieces turned out by the five major western Confederate foundries were smoothbore cannon, mostly of the U.S. Model 1841 6-pounder and 12-pounder howitzer type. These were the tried and tested weapons of the day, and Confederate authorities seemed reluctant to advance to more modern types. Technically, a gun was a long-barrel cannon designed to hurl solid shot with a heavy charge of powder over a long range at a low angle of elevation. The range of a 6-pounder was 1,500 yards. Howitzers had first been used by the French around 1800. They were light-weight, short-barrel smoothbores intended to lob frangible projectiles, such as shell and case shot, among massed troops. A chamber at the bottom of the bore of a howitzer made possible the concentration of small powder charges. The range of the 12-pounder was about 1,000 yards.[53]

The greater distance and accuracy that rifled cannon afforded over smoothbores had long been recognized. Unfortunately, rifled guns had several drawbacks. Fuzes for elongated rifle projectiles remained imprecise, so shells might burst prematurely in the air or bury themselves in the ground before exploding. Canister, the most deadly type of projectile at short range, was not as effective when fired from a rifled gun. Also, in the thickly wooded terrain in which many Civil War battles were fought, the added range of rifles was of little value. The concept of forward artillery observers was unknown, and the cannoneers needed to see what they were shooting at. In thick terrain, smoothbores were more effective because they could fire larger projectiles and more canister with deadly effect.[54]

In addition to these fundamental difficulties, Southern foundries experienced some special ones. Most of the rifled guns turned out in western plants were nondescript, bronze 6-pounder rifles and 3-inch rifles. The rifling, length, and dimensions often varied from foundry to foundry. They also lacked the refined machinery necessary for precision rifling. The quality of the iron ore used in the manufacturing process was often so poor

The T. M. Brennan foundry, in Nashville, which had turned out dozens of field pieces for the Confederate government, in 1864 while the city was under Federal occupation. (National Archives)

that weak castings resulted. Success varied in early attempts by several of the foundries to copy a version of the 10-pounder Parrott rifle, a banded-iron, rifled gun that had been invented by Northern industrialist Robert P. Parrott.[55]

The production of bronze cannon was predicated on the availability of copper, and shortages were experienced at an early date. Therefore, General P. G. T. Beauregard issued a call to the citizens of the Mississippi Valley for bells to be melted down for cannon. He climaxed his appeal with the words: "Who will not cheerfully and promptly send me his bells under such circumstances? Be of good cheer; but time is precious." Bragg considered this move to be sensationalistic and unnecessary, but the public fully endorsed it, and courthouses, factories, public institutions, churches, and plantations quickly responded. Scrap-metal drives were conducted and wagon loads of andirons, candlesticks, gas fixtures, and even doorknobs were collected and sent to the foundries. Enthusiasm apparently even exceeded practicality, for one Mobile foundryman stated that many of the household utensils and ornaments that were received were simply worthless. "There is no gun metal in them and we are daily refusing such articles," he wrote.[56]

●

Such were the men who made up the artillery of the Army of Tennessee and such was the manner in which they were organized, trained, and equipped. It was not an imposing start. Southerners, especially those in the west, were simply not as adept in artillery techniques as their Northern counterparts. They lacked the background in, skills for, and exposure to this branch of the service that they did possess for the infantry and cavalry. Heavy industry and refined machinery, so vital for the manufacture of quality ordnance, were also limited. It remained to be seen if valor and enthusiasm could overcome such deficits.

Chapter 2

"The Battery Was the Common Target"

On September 14, 1861, General Albert Sidney Johnston arrived in Nashville to assume command of the immense Department No. 2, which stretched from the Alleghenies to northwestern Arkansas. General Leonidas Polk, commanding the left flank, had already broken the fragile Kentucky neutrality and moved 11,000 troops to Columbus. Johnston completed the task. Almost every armed man in middle Tennessee was placed under General Simon Buckner and transported by rail to Bowling Green, seventy miles north of Nashville. In east Tennessee, about 4,000 troops under General Felix Zollicoffer advanced to Cumberland Ford, in eastern Kentucky.

Johnston's supply of field artillery was woefully inadequate. Despite pleas to the secretary of war, Zollicoffer still had only one battery: Rutledge's Tennessee. Buckner's pathetic artillery included only two incomplete batteries: Byrne's Kentucky with three guns and Porter's Tennessee with two pieces. Polk counted six batteries in his corps. Stationed at Fort Donelson on the Cumberland River was Maney's Tennessee Battery, an under-strength outfit consisting of forty men, four guns, and no horses.[1]

Convinced that the major Union thrust would come in the center against Bowling Green, Johnston became preoccupied with matters in that sector. General William Hardee's brigade from Arkansas and four regiments from southwestern Virginia were put on trains for Bowling Green. Kentucky recruits were enrolled, and all available troops in Nashville were sent north. Several cavalry outfits were also received, including B. F. Terry's Texas Rangers and Colonel Nathan Bedford Forrest's independent Tennessee battalion.[2]

The artillery also continued to expand. Major Francis A. Shoup's battalion, consisting of three four-gun batteries, accompanied Hardee's brigade. Byrne's battery received three additional cannon, and H. B. Lyon and Robert Cobb organized another Kentucky battery. The Confederate government furnished two 12-pounder howitzers and four 6-pounders, but the company's horses were unfit. Captain William Harper's Jefferson (Mississippi) Flying Artillery, on the way to Virginia, was diverted to Bowling Green. In late December, John H. Guy's Goochland (Virginia) Light Artillery boarded railroad cars at Dublin, Virginia, for assignment to Johnston's army.[3]

Other batteries were in the process of formation, but the problem, as always, was a shortage of ordnance. Confederate officials had awarded a number of contracts for field guns in the fall of 1861, but some time would elapse before the foundries could tool up and make deliveries. Meanwhile, Johnston would need to make do. In October, Buckner requested field pieces for the Bowling Green fortifications, but none were forthcoming. By November, John W. Eldridge's Tennessee Battery was still in Memphis waiting to be equipped. Two batteries were at Clarksville, one of which had no guns or caissons; the other possessed six cannon but its ammunition consisted of only sixty rounds and harnesses were available for only four teams. In Knoxville, Captain George Monsarrat's personnel strength was sufficient to form two companies of light artillery, but his guns numbered only four and his caissons three.[4]

More officers had to be found for the expanding army. In the artillery, two lawyers-turned-soldier emerged in leadership positions. In the Bowling Green corps, the prominent figure was Major Francis A. Shoup. This twenty-seven-year-old West Point graduate and former U.S. Artillery officer had been garrisoned at Key West and Fort Moultrie but had never seen combat. He later resigned from the army and, when the war began, he was practicing law in Florida. Although he was young and inexperienced and years later conceded that he was "ignorant of war" despite his background, he made an excellent drill officer, which was sorely needed at Bowling Green.[5]

The other officer was Captain Smith P. Bankhead, of Polk's corps. A graduate of a Virginia military school, he was the son of a regular army general. When the war began, he was practicing law in Memphis. Polk soon appointed him as his artillery chief, and the newspapers singled the captain out as one of the bright new stars of command.[6]

A dearth of ordnance and a shortage of qualified leaders were not the only problems confronting the fledgling artillery corps. The most serious long-range one dealt with organization.

Johnston did little to structure his command. He designated Hardee's and Buckner's divisions as the "Army of Central Kentucky" and placed it under the immediate command of Hardee. The "army" was in essence a corps, as was Polk's, at Columbus.

This sort of organizational hodgepodge was clearly evident in the artillery, where the structure bordered on the ludicrous. The number of guns per battery varied between three and seven. No administrative guidelines were established. In Hardee's corps, no artillery was available to Buckner's division, but five batteries were assigned to John Bowan's brigade! A similar situation existed in Polk's corps. Only one battery was attached to the 1st Division, which was actually only brigade-size; four were assigned to the 2d Division, of the same size.[7]

If any consistency existed, it was provided by the general brigade-battery structure that was adopted. Under this concept, batteries were assigned to, received rations from, and operated with specific infantry brigades. Despite the long use of this system in the old army, it proved to be an unfortunate choice. The brigade-battery organization was essentially an obsolete one in which the artillery was considered to be simply an extension of the infantry. The drawbacks were numerous. Infantry officers were given close supervision over an arm they did not really understand and could not properly control. Possessive brigadier generals often resented any attempt to send their batteries elsewhere, regardless of the need. The scattering of batteries throughout the army created uncertain lines of authority between infantry and artillery officers. Most important, the brigade-battery structure discouraged the massing of guns in battle.[8]

A far more viable model would have been the battalion organization. A relatively new structure (that had not even been mentioned in U.S. manuals until 1860), it was primarily envisioned for administrative purposes. Batteries still did not operate together as a tactical unit. Some time would pass before the battalion would evolve, but creative artillery officers in the Virginia army, such as E. P. Alexander, were quick to see its potential. No such vision was evident in the western command.[9]

Johnston's raw troops were soon to be tested. On November 7, 1861, a Union force under General Ulysses S. Grant attacked a Confederate brigade at Belmont, Missouri, opposite Columbus. A six-gun Rebel outfit, Watson's Louisiana Baterry, was on line. Bad luck seemed to plague it from the start. The supply of ammunition was low and, as the limited battle extended into the early afternoon, it was exhausted. At 2:00 P.M. a major Union thrust shattered the Southern line; Watson's battery was overrun and forty-five horses were killed. One of the officers, Lieutenant C. P. Ball, was seriously injured when an out-of-control caisson ran over him.

As the Federals advanced toward the river, they met the fire of heavy artillery and Smith's Mississippi and Jackson's Tennessee batteries. One of Jackson's feeble Parrott guns, made by a Memphis foundry, burst on the second round; three men were killed and one wounded. The Confederates received reinforcements, but no additional artillery could be moved up because of the terrain of the riverbank. Nevertheless, the Yankees were driven back and four of Watson's guns recovered.[10]

The next action came on Johnston's opposite flank. On January 19, 1862, Zollicoffer's command of George Crittenden's division was routed at Mill Springs, in southwestern Kentucky. A driving rain and thick forest cover all but immobilized the artillery. Arthur M. Rutledge's and L. W. McClung's Tennessee batteries barely fired a shot. During the pell-mell retreat that followed, all twelve guns and caissons were abandoned, as well as forty-five of McClung's horses.[11]

In both actions, the artillery had been given little opportunity to show what it could do. Worse yet, all three batteries would now need to be reequipped. Johnston was soon writing Chief of Ordnance Josiah Gorgas, in Richmond, requesting "a field battery of Anderson [Tredegar] guns to fill the place of those lost by General Crittenden."[12] It was an ignominious beginning for the western long arm.

●

By January 1862 the Federal buildup in the west had become alarming. Johnston's 45,000 scattered and poorly armed troops in western and central Kentucky faced a force nearly 125,000 strong. The general had 14,000 men at Bowling Green, 5,500 at forts Henry and Donelson, 8,000 at Clarksville and vicinity, and 17,000 at Columbus.

On February 6 a Union army under Grant breached the Confederate defenses at Fort Henry, on the Tennessee River. Attention now focused on nearby Fort Donelson, on the west bank of the Cumberland. By the 13th, Johnston had funneled 17,000 troops there under the command of John B. Floyd. Commanding the river to the north, the Confederates had mounted 13 heavy guns. Within the fort itself were 2 nondescript field pieces. On the land side were 6 field batteries, consisting of 475 men and 31 guns: Porter's Tennessee (113 men and 6 guns), Graves's Kentucky (70 men and 6 guns), Maney's Tennessee (100 men and 4 guns), French's Virginia (58 men and 4 guns), Green's Kentucky (76 men and 7 guns), and Guy's Virginia (58 men and 4 guns).[13]

Several of the Army of Tennessee's future high-ranking artillery officers served at Donelson. The popular, twenty-three-year-old Captain Rice Graves, who had resigned from West Point at the beginning of the war, would later be promoted to major and be appointed as a division artillery chief. Captain Thomas K. Porter, an Annapolis graduate, would likewise receive a major's commission and lead an artillery battalion at Chickamauga. Eighteen-year-old Lieutenant John W. Morton, of Porter's battery, would become chief of N. B. Forrest's horse artillery.[14]

Floyd encountered many problems with his new command, not the least of which dealt with the artillery. The heavy guns were manned by detailed infantry whose training was minimal. Indeed, only four officers were present who enjoyed any sort of expertise in the handling of large seacoast-type cannon. Two of the guns were old 32-pounder carronades, which would be effective only against wooden gunboats at close range. The most powerful cannon, a 10-inch columbiad, needed repair. Battery emplacements on the land side were incomplete. A series of ridges beyond the Confederate line were some 800–1,500 feet higher in elevation. If occupied by Union rifle guns, the river defenses could be taken from reverse. A number of ineffective friction primers added a dismal finishing touch.[15]

Grant's two divisions (17,000 troops and seven batteries) were well up to the fort by February 13. The armies spent the day in establishing their positions and engaging in long-range artillery duels, during which Graves's battery disabled a howitzer in Battery D, 1st Illinois Light Artillery. Meanwhile, Lew Wallace's 3d Division was coming up the Cumberland on transports to reinforce the Northerners.

A brief action occurred on the 13th, when the Federals made a foray against the Confederate center, especially targeting Frank Maney's annoying guns. "The battery was the common target," Wallace stated. The cannon were planted in the vertex of a V-shaped fortification, which was bordered by two steep ravines. Before the Union infantry cleared the woods, the Tennessee gunners opened with a rapid shelling, while Graves's and

Porter's batteries joined in an enfilade fire. Maney's cannoneers, silhouetted against the sky, were rapidly picked off by sharpshooters. So many fell, including Maney and his two lieutenants, that the survivors were able to work only two of the four guns. The attack was repulsed, but at a high cost to the artillery.[16]

That night, the mercury plunged to ten degrees and the ground was blanketed with two inches of snow. Throughout the 14th, the opposing armies seemed paralyzed by the bitter cold. The scene now shifted to the river batteries. At 3:00 the Federal fleet, including two ironclads, steamed toward the fort. It opened fire at a mile's range, but the shots fell short. As the distance was slowly closed to 400 yards, the Rebel "heavies" returned the fire. For an hour, a deafening roar thundered along the Cumberland bluffs. "The air above and around us was full of shot, solid, case and shell, while the river below was almost a continuous spray," an artilleryman was to recall. So awesome was the Yankee fire that Floyd wired Johnston that the fort could not possibly hold for twenty minutes. To everyone's surprise, however, the river batteries even drove the crippled fleet back downriver.[17]

Despite the success of the shore guns, a threat still existed from the land side. The force was now in danger of being trapped by the increasing Union buildup. The Confederate command decided to drive back the Union right wing, which would reopen the Nashville Road. Troops were taken out of the rifle pits and massed to the left.

Before daybreak on the 15th, Gideon Pillow's ad hoc division attacked on the left, supported by Buckner's division in the center. A section of Green's Kentucky Battery moved forward to an open field on a ridge and became hotly engaged. A shot from the enemy's artillery that burst in its midst killed and wounded several men. The remainder of the crew panicked and fled to the rear. Pillow obtained enough volunteers from Guy's Virginia Battery to man the abandoned guns, and he personally directed their fire.[18]

By early afternoon, the Union right had crumbled, which left only a single battery to command Wynn's Ferry Road. The blue cannoneers were sabered at their guns by Bedford Forrest's charging troopers. Even though the Charlotte Road was now completely in Confederate possession and the avenue to escape open, Pillow incredibly ordered his troops back into the trenches.

Buckner's men returned to find that the skeleton force left behind during the attack was hastily falling back before an advancing Federal division. Unable to repel it, the Southerners occupied a hill overlooking their original position. There, Buckner "skillfully placed his artillery where it would do the most damage."[19]

A section each of Graves's and Porter's batteries were placed in position under a withering fire. All of Porter's horses were shot down, and the guns needed to be rolled into line by hand. Within minutes, Porter and thirty-three of his forty-eight effectives fell. Turning command over to young Lieutenant John Morton, the captain said: "Don't let them have the guns, Morton!" "No, captain, not while I have one man left," came the reply. Night ended the fighting.[20]

The next day, the Confederate command was surrendered. Although a dozen or so of Porter's men had escaped the night before with Forrest's cavalry and both French's and Guy's troops managed to board steamboats and flee with Floyd and his Virginians, the fate of most of the cannoneers was captivity.[21] The defeat at Fort Donelson was a staggering blow. Regarding the artillery, a large quantity of ordnance was surrendered, including thirty-three field pieces. Because of these losses, coupled with those at Belmont and Mill Springs, Johnston's long arm was now reduced by fully a third.

Johnston now pulled Hardee's corps back to Nashville, while the newly arrived General P. G. T. Beauregard, his second in command, took charge of withdrawal operations of Polk's corps at Columbus. Every one of the 140 field and heavy guns mounted there was saved. The heaviest were taken downriver to New Madrid and Island Number Ten. News from Johnston's front was not so encouraging. When he evacuated Nashville, he abandoned twenty-four siege guns and sixteen iron 6-pounder field pieces. Most of the latter were apparently unfinished guns that had been cast at the T. M. Brennan foundry. An eyewitness reported seeing "about a dozen large cannon still lying at this foundry, which the sudden flight of the rebels prevented them from rifling and carrying away."[22]

●

During the first year of the war, the Confederate field artillery was not a significant tactical factor. In the actions at Belmont, Mills Springs, and Fort Donelson, the batteries did little or no

Chapter 3

"Wake Him Up with a Few Shells"

Throughout March 1862, Corinth, Mississippi, was alive with activity. Troops from across the western Confederacy were massing there in a determined effort to arrest and roll back the relentless Union drive. Polk's corps, from Columbus, had arrived with 10,000 troops. During the preceding weeks, Beauregard had revamped Polk's command into a more organized system of brigades and divisions. He also adopted guidelines for the artillery: the apportionment of three guns per 1,000 infantry; uniformity of calibers within each battery; and the designation of at least four or six guns as the standard composition of each battery. Polk's reorganized artillery comprised the batteries of Smith's Mississippi, Polk's Tennessee, Bankhead's Tennessee, and Stanford's Mississippi. The four companies totaled 446 men, 347 horses, 24 guns, and a like number of caissons.[1]

Meanwhile, Johnston's troops had slogged over rain-soaked roads through south-central Tennessee. The trip from Murfreesboro was tediously long. At Decatur, Alabama, Johnston planned to move his artillery across the Tennessee River by using the railroad bridge. This proved to be impractical, however, and the guns had to be loaded on railroad flatcars—a slow process. From Decatur, some of the artillery moved overland to Courtland, Alabama. Heavy rains continued to fall, and the roads turned into liquid mud. At least ten days to two weeks would probably be required before the artillery could move over them. It would need to move by rail over the final leg into Corinth.

Preparations were hurriedly made. A special platform was constructed at Courtland for the loading of guns and caissons. The rail system was so overtaxed that some of the batteries had to wait a week before transportation could be furnished. At Burnsville, Mississippi, twelve miles southeast of Corinth, the train carrying Captain Charles Swett's Warren (Mississippi)

Light Artillery collided with the eastbound passenger train. Several cars were smashed, but the men and guns escaped injury and damage. Swett's battery rolled into Corinth on March 23, twenty-six days after it had left Murfreesboro.[2]

Johnston's ranks had been severely reduced by sickness, straggling, and desertion. He arrived at Corinth with 23,000 troops, only 16,000 of whom were effectives. His artillery, 13 batteries with about 44 guns, was undermanned. In Captain Robert Cobb's Kentucky Battery, 121 men were on the roll, but sickness, furloughs, and noncombatants reduced the number of effectives to 98. Major Francis Shoup's battalion of 3 batteries had dwindled to barely 150 effectives.[3]

General Bragg's Corps, 10,000 strong, arrived from Pensacola and Mobile. His artillery included Captain Isadore Girardey's Washington Artillery, a crack six-gun battery from Augusta, Georgia. A newly organized Florida battery was led by an ambitious twenty-two-year-old captain named Felix H. Robertson. Completing the list were two Alabama batteries, commanded by Captains William H. Ketchum and Charles P. Gage, whose personnel represented the cream of Mobile society. Captain Charles Lumsden's Alabama Battery, stationed at that city, had received a promise to be assigned to Corinth, but at the last minute was bumped by Gage's company. Lumsden's men were convinced this was attributable to "political pull."[4]

General Daniel Ruggles arrived from New Orleans with 5,000 infantry and three batteries: Captain G. Ducatel's Orleans Guard Artillery, Captain Samuel G. Bain's Vaiden (Mississippi) Light Artillery, and Captain W. Irving Hodgson's famed Louisiana Washington Artillery (Fifth Company). Hodgson's battery left New Orleans with a full complement of men and guns but no horses. They were to receive them at Grand Junction, Tennessee, only weeks before they would fight in battle.[5]

By March 23 the unprecedented concentration had been achieved. Some 40,000 effectives had been massed. Johnston's enlarged artillery corps now comprised twenty-three batteries, about 122 guns, and 2,000 men. Two-thirds of the companies had six guns and one-third four guns.[6]

Many of the men did not care for Corinth. A Tennessean noted that a hole dug two feet deep in any direction would bring "terribly unwholesome water" bubbling up. About 10 percent of the artillerymen were stricken with illness. The horses almost refused to drink the foul water. Because the mud contained acid minerals, their hair fell out. Each night, the animals were carefully washed and groomed, but the problem persisted.[7]

Everyone sensed that a big fight was nearing. Even now, Grant's army was only twenty-five miles north, encamped at Pittsburg Landing, on the Tennessee River. Johnston faced a serious predicament. If Don Carlos Buell's Union army in Nashville made a move into northern Alabama, Corinth would be outflanked. If he moved to unite with Grant, the Confederates would be facing 70,000 troops. If the latter were to be the case, a strike was imperative to prevent it.[8]

The difficulties involved in molding the assembled "mob," as Bragg referred to it, into a cohesive fighting unit were legion, and barely two weeks were available for this purpose. The problems of the artillery were the same as those facing the entire army: organization, command, logistics, and tactical planning.

Beauregard was assigned responsibility for organizing the force, and Johnston accepted his proposals in their entirety. The troops, christened the "Army of the Mississippi," were unevenly divided into four "corps" under Hardee, Bragg, Polk, and Breckinridge, though the latter two were actually of division size. It would prove to be a cumbersome arrangement. Beauregard unfortunately failed to adopt a battalion structure for the artillery. He retained the old policy of assigning each battery to a brigade of infantry. His rationale was that the nature of the terrain and the inexperience of the officers made it necessary to

Cannoneers of the Washington Artillery (Fifth Company) of New Orleans in their camp near Carrolton, Louisiana, only weeks before they were to fight at Shiloh. (Confederate Memorial Hall of New Orleans)

subdivide the batteries in order "to obtain even a partial benefit from their presence in the field."[9] Yet, artillery was placed under infantry officers, many of whom were equally as inexperienced. At any rate, it is difficult to see how battalions used as tactical units could have been any less effective than what resulted from the prevailing organization.

The corps contained no uniform number of guns. Although most of the brigades had a single battery attached, several had two or three. This meant that Bragg's corps, which was the largest, averaged two guns per 1,000 effectives, and Breckinridge's corps, which was really only a division, averaged five per 1,000 effectives.

General Bragg, who had been an artillery officer for nineteen years, was not consulted concerning the arrangement or assignment of the guns. He was not satisfied with the organization. He later complained that, just before the battle, all the batteries were "placed under the nominal orders of the Corps Commanders, a trust it was simply impossible for him to execute."[10] Yet, even if Bragg had been given the opportunity, he probably would not have made any significant changes. When he later rose to command of the army, he rigidly clung to a brigade-battery structure.

Another problem was command. Assigned to each corps was a tutorial chief of artillery: Captain Smith Bankhead for Polk's corps, Major James Hallonquist for Bragg's, and Major Francis Shoup for Hardee's. No single officer directed operations. Shoup was senior, but he readily admitted that his authority in no way approached that of an army chief of artillery. Nor were the specific battlefield functions of the chiefs well defined. As a result, they were initially wasted in the morning assault at Shiloh in a "do anything but do something" policy. Shoup spent the morning in the menial task of rounding up captured cannon. Bankhead even opted to relinquish his staff position so that he might personally command his own Tennessee battery.[11]

Supplies were also low. Captain Felix Robertson's Florida Battery left Pensacola with four 12-pounder Napoleon guns, one caisson, and 231 rounds of ammunition. At Montgomery, it was issued a battery wagon and traveling forge. Once in Corinth, Robertson barraged the ordnance officer with requests for items "absolutely necessary for the full equippage of this company." The Vaiden Light Artillery was so poorly equipped that it was to be unable to participate in the upcoming battle.[12]

The armament was also not of the best quality. Most of the guns were of Southern manufacture. About 85 percent of them were smoothbore 6-pounders and 12-pounder howitzers. Earlier, Beauregard had written Gorgas, in Richmond, in an attempt to modernize his artillery: "I desire to have 12-pounder Napoleon smoothbore and 6-pounder (caliber) rifle guns, which I am advised by General Bragg can be manufactured in New Orleans, where Leeds & Company have the proper models and all necessary experience."[13] The request was too late to be of any assistance.

For most of the cannoneers, this was to be their first battle. They were inexperienced and, in some cases, inadequately trained. Major Shoup later noted that, during the Battle of Shiloh, several batteries used maneuvers that had never even been practiced. Indeed, because of the shortage of ammunition, some of the gun crews had not even fired their pieces.[14]

On the night of April 2, Johnston found that his preparation time had expired. Word was received from Frank Cheatham's division at Bethel, twenty miles north of Corinth, that he was being menaced by Lew Wallace's division from Crump's Landing, four miles downriver from Pittsburg Landing. Another report was that Buell's army had left Columbia to join Grant. Johnston had to move quickly. He issued orders for the army to move out at 6:00 A.M. on the morning of the 3d.

Special Orders No. 8, which described the marching and battle plans, was chiefly Beauregard's conception. It contained grave errors. Beauregard envisioned a surprise attack, in which the corps would be arranged in unwieldy tandem lines rather than abreast. The poor artillery alignment called for the batteries to be scattered throughout the army with their respective brigades. Batteries were ordered to be placed in column, section front, in the rear of brigade intervals.[15]

The initial assault plan included no coordinated use of artillery. The prebattle instructions to chiefs of artillery to "mass their batteries in action and fight them twelve guns on a point" was too open ended to produce sufficient results. The brigade-battery organization simply did not lend itself to the massing of guns in battle. As a result, the artillery was not committed in mass. When batteries did cooperate, it was more because of the circumstances than design. The morning assault at Shiloh was characterized chiefly by individual batteries operating on their own. Adjutant General Thomas Jordon, a contributor to the battle plan, later admitted that batteries were "too often employed singly."[16]

The attack order stated that the rifle cannon should "fire mainly on the reserves and second line of the enemy" and only "occasionally will be directed on his artillery." Yet, the doctrine of the day stated that artillery on the offensive should concentrate on the enemy's cannon, not his infantry. The idea was to neutralize the enemy's defensive capability quickly. A practical matter was also involved: unlimbered batteries presented a far larger target zone than a line of infantry.[17].

As the troops prepared for battle, the army scurried with activity. A Mississippian later recalled that his battery was "ordered to get ready to move" and that "we were busy all day cooking rations." Orders prescribed that all field guns be issued 200 rounds of ammunition. A badly needed supply of shells from the Skates & Company foundry, of Mobile, arrived at the Corinth rail depot just before the army pulled out.[18]

Two batteries, Captain Samuel C. Bain's Vaiden Light Artillery and Lieutenant W. W. Carnes's Tennessee Battery, were assigned to remain in the Corinth garrison. Carnes was chagrined to learn the news. His seventy-five cannoneers were considered to be too few to man the company's six field guns adequately. Long after the army was out of sight, Carnes pondered a way to join the action. He received permission from an ordnance officer to turn in two of his cannon. Thus reduced to four guns and, in his own mind, having resolved the manpower shortage, he hastened with his battery to the field. They were to arrive in time to see their comrades plodding slowly back to Corinth.[19]

The march to Pittsburg Landing was chaotic. Hardee's corps, which spearheaded the column, did not even leave until late afternoon of the 3d. For the artillery, the journey was especially grueling. The country roads were ill suited for the passage of cannon and caissons. Worse yet, rain began to fall heavily on the afternoon of the 4th and continued throughout the next morning. The infantry began to deploy that same morning, but the attack was stalled by more delays. The artillery was partially at fault. Polk's and Breckinridge's batteries were bogged down in the mud and blocking the roads. Because all the infantry was not in position until late afternoon, the attack had to be postponed until the next morning. Late that night, batteries were still coming up.[20]

●

April 6 dawned sunny and clear. As early as 3:00 A.M. the horses in some of the batteries were already hitched.[21] About 6:30, after having skirmished for an hour and a half, the long-awaited advance began. The initial assault smashed against the advanced Union divisions of William T. Sherman and Benjamin Prentiss. Patrols had sounded the alarm, but the drowsy Federals were totally unprepared for battle.

Beauregard noted that "at 7 o'clock the thunder of artillery announced the serious opening of the conflict." On the Confederate right, R. G. Shaver's and A. H. Gladden's brigades came storming through the thickets east of the Pittsburg-Corinth Road and struck Prentiss's terrified troops. The six guns of the Warren Light Artillery and the four of Captain William L. Harper's Jefferson (Mississippi) Flying Artillery hurriedly unlimbered in support. The Yankees fell back in confusion, but not before several of the cannoneers fell.[22]

On the left, General Pat Cleburne ordered Captain John Trigg, commanding an Arkansas battery, to "wake him up with a few shells." The first round cut off a treetop and sent it crashing to the ground. The battery continued firing, but most of the rounds went wild. Major Shoup concluded that "it was random work, under excitement, and the execution was not much."[23]

Large portions of the Union line were swept away. The rapid movement of the infantry, coupled with the rugged terrain, made it extremely difficult for the batteries to maintain pace. The soft and muddy ground further impeded mobility. "It was not a good place for a fight," complained a Louisiana artilleryman. "There were very few open and cleared places, the land being hilly and covered densely with trees and undergrowth." One general noted that Captain Charles Gage's Alabama Battery was forced to cut its way through "thickly wooded country over ravines and hills almost impassable to ordinary wagons." One of Gage's men wrote that "it was down one hill and up the other and at the bottom of the hills were the ravines, and they were so boggy that a man could hardly cross them, and, in some cases, we had to build bridges so as to enable our battery to cross."[24] The result was that many batteries became separated from their brigades almost from the beginning.

After the initial shock, the Federals fought stubbornly and the Rebel advance slowed. In the confusion, units became tangled and, in some cases, wandered aimlessly about. Casualties mounted in the thick underbrush. Cleburne's brigade advanced without artillery support and was pulverized by Sherman's batteries.

The only significant concentration of artillery during the

morning attack came about 7:30. Major Shoup's battalion of three four-gun Arkansas batteries, Bankhead's Tennessee Battery, and the Louisiana Washington Artillery, totaling twenty-four guns, deployed on a crest near Shiloh Branch to the west of the Pittsburg-Corinth Road and began lobbing shells into the Federal camps. These pieces were later to attempt to knock out Samuel Barrett's Battery B, 1st Illinois Light Artillery, at Shiloh Church. Tactically, the situation was ideal, but the inexperienced gunners fired too high and the effect was minimal.[25]

As Prentiss's shattered division streamed northward, General Stephen A. Hulbert's division attempted to patch the line in a peach orchard west of the Hamburg-Savannah Road. Even before his troops established position, Rebel artillery opened fire. One of these batteries was a Florida outfit commanded by Captain Felix Robertson. A Texan by birth, he was destined to become a significant and controversial figure in the western long arm. This was his first time in combat, but he was to leave his mark. His gunners trained their four Leeds & Company 12-pounder Napoleons on the forming Union line. An early round wounded one of Hulbert's brigadier generals. Another shell struck a caisson in the 13th Ohio Battery and caused a huge explosion. The panic-stricken Yankee gunners abandoned all six guns without firing a shot. Hulbert was so enraged that he had the battery disbanded and the commanding officer, Captain John Myers, dismissed from the service. Thus, in a single shot, one artilleryman's career began and another's ended.[26]

Several Confederate batteries suffered severely during the morning attack. The problem was essentially the same in each case. In a defensive posture, Civil War artillery was still a potent force, but the advent of the rifle musket profoundly altered its offensive use. The rifle musket was deadly accurate up to 400 yards. No longer could gun crews hope to maneuver close to enemy lines and make gaping holes with blasts of canister. The crews that tried it would pay dearly.[27]

Several Rebel batteries attempted Napoleonic tactics during the morning assault and the results were predictable. At 9:00 Captain Marshall Polk's Tennessee Battery unlimbered in Rhea Field, to the east of the main Corinth Road. A gun crew was ordered to move close to the enemy lines and blast away. It moved forward, but had barely positioned itself before several men were killed or wounded and all the horses disabled; the gun had to be abandoned. Captain Polk's infantry support, Bushrod Johnson's brigade, suddenly fell back in confusion, which left the entire battery exposed to deadly rifle and artillery fire. "At this time it was reported to me that Captain Polk had his leg broken, more than half his battery was disabled, and but one gun was being discharged," observed a colonel. The battery was wrecked. Lost were 24 of 102 men, 30 of 81 horses, 2 guns, and all 6 caissons. Young Polk, who only a few years earlier had been a student in a North Carolina college, was taken prisoner.[28]

About 11:30 Captain Isadore Girardey's Georgia Battery was operating on the Confederate right. Union defenders were screened by a thick undergrowth and offered stiff resistance. The Georgians maneuvered to within 100 yards and began blasting out tins of canister. Sharpshooters soon zeroed in, however, and within minutes seven men fell wounded. Girardey admitted that his losses would have been higher but for a timely assault by the 2d Texas.[29]

About noon, the divisions of Sherman and McClernand launched a counterattack against the Confederate left. Both sides took heavy losses in a stubborn fight that lasted forty-five minutes. Captain Robert Cobb's Kentucky Battery galloped past Shiloh Church and was ordered to deploy in Wolff Field. It was subjected to a withering fire and cut to pieces. "Cobb's battery wheeled into line and returned their fire [while] we hurried to take our position," noted a Kentucky infantryman. "Just then one of the enemy's shells killed two of Cobb's men and completely carried away both hands of another who wrung the bleeding stumps and said, 'My Lord, that stops my fighting.'" The battery was overrun, but was later rescued when the Federals were driven back. Before the bloodletting was over, thirty-seven artillerymen and seventy-eight horses had been killed or wounded. Cobb retired his wrecked battery with mules.[30]

At 12:30 the Louisiana Washington Artillery unlimbered across the road from where Cobb's men had just been mauled. Within minutes, snipers dropped eleven men and a number of horses. "Here for the first time we were placed face to face with them and for the first time found out the danger of sharpshooters, who were not more than 200 yards off behind the trees, aiming deliberately at us," lamented one of the New Orleans gunners. Soon the fight became "too hot for us," he confessed, and the battery was ordered back.[31]

The lackadaisical direction given the artillery was sorely felt as the battle progressed. Brigadier generals, preoccupied with infantry operations, left the artillery to fend for itself. By noon, the divisions of Sherman and McClernand had been swept away from the Shiloh Church vicinity and a second defensive line along the Purdy-Hamburg Road. Twenty-three cannon were captured in the process. The Confederates now had eleven batteries (about fifty-eight guns) employed on the left, not counting Polk's and Cobb's batteries, which were knocked out during the morning attack. In comparison, Sherman and McClernand had only sixteen guns remaining on the line. Yet, Rebel batteries continued to be employed in piecemeal fashion or, in some cases, sat idly by.

Several vicious battery duels occurred as the battle progressed. For fifteen minutes, Captain Thomas Stanford's Mississippi Battery engaged a Federal battery at a range of 600 yards. Shells came crashing in among the Mississippians and killed or wounded four men and several horses. "Before we could fire a gun a shell blew up one of our ammunition chests; another cut off the splinter bar of the third detachment; another almost cut our wheel rider (Bowen) in two. He was killed instantly. William Jones had his right arm shot off," wrote one of Stanford's men. The Union guns were finally silenced but, as a Mississippi cannoneer admitted, "it was a hot time for a little while." Captain Harper's Mississippi Battery engaged some Yankee guns a scant 400 yards away. So close were the shiny bronze pieces that they could "be distinctly seen glittering in the sun."[32]

Grant held a commanding edge in rifled guns but their added range was largely neutralized by the heavily wooded terrain, which limited visibility. Still, in a one-on-one duel at a range of more than 1,000 yards, a smoothbore battery was at a serious disadvantage with piercingly accurate rifled cannon. Over by Duncan Field, Captain Melancthon Smith's Mississippi Battery became engaged in a lopsided duel with Emil Munch's Minnesota Light Artillery of grooved guns. Before Smith's men could even unlimber, several horses were struck to the ground by shell fragments. Smith's men toughed it out for an hour before withdrawing. Lieutenant James C. Thrall's section of Hubbard's Arkansas Battery did not last nearly that long when it exchanged blows with a Parrott battery. After firing only three or four rounds, Thrall pulled his smoothbores back and admitted that "it was a little more than I felt disposed to contend with."[33]

By late morning, the focal point of the battle had shifted to the Confederate right center. Here, along an old sunken trail bordering Duncan Field, the divisions of Wallace and Hulbert, together with the remnants of Prentiss's shattered command, made a stand. The original Confederate plan of a sweeping right flank movement had by now been abandoned, and by mid-afternoon the bulk of Johnston's army had been thrown into the fight in the center.

For several hours, General Bragg, directing operations in that sector, butted his brigades in near-suicidal, frontal attacks against the Federal salient, dubbed the "Hornets' Nest." In just such a defensive posture, Civil War artillery performed at its peak efficiency. Curiously, Bragg himself had used his own battery in just such a manner at Buena Vista during the Mexican War and estimated he had inflicted nine-tenths of the total enemy casualties. The old artilleryman had learned little. The sight of Union artillery mowing down his infantry apparently failed to jog his memory.[34]

Bragg received urgent requests for artillery support, but all were unanswered. "I . . . sent Mr. Robert Pugh to the General after the first assault for artillery; but the request was not granted, and in place of it he brought me orders to advance again on the enemy," wrote Colonel R. L. Gibson. Time and lives would have been saved had Bragg immediately enfiladed the enemy's flanks with artillery fire. Instead, he concentrated on the old army tactic of overwhelming the enemy with the bayonet.[35]

By mid-afternoon, it had become evident to Brigadier General Daniel Ruggles, commanding a division in Bragg's corps, that the Hornets' Nest could not be overwhelmed by infantry alone. About 3:30 Ruggles summoned his staff officers and ordered them to "bring forward all of the field guns they could collect from the left toward the right as rapidly as possible." Stanford's Mississippi and Byrne's Kentucky batteries and a section of Ketchum's Alabama Battery were already in the vicinity and had, in piecemeal fashion, been lobbing shells into the Hornets' Nest. Within the next hour, aides succeeded in rounding up an additional seven batteries.[36]

Two separate concentrations apparently developed. On the left, a section of Ketchum's battery was already engaged along the main Corinth Road when other companies began assembling. Captain Smith Bankhead wrote: "As I [Bankhead's battery] went into action Captain Stanford formed on my right. I found the [Louisiana] Washington Artillery already in position on my left and firing rapidly. Captain Robertson's 12-pounder [Napoleon] battery formed on the right of Stanford, with Captain Rutledge on his right." Bankhead was aware of another group of batteries farther to the right but, he noted, "by whom commanded I am unable to state."[37]

The commander in that sector was Major Shoup, who for some

time had been massing guns in a nearby skirt of woods. Lieutenant James Thrall, leading a section of Hubbard's battery, wrote: "Captain Burns' [Byrne's] battery formed on my right, Captain Swett's [Mississippi] battery, and Captain Trigg's and Roberts' [Arkansas] batteries formed on my left." When all was in readiness, these batteries were advanced and deployed simultaneously.[38]

Not until close to 4:30 did Bankhead's and Shoup's artillery groups became consecutively engaged. Some fifty-three guns were assembled, mostly of the 6-pounder and 12-pounder howitzer type.[39] The range was 500 yards across an open field, ideal for the short-range howitzers. The results were astounding. The crash of massed artillery reverberated for miles, and smoke quickly filled the air. One Union officer thought the barrage sounded like "a mighty hurricane sweeping everything before it." A captain in the 2d Iowa wrote that the "shells and shot [that] passed over us terrifically at about the height of a man's head from the ground while sitting down . . . continued so long that it was a relief when the Rebels began to advance upon us." A Confederate officer gloated that "no one who observed the effects of that firing could but be agreeably surprised at its results."[40]

The Confederate artillery also suffered some losses. When a Yankee battery zeroed in on Robertson's position, one of his troops was literally blown apart by a Parrott shell. The situation became so critical that Robertson ordered a retreat, but so many horses were disabled that two guns had to be temporarily abandoned.[41]

The concentrated artillery fire proved to be too much. Within minutes, the Federal batteries began withdrawing, and Hulbert's troops began streaming toward the landing. At 5:30, by which time Wallace had been mortally wounded and his command virtually surrounded, Prentiss surrendered the remaining 2,200 troops. "The fire opened beautifully but almost immediately the blue coats . . . began to break to the rear, and we soon saw white flags," Shoup was to recall. "I remember a distinct sense of disappointment, feeling that if they had only stayed a little while we should have punished them handsomely."[42]

Ruggles's fifty-three guns had neutralized the Federal artillery and hastened, if not caused, the demise of the Hornets' Nest. Yet, the action was too late to alter significantly the outcome of the first day's battle. Five hours earlier, the same potential had existed, but the delay had taken its toll. Nearly an hour and a

half had been required to assemble all the cannon. This was
primarily because of the brigade-battery organization, which
scattered batteries throughout the army. Too much valuable
time was lost in massing the guns. Ruggles's barrage, though
effective in its own right, was not significant in the tactical
outcome of the battle.

The barrage soon became the subject of postbattle magnifica-
tion. Interestingly enough, the incident was not mentioned in
any of the After Action Reports nor in the letters and diaries of
four artillerymen whose batteries participated. It came to light
in Ruggles's amended report and several affidavits compiled at
his request nearly a year later. These reports, which glorified
him as the "controlling genius on that occasion," came at a
sagging time in his career. The overall significance of the event
may have taken on more importance in retrospect. After the
war, Major Shoup candidly wrote that at the time he did not
think "that this artillery fire had much to do with the enemy's
confusion." He also wrote: "By the way, I find in the *War Records*
that General Ruggles claims the credit of making this concentration of artillery. I remember that he was there at the time,
but I thought he was a spectator, and I was really under the
impression that I conceived and executed it myself."[43] In any
event, the surrender of the Hornets' Nest seemed to teach the
Confederates a lesson, and they began employing their artillery
en masse.

Afterward, Major Shoup moved his composite battery group of
some twenty-odd guns down the main road leading to Pittsburg
Landing. Only three-quarters of a mile from the river, he encountered General Breckinridge, who was forming two lines of
infantry for one final push. Federal flags could plainly be seen
500 yards down the road. Shoup ordered a barrage to "shake
them up." After replenishing their caissons from nearby stacks
of captured ammunition, the gunners began a furious cannonade. At 6:00, as the supply of shells dwindled, Shoup sent a
message to Breckinridge: "If you are going to charge, now is
your time." As the infantry moved past the row of cannon, a
courier suddenly galloped up. Beauregard, who had succeeded
the mortally wounded Johnston, had issued orders to break off
the engagement and retire to safety.[44]

The attack probably would not have succeeded. Throughout
the afternoon, Grant's chief of artillery, Colonel J. D. Webster,
had been massing guns just above the river landing. Some fifty

of them, including two batteries of siege cannon, stood poised along a one mile semicircular perimeter. Many of them were small-bore rifled guns, which were not highly effective in firing canister. Still, the barrier was formidable. About 5:30 Bragg ordered the remnants of James Chalmers's and John K. Jackson's brigades across a deep ravine with instructions to "drive them into the river." Encountering a murderous fire, the Confederates were forced to withdraw. Gage's battery supported the assault from a prominent ridge, but was severely hit by cannon fire and was forced to retire.[45]

At dusk, Captain Thomas Stanford attempted a daring feat. Cautiously, he moved his Mississippi battery down a hill near the river and prepared to shell the Federal gunboats anchored in the Tennessee River. Even though the naval fire proved more demoralizing than deadly, it was more than he was willing to take on. Because it was now dusk, he feared the sailors would spot the flash of his guns and obtain the range. The battery withdrew quietly.[46]

A cold rain on the night of April 6 added to the misery of both armies. Hundreds of Southern soldiers spent the night skulking in the rear, seeking the comforts of Yankee tents or plundering the camps. Some of the batteries were pulled far back into rear positions. Although fatigued, largely unorganized, and thoroughly soaked, the Southerners were confident they would finish Grant off the next day. But, even then, the decisive factor of the battle was taking place. During the night, massive Union reinforcements arrived: Buell's Army of the Ohio, 20,000 strong, and Wallace's belated division from Crump's Landing.[47] Preparations were being made in enemy headquarters for a general counterattack. At dawn, the tables would turn.

•

At daylight on April 7, Colonel Preston Pond discovered too late that the main Confederate line on the left had been pulled back the previous night. His brigade was thus exposed and alone as Lew Wallace's fresh division rolled forward. Faced with a perilous situation, Pond withdrew his troops and left Bill Ketchum's Alabama Battery to cover the retreat. This mission was performed so ably that one Federal officer commented that "the enemy's battery was exceedingly well served." Although it sustained losses in both men and horses and needed to abandon one gun that became stuck in the mud, the later rumor that

"Capt. Ketchum is killed, and all his men either killed or captured" proved to be false. After being engaged in several positions, the battery withdrew intact. Pond later credited it with
saving the brigade.[48] This scene was to be repeated many times
during the day as the gray artillery plugged a crumbling dike.
The near-sacrificial rearguard actions of some batteries may
well have prevented a general retreat from degenerating into a
rout.

At 11:00 the Louisiana Washington Artillery, posted on the
edge of a cotton field on the Purdy-Hamburg Road, lost its infantry support and was suddenly confronted by several Federal
regiments. The New Orleans gunners, supported by two pieces
of McClung's Tennessee Battery, braced for the assault. They
"poured some sixty rounds into the enemy," but this did not stop
the blue mass. Three of the six guns were overrun, and vicious
hand-to-hand fighting ensued.[49]

One of the artillerymen described the scene:

> We were left entirely unprotected. The Crescent reg-
> iment was called up for our relief, to meet the advancing
> enemy now not more than a hundred yards off, when we
> were ordered to get out of the way, but the order was too
> late by five minutes. The balls were falling around us
> like hail, and before we could get ready three horses at
> my piece and the same number at two others were
> killed, our sergeant was killed and Lieut. Slocomb
> wounded, and we had to run leaving these three pieces
> on the field. The enemy came up to and even passed
> them almost routing the Crescent regiment, which
> receiving heavy reinforcements rallied and drove the
> enemy back.[50]

The battery had been saved from annihilation, but it sustained severe damage. As Captain Hodgson gazed over the
wreckage, he saw strewn over the ground the bodies of eight
dead and wounded cannoneers and the carcasses of twenty
horses. For want of animals, he was forced to abandon three
caissons, a wagon, and a traveling forge.[51]

To the west on the eastern Corinth Road, Captain William
Harper's Mississippi Battery barely escaped. It was already low
on manpower. On the morning of the 6th, it mustered only seventy effectives. That number was now further reduced by eight
casualties, including the captain, and a hospital detail of four.
The four gun crews were consequently down to six men apiece

rather than the prescribed eight. When the Federals were only fifty yards away, they let loose a volley that dropped five horses. One cannon had to be abandoned, but miraculously no casualties were suffered.[52]

Over by Duncan Field, Captain Edward Byrne's Kentucky Battery also had its hands full. Since late morning, it had been dueling with a Federal battery. Because the guns were posted on a ridge, at each recoil they went reeling down the slope. They then needed to be rolled back into position and resighted. By early afternoon, the men were exhausted and fully a third of them were out of action. Only by receiving infantry reinforcements from Trabue's brigade was the battery able to remain in service.[53]

Matters grew steadily worse. The Southerners were simply caught off guard by the sheer weight of the Union onslaught. In the early afternoon, the Confederate line by Sherman's Review Field began to crumble under the pressure. The hasty retreat left Stanford's battery, unlimbered on the Purdy Road, virtually alone to contest the advance. The gunners nervously stood by their pieces until the charging Federals were barely 300 yards away and then unleashed volcanic volleys of canister. "Large gaps were made by every gun at each discharge," Stanford noted. "Three regimental flags being in full view, I gave the order to point at them, and soon had the satisfaction of seeing two of them to the ground, both being raised again. One was again cut down."[54]

One of Stanford's men described the panic. "The enemy came upon us like an avalanche," declared John Magee. "We stood firm, pouring the canister into them until they got within 75 yards and then the captain gave the order to limber up. Most of the horses were killed, and those living were so badly tangled it was impossible to get them in order under the heavy fire of minié balls coming in around us." The cost was high. Stanford lost twenty men, four guns, and all six caissons. The battery was virtually destroyed, but precious time had been bought for the infantry to form a second line.[55]

Unable to stop the relentless Union drive, Beauregard at 2:30 ordered a general retreat. About 2,000 infantry and fifteen cannon were assembled and posted on an elevated ridge just south of Shiloh Church. The army then began an orderly retreat. Frantic efforts were made to carry away as many of the captured guns as possible, a task complicated by the shortage of animals. Captain Melancthon Smith left behind three of his own cannon in lieu of three better Union James rifles.[56]

The rear of Beauregard's army passed the row of cannon at 4:00. Major Shoup suddenly realized that the artillery was now totally alone on the field. "I looked to the rear and there was not an infantryman or calvaryman in sight," he wrote. Prolonges, ropes with hooks attached between the gun carriage trails and the limbers, were rigged so that the guns might be withdrawn while firing. They were alternately pulled back in this fashion. Shoup later recalled that "we were very much absorbed in a movement we never before had had a chance to practice on the field."[57]

While the batteries were being slowly retired, Shoup rode on ahead and began searching for the column. A harrowing moment occurred when he came to a fork in the road but found no guide to give directions. He galloped down the most promising road, but, after riding some distance, found no infantry at all. A sudden panic came over him. "There I was, abandoned by the army and at the mercy of the enemy, with all those guns!" he wrote. He quickly doubled back, took the other road, and eventually found the column. His artillery was saved.[58]

Bad roads, which by now were quagmires of mud, and the shortage of artillery horses nearly led to disaster on the retreat. At 7:30 on the morning of April 8, Bragg informed Beauregard: "Our artillery is being left all along the roads by its officers; indeed I find but few officers with their men." By 2:00 the situation had further deteriorated. At that time, Bragg informed Beauregard: "The roads are horrible and unless we can mend them it is impossible for the artillery to get in." By that time, extreme measures were being taken, including the dismounting of 200 cavalry troopers and using their mounts to haul the guns. By late afternoon, some of those belonging to Breckinridge were still at Mickey's farmhouse because not enough horses were available to haul them. Byrne's battery did not reach Corinth until the 10th. Had the Federal pursuit been strong, Beauregard would undoubtedly have lost much of his artillery. The Confederate retreat, however, was effected with a minimum of interference.[59]

The fierceness of the fighting at Shiloh was reflected in the casualties. Beauregard lost a fourth of his army. For all practical purposes, Cobb's, Stanford's, and Polk's batteries were wiped out. Several others suffered nearly as much. The Louisiana Washington Artillery lost 26 men and 30 horses, Bankhead 20 men and 37 horses, Robertson 19 men and 23 horses, and Smith 14 men and 23 horses. Overall artillery casualties totaled about 300, or 15 percent.[60]

The Confederates captured some thirty-three guns during the April 6 assault. Many of these were recaptured by the enemy on the 7th, however, and the Confederates could not haul away some guns for want of horses. They also lost a number of their own on the second day. Thus, the net gain total was considerably altered. The Southerners came out probably four guns ahead, if that many. But, to their advantage, many inferior Southern-made cannon were exchanged on the field for superior Northern guns. In no other battles of the Civil War did so many pieces exchange hands. A peculiar situation thus existed at the battle's conclusion, by which time many Confederate batteries were armed with Yankee guns and vice versa.[61]

Shiloh taught two lessons regarding the artillery—one tactical and the other organizational. The axiom that Civil War artillery was essentially defensive in nature was reaffirmed. Old tactical theory regarded the artillery as both an offensive and defensive arm, but battles such as Shiloh proved that warfare was undergoing a transition.[62] Artillery used on the tactical offensive was now limited in its effectiveness. Ruggles's barrage notwithstanding, the real hero of the first day's battle was the blue artillery. The determined stands made by the batteries at Shiloh Church, the Hornets' Nest, and Grant's last line likely prevented the Union army from being overrun.

Artillery on the offensive could only be used effectively if it was concentrated. Even then, the technology associated with such aspects as explosives and fuzing placed limits on its potential. After wasting their artillery in unorganized, piecemeal attacks in the morning, the Confederates finally did mass their batteries in an effort to crush the Hornets' Nest. Ruggles's barrage was the largest concentrated use of field artillery on the North American continent up to that time.[63] After that, the Rebels seemed to have learned their lesson and began employing their artillery in large ad hoc battery groups. In future battles, however, this principle was not to be employed.

Shiloh demonstrated the inability of the brigade-battery organization to deliver massed fire rapidly. As long as batteries were assigned to brigades and scattered throughout the army, their full potential could never be realized. Unfortunately, the Confederates did not seem to grasp the relationship between effective organization and the tactical massing of guns. It was a lesson not really learned until the end of the war—like linear tactics versus rifle muskets. After Shiloh, the antiquated brigade-battery structure was retained.

Chapter 4

"Our Artillery Told Fearfully on the Enemy"

Beauregard's shattered army fell back to Corinth, where it began to recuperate and prepare for the expected advance of the combined Union force, now under the command of General Henry Halleck, that totaled 125,000 troops. Even with the addition of Earl Van Dorn's Army of the West, the Confederates still numbered barely 50,000. The corps of Polk, Hardee, and Bragg were placed in a three-mile semicircle north of Corinth; Van Dorn was assigned to the east flank; and Breckinridge's Corps was held in reserve.[1]

While preparations were underway for yet another fight, the Southern commander pleaded for reinforcements. Additional regiments were sent from east Tennessee as well as the South Carolina and Georgia coasts. Beauregard maintained the essential structure of his army, but shifted around a number of regiments. The makeup of the artillery changed considerably. Polk's Tennessee Battery was disbanded, twenty-three of the men transferring to Carnes's battery, and Rutledge's company merged with McClung's. The Vaiden Light Artillery was assigned to man siege cannon. Gage's Alabama Battery was transferred back to Mobile and the Pettus Flying Artillery to Vicksburg. Several accessions offset these losses. Lumsden's and Waters's Alabama batteries were sent up from Mobile. In addition, the Orleans Guard Artillery, Eldridge's, Baxter's, and Baker's Tennessee batteries, and Watson's Louisiana Battery—all of which had been on detached duty at various outposts—arrived and were given assignments. On May 26, Beauregard's army included twenty-three batteries.[2]

Several of them used the brief respite to reorganize and elect new officers. In some, such as Swett's Mississippi Battery, the men affirmed their leadership. This expression of confidence was lacking in the Louisiana Washington Artillery. A private stated that the men were disgusted with the performance of Captain Irving W. Hodgson and that "very few in the company would be willing to go into another engagement without [Lieutenant Charles] Slocomb." Hodgson soon resigned on account of illness, and Slocomb was quickly promoted to captain.[3]

At least one election turned out to be rigged. In Stanford's battery, Sergeant W. H. Brown was elected by a three-fourths vote to fill a vacancy for second lieutenant. But, because of bad blood between Brown and Captain Thomas Stanford, the officers contrived the vote so that another man was commissioned. The truth later came out (one lieutenant resigned in disgust over the sham), but the results were never challenged.[4]

Beauregard revamped his organizational guidelines for the artillery. All six-gun batteries were reduced to four. Any excess lieutenants were to serve in other batteries or with siege artillery until the next battle, when they would replace casualties. Uniformity of calibers was established within each battery—either four rifles or four smoothbores. The standard of six horses per gun was maintained, and, in case of deficiencies, cavalry troopers were to be dismounted and their horses turned over to the artillery.[5]

By the end of May, the Confederates had determined that they could not hold Corinth. The army began to slip out of town quietly on the 30th. By June 9 it held a new line at Tupelo, fifty-two miles to the south. Shortly thereafter, Beauregard was removed from command by the Richmond government and replaced by General Braxton Bragg.

During July, Buell's Army of the Ohio plodded slowly along the Memphis & Charleston Railroad toward Chattanooga. Hampered by cavalry raids, this advance soon bogged down. The initiative now shifted to the Confederates. Bragg decided to move his army to Chattanooga and join Kirby Smith's Army of East Tennessee. The combined force would then move to defeat Buell in middle Tennessee and invade Kentucky. Van Dorn's army and Breckinridge's division, buttressed by a brigade of Louisiana troops and a number of newly organized Mississippi and Alabama regiments and some Fort Donelson exchanges, would remain in Mississippi to confront Grant, now commanding in that sector.

The logistical complexities involved in such a move were enormous. An immense amount of artillery ordnance was in storage at the Grenada depot. On hand were thirty-eight field pieces, including twenty-three 6-pounders and three 12-pounder howitzers, five siege guns, fifty-four limbers, eleven extra gun carriages, twenty-five caissons, and three traveling forges.

Many of the cannon were listed as "old style" iron pieces, and a number of the caissons were damaged. Still, all needed to be removed. Bragg's Prussian-born army chief of ordnance, Colonel Hypolite Oladowski, issued two hundred rounds to each field piece before leaving Tupelo, and fifty rounds per gun were forwarded to the new depot at Dalton, Georgia, outside Chattanooga. Ordnance authorities in Richmond were advised by wire that "some gun carriages, implements and harness it will be necessary in a very few months to replace by new."[6]

On July 23, Bragg's army left Tupelo en route for Chattanooga. The infantry was loaded on rail cars and moved south to Mobile, then east to Atlanta and north to Chattanooga. The artillery was ordered to follow the more direct dirt roads "via Aberdeen, Columbus, Miss., Tuscaloosa, through Will's Valley to Gadsden, Ala., and Rome, Ga. The batteries may be sent by rail from Randolph via Talladega, the horses by the ordinary roads, meeting the batteries at the terminus of the railroad."[7]

The journey was fraught with difficulties almost from the beginning. On the second day out, the horses in Captain Carnes's battery balked at crossing a creek and held up the entire battalion. By July 25 his exhausted animals were rapidly giving out. He consequently took his cannon and caissons to Artesia and loaded them on railroad flatcars to go by way of Mobile.[8]

Other problems were encountered, including a number of poor bridges. A horse and driver in Stanford's battery fell completely through a rotten trestle. Several advance work parties were sent out to repair roads and bridges. At Wilsonville, Alabama, the guns and caissons were loaded on railroad cars to cross the Coosa River. They were then unloaded and the teams hitched up again to continue the journey.[9]

Discipline could have been better. In Aberdeen, Private John Magee, of Stanford's battery, wrote that "there was some lewd women in town—some of the boys were about them all night." In another town, he noted that "many of them [officers] got drunk and behaved very badly," and in Talladega several artillerymen "got tight and wanted to fight." An altercation between a soldier in the Washington Artillery and one in the Jefferson Artillery led to the latter's death.[10]

For the most part, however, the trip was orderly and apparently even enjoyable. All along the route, "many pretty girls [were] eager to see the cannon." At Aberdeen, a "rich and varied banquet set by the citizens awaited the column," wrote a Tennessee soldier. At Blue Mountain, Alabama, "the boys enjoyed themselves hugely," Magee noted, though the women were "not very good looking." At a girl's school, the student body was entertained by "firing a blank shot from Smith's battery." Captain J. W. Eldridge made a speech, and the officers danced with the ladies to the tune of a fiddle.[11]

The column usually made anywhere from fifteen to thirty miles a day. Rome, Georgia, was not reached until August 13–15. There, the guns, carriages, and cannoneers were loaded on rail cars for the final leg into Chattanooga, while the horses and drivers continued overland. Each train carried only two batteries because the ordnance was so heavy. Twenty-four days were required for the entire column to complete the 432-mile trip.

Once in Chattanooga, the men went into camp for a brief rest. On August 16, Magee wrote: "In camp—artificer fixing up gun carriages—some washed clothes. Got our bread baked by a lady—about 11 o'clock the horses came in. We then hitched up and changed our camp only a few hundred yards. Boys all well and in good spirits."[12]

Additional artillery had joined along the way. Semple's Alabama Battery from Tuscaloosa met the column at Blue Mountain. Magee thought that these soldiers were "gay boys—some of them right good musicians. Played several tunes on a fiddle and banjo." Captain Henry Semple was frustrated by the laxness, however. "You have no idea of the trouble and vexations of a march when 110 horses have to be watched and 128 men who become as children as soon as they get in the army," he wrote his wife.[13]

Another new outfit, which joined the command at Chattanooga, was Captain Joseph E. Palmer's Georgia Battery. Along with the other three companies of the newly organized 14th Georgia Artillery Battalion, this battery had been assigned to a camp of instruction at Calhoun, Georgia. Several officers were sent down from Chattanooga to select the best-drilled unit to accompany Bragg's army. "Boots and Saddles" was sounded and all four companies were ordered out and put through various maneuvers, at the end of which Palmer's crack group was chosen.[14]

Before leaving Chattanooga, Bragg reorganized his army into two wings under Hardee and Polk. Each wing, or corps, consisted of two divisions. The general made no changes in the artillery structure and retained the brigade-battery organization. His former corps artillery chief, Major James H. Hallonquist, was promoted to lieutenant colonel and appointed as army chief of artillery.[15]

While Bragg waited for his artillery to move up, Kirby Smith's army, reinforced with two of Bragg's brigades, moved into Kentucky. On August 30 it captured the Federal garrison at Richmond and then moved on to Lexington, where it remained in control of central Kentucky throughout September.[16]

Because Smith was determined to act independently, Bragg was forced to alter his original plan. He would now bypass the Northerners in middle Tennessee and keep his army between Buell's and Smith's. Once in Kentucky, the two Confederate armies would unite. On August 28, Bragg's troops crossed the Tennessee River and began the march north. The journey through the rugged valley of the Tennessee was an arduous one for the artillery. Crossing the southern slope of Walden's Ridge proved to be a major project. Ten horses were attached to each gun, and infantry was detached all along the road to help tow them up the steep grade.[17]

By September 13, Bragg's divisions were at Glasgow, Kentucky. Buell's army, which moved to intercept, was at Bowling Green. Capturing a brigade-size force at Munfordville on the 17th, Bragg swerved eastward to link up with Smith. In early October, Buell launched a counteroffensive from Louisville that caught the Confederates badly scattered. Three Union corps concentrated at Perryville against Hardee's corps and Cheatham's division of Polk's corps. Bragg thus had 16,000 troops confronting Buell's 58,000. Unaware of the overwhelming force in their front, the Southerners took up a "defensive-offensive" position on the steep eastern ridge of Chaplin's Creek, a stream west of Perryville.

•

Throughout the morning of October 8, St. John Liddell's advanced brigade, supported by Swett's Mississippi Battery, was driven back by a heavy force of Federals west of Perryville. Shifts were made in the Confederate line so that Cheatham's division held the right, Buckner's the center, and Anderson's the left. Bragg arrived on the field and decided to attack the Federal left. Two of Anderson's brigades and one of Buckner's were moved to fill the gap between Buckner and Cheatham.[18]

About noon, General Sam Wood, whose brigade formed the

right of Hardee's corps, spotted Federal artillery in the woods across Doctor's Creek. He sent an urgent message to Polk to hurry up some guns. Carnes's Tennessee Battery happened to be nearby because one of its teams had become tangled in a farm gatepost. It was ordered to occupy the gap between the lines of Cheatham and Hardee. The twenty-two-year-old Carnes wheeled his Memphis battery into position on the edge of some heavy timber, which was fronted by an open valley. Peering through his field glasses, he quickly spotted a Federal battery. At 12:30 the order to commence firing was given. "Our attack brought a fearful response from across those fields, for within a few minutes we were under the fire of four six-gun batteries at different points opposite," Carnes stated. "All seemed to be using rifled guns, as, though the distance was extreme for us, none of their shots fell short, but fortunately for us, most of them went high overhead, cutting off tree limbs that fell on us."[19]

Darden's Jefferson (Mississippi) Flying Artillery now entered the fight, and for the next hour a fierce duel raged. Stanford's Mississippi Battery of rifled guns soon replaced Carnes's smoothbores. Federal artillery zeroed in on it before the guns could even be unlimbered. "The Yankees had perfect range on us," declared one of the men. "Had one of our ammunition chests to explode. Pitt McCall and Charles Boycroft killed and several wounded before we could fire a gun."[20]

At 1:30 the duel ceased. Half an hour later, Cheatham's division rose onto the steep bluffs across the creek and attacked the raw troops of James Jackson's division. Daniel Donelson's and George Maney's brigades were smashed by Union artillery fire. It seemed as though the Confederate attack would fall apart. Cheatham's troops pushed onward, however, overran an advanced Federal battery, and routed William Terrill's brigade. The Union line was driven back two miles when General Alexander McCook, commanding the Federal left, sent in an additional brigade, which checked Cheatham's advance.[21]

Major Melancthon Smith, heading Cheatham's artillery, moved Turner's Mississippi Battery from the river bottom at Walker's Bend to the woods on top of the bluff. The artillerymen galloped over a narrow farm trail, which they were forced to stop and repair at places. Once on the bluff, Cheatham ordered the battery to the extreme right to a hill overlooking the enemy. The guns were positioned and opened with an enfilading fire with canister and spherical case at a range of 250–300 yards. A young cannoneer heard a voice shout: "Let me have my hand at them."

Looking up, he saw General Cheatham. The youth stood aside while the division commander "fired several rounds, pointing the gun and directing the fire apparently with as much pleasure as a boy shooting at rabbits."[22]

Hardee, meanwhile, had concentrated his attack against the Federal center, where the enemy line crossed the Mackville Pike. The Southerners were obliged to advance in full view of Federal artillery on the ridge west of the creek. Tom Jones's brigade was shattered and forced back. As that of Bushrod Johnson reached Doctor's Creek, the scene became one of total confusion because of the oblique wheel it was ordered to make. The Washington Artillery accidentally fired into two of Johnson's Tennessee regiments. Compounding the error, Southern infantry fifteen minutes later fired on the New Orleans battery![23]

After severe fighting, Buckner's division pushed the Federals back past the Henry Bottom house and up a slope to a second defensive line. There, the Union artillery attempted to stem the tide. Pat Cleburne's brigade, supporting Wood's regiments, smashed McCook's right, however, and sent the Yankees streaming back to open ground astride the Mackville Pike, near the intersection of the Benton Road.

Now the Confederates brought up their own artillery from the creek bottom to batter the Union line. At 3:30 the Washington Artillery, Darden's Mississippi, and Calvert's Arkansas batteries, twelve guns in all, were assembled above the Bottom house and opened fire. The 1st Michigan and 5th Indiana batteries responded, and a forty-five-minute duel ensued. "Balls and shells continued to fall thick and fast from the enemies' guns," explained Bushrod Johnson, "while our batteries replied with great rapidity until after dark." Union General Lovell Rosseau wrote that "the air seemed full of them [shells]" and that he saw "as many as four or five burst at a time."[24]

Massed Federal infantry and artillery clung to the vital junction of the Dicksville-Springfield and Perryville-Mackville roads. The brigades of Cleburne and Wood were stopped as Union reinforcements began to arrive near the Springfield Pike. Night soon ended the fighting.[25]

Artillery casualties at Perryville were extremely light, especially in proportion to those of the infantry. Cheatham's division, for example, suffered a staggering 1,451 casualties. Yet, in the three batteries attached to those brigades, the number was only 11. Apparently the heaviest artillery loss came when a detachment of 12 men and two caissons from the Washington Artillery, sent to the rear for ammunition and water, stumbled onto a Federal regiment on the Danville–Mackville Road and was captured.[26]

That night, Major Smith ordered Lieutenant William Turner to send his teams and limbers to the field to haul away the abandoned enemy cannon. The lieutenant was able to remove five prized 12-pounder Napoleon guns (two of which he kept for his battery), one 12-pounder howitzer, one Parrott rifle, two limbers, and two caissons. Two disabled caissons were left on the field.[27]

For the most part, the Confederate artillery received high marks for its performance at Perryville. General Joseph Wheeler, commanding the cavalry, observed: "Our artillery, handled with great skill, told fearfully on the enemy, who sought, when practicable, to take shelter behind stone walls and fences. Fortunately we were enabled many of their temporary shelters with a well directed fire from our batteries."[28] The late afternoon artillery concentration at the Bottom house played a significant role in driving back McCook's corps. "Seldom if ever were the guns of Bragg better served," observed one historian.[29] Once again, as at Shiloh, the key to effectiveness had been the massing of brigade batteries.

●

Early on the morning of October 9, Bragg, now thoroughly alerted to his precarious situation, ordered a retreat. The next day, he made a belated union with Kirby Smith's army at Harrodsburg. Bragg soon gave up any plans of making a stand anywhere in Kentucky and ordered a retreat through Cumberland Gap to Tennessee. The artillery was plagued with problems all along the way. Smith's battery, armed with two captured 12-pounder Napoleon guns, now lacked sufficient teams to haul its own 6-pounder section. The latter pieces were consequently dumped in an old well. Lumsden's battery was likewise obliged to bury several guns, in an apple orchard near Dick's Creek. At Bryantsville, the only forage wagon in Semple's battery broke down and caused the 125 animals in that company to go forty hours without corn.[30]

Further complicating matters, Captain J. H. Calvert, commanding an Arkansas battery, was up to his old habits. He was drunk on October 9 during the march from Harrodsburg to

Bryantsville. While in a stupor on the 15th, he struck one of his sergeants with a sword. On the 17th, Captain Semple reported that his Alabama battery had been ordered to march in the rear of Darden's battery. Calvert replied that "he knew his place and intended to have it and that he did not give a damn about the order." When Semple said he would report the matter to his superior, Calvert replied that "he intended to go on after Darden and might refer it to whom he pleased." Calvert then began swearing and forced his teams to drive Semple's men off the road. Formal charges were placed, and the Arkansas captain was later cashiered from the army.[31]

By November the army was once again in Tennessee. If the artillery had not significantly decreased in numbers during the campaign, it certainly had not increased. Although Kirby Smith organized one new battery of Kentucky recruits, Bragg's artillery had done little or no recruiting. Indeed, the one artillery company that might have attracted prospects, Cobb's Kentucky Battery, was with Breckinridge's division in Mississippi.

Chapter 5

"To Sacrifice One Arm for the Safety of Another"

Even as his retreating army plodded through Cumberland Gap, Bragg was envisioning an offensive in middle Tennessee. Already General John C. Breckinridge's division, transferred from Mississippi, and N. B. Forrest's partisan cavalry brigade were posted at Murfreesboro. Bragg sold the idea to the Richmond government when he was summoned there in late October. Soon his four divisions were boarding cars at Chattanooga for the Murfreesboro front. Several weeks later, Kirby Smith and two divisions from his Army of East Tennessee, also left Knoxville for the rich valleys of middle Tennessee.[1]

As usual, the artillery was not afforded the luxury of a train ride. Because of the overtaxed transportation system, it was required to move overland. A blanket of snow covered the ground as the caravan pulled out of Knoxville. The route was via Kingston to Washington, over Walden's Ridge to Dunlap, south to Jasper, over Cumberland Mountain, and across to Tullahoma. It was a grueling 185-mile journey, much of it over rugged mountain terrain, that required fifteen travel days.[2]

The men suffered terribly. "We have the usual troubles of soldier life, and in addition have had a march of fourteen miles through a driving sleet and snow," complained the captain of an Alabama battery. "The snow remains after four days still, in shady places, and the weather, though milder today, has been very severe. Tents frozen in the morning so stiff as to stand without poles or ropes. I have lost two men by death since the campaign commenced, both of whom died from exposure and insufficient medical arrangements and want of tents in our first snow at Knoxville."[3]

Once again, Bragg was faced with a reorganization. On November 22 he restructured his infantry into three corps under Hardee, Polk, and Smith. The cavalry was also revamped and placed under Joseph Wheeler. Bragg rechristened the force

as the "Army of Tennessee," a name it would retain for the war's
duration. Its strength was about 47,000, including some twenty-eight batteries of artillery.

The new structure soon disintegrated. On December 12, Patton Anderson's division was broken up and the troops dispersed between Hardee and Polk. Three days later, Carter Stevenson's division was ordered to reinforce General John C. Pemberton's army in Mississippi. The new organization gave Polk the divisions of Jones Withers and Frank Cheatham, and Hardee was assigned those of John Breckinridge, Pat Cleburne, and J. P. McCown. Kirby Smith returned to east Tennessee.[4]

McCown's division was new to the Army of Tennessee. Two of his batteries, Humphreys's Arkansas and Douglas's Texas, had served in Earl Van Dorn's old Army of the West and fought at Pea Ridge. The Texas battery was actually a militia outfit that dated back to 1859 and had been organized as the "Dallas Light Artillery." Its original thirty-five members were so prominent that its function was as much social as military. The state of Texas presented the battery two 12-pounder howitzers, and the captain, John J. Good, drilled the men from a manual. McCown's other battery, Captain W. A. McTyre's Eufaula Light Artillery, had been organized in late February 1862. It had been in active service only seven months and had never engaged in more than minor skirmishes.[5]

The hastiness with which the Murfreesboro campaign had been undertaken soon became evident. The army was simply in no condition for a second offensive. Its commander seemed to ignore several key problems. The organization had been hastily effected without much imagination and forethought. According to one modern author, the infantry suffered from "complete disorganization" and "serious problems remained" with the cavalry.[6] Bragg also continued his traditionalist view of the artillery, that is, as merely an extension of the infantry. A superior organization at this time would have partially offset the Southerners' inferiority in quality and quantity of guns. This did not occur. The old brigade-battery structure was retained.

The army was also subjected to a severe manpower crunch. Throughout October and November, its ranks were thinned by desertions and sickness. Bragg lamented that some of his regiments were down to 100 men. The artillery suffered similarly. In late December, Cheatham's four batteries mustered only 295 men present for duty. A number of companies would fight the upcoming battle with less than 75 effectives. Major Rice Graves,

Breckinridge's artillery chief, wrote that "the companies are not so thoroughly and efficiently drilled as could be wished, from the fact that they are very short of men, the drivers and cannoneers frequently having to take each others places."[7]

Problems were also encountered with the stock. On the surface the supply seemed adequate. In late November, Withers's batteries averaged seventy-one horses and twenty-three mules apiece. In Breckinridge's batteries, ten to twelve surplus horses per company were even available as replacements. The trouble was that many of the animals counted on paper were in an unserviceable condition. Disease and strenuous overuse, especially after the long overland trip from Knoxville, were taking an increasing toll. Captain Henry Semple reported that so many of his animals were run-down that his caissons were being drawn by two rather than three teams. After an inspection of Cobb's and Eldridge's batteries, most of their horses were condemned.[8]

Bragg's armament continued to be dominated by the two staples of the Confederate field artillery: the 6-pounder and 12-pounder howitzer. These weapons accounted for probably 85 percent of his cannon. A few 12-pounder Napoleons were also in use. Semple's and Robertson's batteries each had six Leeds & Company Napoleons; Smith's battery, two Yankee Napoleons that had been captured at Perryville. Bragg counted barely a dozen long-range rifled guns.[9]

Despite the problems that persisted at all levels, a business-as-usual atmosphere prevailed at Murfreesboro throughout December. "Mending a wheel, looking at ammunition, making about a half dozen written reports daily (thank God they can't read half of them) fills up the day and as we lack candles bedtime comes at dark," wrote Captain Semple.[10] Much of the time was spent in routine drill. The artillerymen in Breckinridge's division were kept on a demanding schedule. Gun crews rehearsed at their pieces two and a half hours daily. Drivers practiced harnessing and unharnessing an hour and a half and were then put through three hours of battery drill. Officers attended classes on tactics for two hours daily.[11]

At least one battery experienced difficulties during drills, a situation caused, according to a soldier, by an incompetent officer. Captain Thomas Stanford, commanding a Mississippi battery, became ill in late October and was granted a furlough. This left thirty-three-year-old Lieutenant Hugh McSwine temporarily in command. The men were not pleased. On December 1 a private complained: "Drilled on [the] field. McSwine in command. He cannot drill the company. Not fit for an officer, but we cannot help ourselves." Subsequent drills proved to be even worse.[12]

Bragg made few preparations for a possible advance by William Rosecrans, Buell's successor—much less an offensive by his own army. The troops settled in for the winter, and thoughts turned from the Yankees to Christmas. The men in Lumsden's battery eagerly unwrapped packages from home. There was "something for nearly everyone," noted one of the men.[13]

•

While the Confederates settled in for the winter, the Union army in Nashville prepared for battle. Rosecrans had learned that a division (Stevenson's) had been detached from Bragg's army and that Forrest's and Morgan's cavalry brigades were absent on raids. The Union commander decided to move against the weakened Southern army. On the rainy and fog-shrouded morning of December 26, the blue army snaked southeast toward Murfreesboro. Rosecrans's 47,000 officers and men were to engage Bragg's 38,000. The Yankee cavalry was clearly outclassed by that of the Confederates, but the Union artillery was powerful. Twenty-six batteries with about 244 guns (a 50:50 smoothbore-rifle ratio) accompanied Rosecrans's army. Bragg had twenty-four batteries, but, because most of them possessed only four guns, he counted only 106 cannon.[14]

The Army of Tennessee was spread over a forty-mile front when the Union advance began. Bragg now frantically attempted to pull his scattered divisions together to a position some three miles northwest of Murfreesboro. To accomplish this, Wheeler's cavalry would need to buy some time. At the first signs of an advance, a section of Captain J. H. Wiggins's Arkansas Battery of horse artillery was moved north of La Vergne and soon became engaged. So skillfully were the guns used that, according to one Union officer, the entire left wing of Rosecrans's army was "brought to a stand still." Before reaching Stewarts Creek, the Federal spearhead was halted no less than half a dozen times by Confederate roadblocks supported by Wiggins's guns. When the Federals halted and brought up their own artillery, the Southerners would quickly break off the engagement and fall back before becoming deeply committed. For the next two days, Wiggins's cannoneers were alternately engaged in sections in this manner, a tactic that proved to be quite effective.[15]

For several days, the armies skirmished and groped around to determine each other's position. By the afternoon of December 29, Bragg perceived that the main threat was to his right wing on the west bank of Stone's River. Wayne's Hill, a crucial eminence that commanded the river fords on Breckinridge's left and also flanked Withers's right on the west bank of the river, was occupied by several regiments of Roger Hanson's brigade and Cobb's Kentucky Battery. About 7:00 P.M. the enemy, in brigade strength, attempted to storm the hill. A heavy musket fire was delivered at short range. "Fortunately, the cannoneers were ordered to the down and thus escaped without injury, save one detachment which, not hearing the order, remained standing and were all either killed or wounded," Major Graves explained. Confederate infantry reinforcements were rushed forward and the battery was saved.[16]

By the 30th both armies had maneuvered into position in front of Murfreesboro and were using their artillery to "spot" the opposing line. This was basically a type of ineffective gunnery known to artillerymen as "shelling the woods." Occasionally, however, some sharp battery duels occurred. Cobb's guns opened on two enemy batteries across the river at ranges of 1,200 and 700 yards respectively. He was forced to retire his company beyond the crest of Wayne's Hill "to protect it from the fire of the enemy's pieces, of much longer range than mine." Light earthworks were thrown up, and that night Cobb was reinforced with a rifle section of the Washington Artillery and of Lumsden's Alabama Battery. Semple's battery of six Napoleon guns was strongly entrenched on a hill 500 yards to the left rear of Wayne's Hill to command the fords and enfilade Withers's right flank across the river.[17]

Robertson's Florida Battery, positioned on the west side of the river on the Truine Road west of the Smith house, encountered the heaviest action of the day. At 4:00 Robertson opened a cannonade on enemy skirmishers in his front. The 2d Minnesota and 8th Wisconsin batteries quickly responded. One of Robertson's caissons was struck, which caused an explosion. The 21st Illinois made a dash for the Rebel guns, but was repulsed with canister and the support fire of the 154th Tennessee. Fourteen Floridians were killed or wounded. Lieutenant W. A. McDuffie's Eufaula Light Artillery was brought up in support and succeeded in disabling a gun of the 8th Wisconsin Battery.[18]

By the night of the 30th, circumstances had arisen which convinced Bragg that the real threat was not to his right flank but to his left. He therefore devised a plan that called for Breckinridge's divisions to hold the high ground east of the river, while the rest of Hardee's corps (McCown's and Cleburne's divisions) massed to the left of Polk's corps (Withers's and Cheatham's divisions) west of the river. At daylight on the 31st, McCown was to attack, supported by Cleburne. As the Confederates advanced, they were to wheel to the right, which would cause the Federal right wing to jackknife into the angle between the Nashville Pike and Stone's River.[19]

Once again, the gray artillery faced an offensive battle over unfavorable terrain. Further, the role it was to play, other than to offer general support to the infantry, was never established. The only prebattle directive issued to the chiefs of artillery instructed them to "pay special attention to posting of batteries and supervise their work, seeing they do not carelessly waste ammunition."[20] It seems clear that Bragg simply did not feel that the artillery should have a distinctive role like the infantry and cavalry. Its function in the battle was an afterthought. For example, the Confederate attack was to be made by the left flank, yet a third of the artillery was posted on the right flank, east of Stone's River. By noon of December 31, many of these batteries would be scrambling to cross the river to support the assault.

At least the high command planned for one contingency. At Shiloh, numbers of guns had been captured by the Confederates during the morning attack. Some of them were not removed from the field until the Rebel retreat came the next day. By then, because of a shortage of animals, others had to be abandoned. To avoid a repetition of this, an officer from Carnes's battery was assigned a detachment of men and several teams of mules for the purpose of removing captured cannon and caissons to the rear at once to avoid recapture.[21]

•

A cold drizzle continued on the morning of December 31. At 6:00 Hardee's veterans smashed into the divisions of Richard Johnson and Jefferson C. Davis of Alexander McCook's corps. The Federals were caught unprepared. Many of them were eating breakfast, and artillery horses were in the rear being wa-

tered. Johnson's division was routed and eight guns captured.
The victorious Southerners swept uncontrollably past the
Franklin Pike. By 9:00 McCook had been forced back to a new
line along the Wilkinson Pike.[22]

Meanwhile, Hardee's artillery had been experiencing difficulties. His biographer has stated that "next to controlling Mc-
Cown, employing the artillery gave Hardee the most trouble
during the battle." He was forced to "spend a great deal of time
placing his batteries in position to knock out the enemy's batteries and to give supporting fire to the infantry."[23]

The rugged terrain, coupled with the rapid movement of the
infantry, made it extremely difficult for the batteries to maintain pace. As Douglas's Texas Battery rumbled forward, one of its
caissons struck a log and broke down. Several of the horses also
became entangled and ripped their harnesses. "Some time was
required in righting these things," noted Douglas. As the Southern infantry swept onward, Hardee's batteries began to stack up
along the Wilkinson Pike, unable to follow in the dense cedar
brake and limestone outcroppings.[24]

When Humphreys's Arkansas Battery galloped north toward
the Wilkinson Pike, it entered a gap created on McCown's right
flank. An estimated sixteen Union guns suddenly erupted at a
range of 500 yards. Shells burst around the Arkansas gunners
"tearing down the trees like the whirlwind and scattering them
like lightning." Two of Humphreys's guns were disabled and
eight men and five horses fell. The wrecked battery was quickly
retired to the rear.[25]

As if contending with the Union artillery were not enough,
sheer carelessness on the part of the Rebels created additional
havoc. The Eufaula Light Artillery had not been issued sufficient ammunition before the attack, which kept it out of service
until early afternoon. Two of Humphreys's guns were rendered
useless when it was discovered that their ammunition was too
large to fit in the bore. Two pieces in Swett's Mississippi Battery
were also placed out of commission, one when a friction primer
broke off in the vent and the other when a case shot became
jammed in the bore.[26]

A mistake was also made in not properly supporting John
Wharton's cavalry brigade with artillery. The Rebel troopers
had swung around and were creating havoc on the Federal right.
A wagon train of several hundred vehicles was spotted on the
Nashville Pike. Wharton placed his only artillery, Captain B. F.
White's Tennessee Battery, in position to support a cavalry

charge. At the same time, he sent urgent appeals for additional artillery. None was forthcoming. The troopers overran the wagon train and vigorously pursued the retreating Federals. In the meantime, some 300 enemy cavalry had maneuvered around to Wharton's rear and sighted White's now isolated battery. A quick charge was repulsed by the Tennessee artillerymen, but it was a close call. Not until late afternoon were any additional batteries dispatched to the far left.[27]

The attack was now taken up by Cheatham's and Withers's divisions of Polk's corps. Phil Sheridan's division put up stiff resistance and inflicted severe casualties on the advancing Southerners. Cheatham's brigades were ripped apart by massed artillery fire. Turner's Mississippi Battery advanced to a brick kiln west of the Harding house and opened with an effective fire, in which 200 rounds were expended in forty minutes. At best, however, Polk's artillery support was limited and uncoordinated. Scott's and Robertson's batteries were never even advanced and Carnes's and Barret's batteries were only minimally engaged. Waters's Alabama Battery supported the 10th and 19th South Carolina regiments, but "met a great deal of trouble from the great number of friction primers that were worthless."[28]

By 10 o'clock the Confederate drive had begun to lose momentum. The Federal line now bent back at a right angle at a four-acre eminence on both sides of the railroad north of the Nashville Pike known as the "Round Forest." Here Rosecrans concentrated five brigades and supported them heavily with artillery. Reminiscent of his performance at the Hornets' Nest, at Shiloh, Bragg now attempted to storm the position with near suicidal infantry assaults. Brigade after brigade was hurled back by massed infantry fire supported by more than fifty cannon. "The Confederates had no sooner moved into the open field from the cover of the river bank than they were received with a blast from the artillery," explained a Union officer. "Men plucked the cotton from the boles at their feet and stuffed it in their ears. Huge gaps were torn into the Confederate line at every discharge."[29]

As with the infantry, Bragg committed his artillery in piecemeal fashion. Stanford's battery was advanced to the Cowan house and immediately came under a withering fire. It was "the most terrible cannonading I ever witnessed," wrote a Mississippi gunner. Within minutes, four men and several horses were put out of action and a limber chest was blown to splinters. The battery was quickly pulled back. A section of Lumsden's battery unlimbered on a hill near the Cowan house and fired fifty rounds before withdrawing. Bragg later wrote that he ordered up "our heaviest batteries of artillery and rifled guns" to batter the Round Forrest but to no avail. In reality, nothing like a coordinated artillery effort was ever made. Indeed, when Carnes's Tennessee Battery began firing to cover the retreat of a shattered brigade, Bragg dispatched an aide to "report the name of the battery firing without orders."[30]

The scenario actually provided an excellent opportunity for the artillery. The vertex of the Union angle presented a compact target that was subject to a crossfire. One option was simply to commit simultaneously the guns of Polk's corps north of the Cowan house in a frontal fire similar to that of Ruggles's barrage at Shiloh. A more sophisticated option was to commit Polk's batteries en masse north of the Cowan house, which would form an obtuse angle, with Hardee's artillery running northwest to southeast. The Union position was also subject to an enfilade fire from Breckinridge's rifled guns across the river in the Wayne's Hill vicinity. Bragg neglected these opportunities and continued to misuse his artillery.

Failing to break the back of the Federal salient with either infantry or artillery, Bragg now called upon Breckinridge to send reinforcements from the east side of the river. Throughout the afternoon, these fresh brigades were wasted in repeated isolated assaults against the Round Forest. As Daniel Adams's and John Jackson's brigades were advanced, Breckinridge ordered an aide to "find some artillery." The Washington Artillery and Captain Edward Byrne's battery were rounded up, but groped around for orders after they arrived. Byrne was finally told to "take the best position he could find." After these brigades were repulsed, William Preston's and J. B. Palmer's troops were advanced under a "terrible fire from Yankee artillery for a distance of 400 yards across an open and unprotected hill." During the attack, Preston's attached artillery, Wright's Tennessee Battery, remained parked on the Franklin Road.[31]

During the early afternoon, Hardee's weary troops launched three attacks against the Nashville Road. This was the weakest part of Rosecrans's line, where McCook's shattered divisions were forced to cover a mile-and-a-half stretch. Once again, the Southern artillery was haphazardly used. General Bushrod Johnston frankly wrote: "It was unfortunate that our artillery was not properly moved forward to support us. . . . I do not think that our artillery was sufficiently used on the left. General Liddell's battery [Swett's] arrived on the ground, and he proceeded to put it in position for the work to be done, but he did not succeed in time before the retreat commenced."[32]

On the few occasions when batteries were brought up, they were utilized one at a time, which made easy pickings for massed Union guns. Lieutenant Thomas Key's Helena Light Artillery galloped forward and unlimbered, only to be pulverized by a murderous artillery fire. "Their rifle guns could throw canister as far as ours could spherical case, and in order to prevent annihilation, we were forced to withdraw," wrote Key.[33]

•

Throughout the night of the 31st and New Year's Day, the armies glared ominously at one another as the commanders contemplated their next move. Some maneuvering occurred. Rosecrans abandoned the Round Forest to shorten his line, and Polk quickly moved up into the position. More notably, the Federals crossed the river to the east bank in division strength and occupied a strategic hill that overlooked McFadden's Ford.

During the early morning hours of January 2, the Confederates at last did what they should have done on the early afternoon of December 31. Some twenty-two guns were massed north of the Cowan house in a line stretching for a quarter of a mile. The batteries of Stanford, Carnes, and Turner were positioned north of the railroad. That of Scott was placed in an open field between the railroad and the Nashville Pike. Robertson's six-gun battery rested to the left of Scott in front of the Cowan house. About 9:00 the gray cannoneers opened a furious barrage that struck up along the railroad and the Nashville Pike. The Yankee artillerymen were startled by the sudden eruption and, declared one officer, "they had our range perfectly." Three Union batteries were forced to withdraw after a thunderous twenty-minute duel. Perhaps the most significant aspect of the whole affair was that it demonstrated what could have been accomplished all along by massing artillery. But, as one historian observed, "if the Rebel artillery dominated the morning duel on the west bank, the afternoon fight, when the really significant action took place east of the river, would belong to the Union cannoneers."[34]

Bragg was now becoming increasingly alarmed about the Federal division on the east bank. Polk's corps was exposed to an enfilading artillery fire. Shortly after noon, Bragg informed

General Breckinridge that his division must attack the heights in his front. The latter argued that Union artillery dominated the high ground west of McFadden's Ford and that his infantry would be hit by cannon fire as they advanced. Bragg was unyielding, however, and the attack was scheduled for 4:00.

The artillery was to play a vital role. To distract the Federals and soften up their line, Polk's guns on the west bank were to open a fifteen-minute preliminary barrage beginning at 3:45. In direct support of the infantry, Breckinridge would have Anderson's and Wright's batteries and four guns of the Washington Artillery. As a further supplement, Bragg ordered from Wayne's Hill four guns of Semple's battery and from across the river Robertson's six guns, all ten pieces to be commanded by Robertson. In the Wayne's Hill vicinity, Cobb's battery and a section of Lumsden's battery were in position to deliver an enfilade fire across the river. Byrne's battery would serve as a reserve. The cavalry, which was also to participate in the attack, was supported by White's battery. Bragg was thus committing some fifty-three guns, half his artillery, to this venture. Twenty-six of the cannon would be directly involved in the attack.[35]

Problems arose almost from the beginning, not the least of which related to the role of the long arm. At the very hour of the assault, Breckinridge and Robertson apparently began feuding over exactly what the artillery was to do. According to Robertson, Breckinridge envisioned that the attack would be made by a combination of both arms, the batteries being positioned between two lines of infantry. Robertson refused and maintained that his instructions from army headquarters were "to wait until the infantry had crowned the crest, and then to rush up and occupy it." He further argued that Breckinridge's arrangement would likely crowd the field and cause misdirection of fire so that, in the event of a reversal, every gun might be lost. "General Breckinridge, thinking differently, however, formed his batteries and advanced them simultaneously with his infantry and immediately behind it," wrote the captain.[36]

Because of subsequent events, Robertson has been soundly criticized by modern writers, who describe him as an overly ambitious Bragg crony who was not beyond lying. Inasmuch as the disagreement was not mentioned in Robertson's original report but only in a second report prepared some days later at Bragg's request, one author has even questioned whether or not the incident actually occurred.[37] The objections raised by Robertson, however, whether at the time or after the fact, were valid ones. Breckinridge gambled heavily by calling for a combination attack.

Two facts can be clearly established about the artillery's part in the assault. First, Breckinridge's batteries did advance with the infantry, while Robertson's ad hoc battery group remained in the rear. Second, Robertson was given explicit orders that, once the crest had been taken, Semple's four guns were to be placed on the right of the division, while Robertson's own six would protect the left flank from anticipated artillery fire from across the river.[38]

Even before the attack began, Bragg's massive artillery support began to dwindle. Byrne's battery exhausted its ammunition supply in preliminary, and unnecessary, skirmishing. Because of poor coordination, the calvalry and White's battery never received orders to attack. Thus, seven guns were effectively eliminated before the assault even began. At 3:45 Polk was to begin his diversionary barrage. He did not learn of the attack until 3:30, however, and thus had only fifteen minutes to prepare his artillery. The smoothbores began firing on time but accomplished nothing because they lacked sufficient range to strike their targets.[39]

At 4:00 a cannon, probably from Anderson's battery, boomed a single shot: the signal for the advance. Two long lines of infantry, some 5,000 troops, grimly moved forward in front of Wright's, Anderson's, and Vaught's batteries. Barely half the distance had been covered when Breckinridge noticed that the cavalry was not advancing and that his right was badly overlapped. He was compelled to halt his advance until Major Graves could bring up a battery to cover that sector.[40]

Captain Eldridge Wright's Tennessee Battery moved forward at a gallop. As it cleared an open wooded area and moved into a large cornfield, the lead horse in one of the 6-pounder teams was struck in the head by a minié ball and tumbled to the ground. Before the drivers could stop the team, the carriage crashed into the dead animal, snapped the pole, and placed the piece out of commission. Wright's men managed to unlimber their other three guns and soon became engaged in a fifteen-minute duel with a Federal battery a scant 300 yards distant.[41]

Searching for additional artillery, Graves spotted an uncommitted battery 300 yards in the rear of Wright's position. He rode over and discovered that it was Semple's four-gun detachment under Lieutenant E. J. Fitzpatrick. The lieutenant claimed he had received no orders from Captain Robertson concerning his role in the attack. Graves immediately ordered the battery forward, and the Alabama gunners were soon engaged along side of Wright's Tennesseans.[42]

Meanwhile, Breckinridge's infantry had reached the heights and overpowered the Federals. Going out of control, his troops swarmed over the crest, down the slope, and into the river bottom at McFadden's Ford. As they eagerly pursued the Federals, however, the tightly packed Southern ranks increasingly came within the range of Crittenden's massed artillery on the high ground west of Stone's River. These fifty-seven guns, directed by Major John Mendenhall, suddenly blasted out a wall of flame. The Confederates were staggered and began to reel back.[43]

For the time being, the Rebel artillery could do little to respond. Wright's and Semple's batteries were committed on the right, and Vaught's and Anderson's batteries were in motion. Cobb's battery was on Wayne's Hill, on the far left rear of the division, but his smoothbores lacked sufficient range to reach Crittenden's artillery. The rifle section of Lumsden's battery, commanded by Lieutenant E. Tarrent, was moved to an open field near the river in front of Wayne's Hill and fired four rounds. This drew heavy fire upon Cobb, however, and Tarrent was forced to cease fire. For some fifteen minutes, the Northern artillery, virtually unopposed, pounded the Rebels at the estimated rate of a hundred rounds per minute.[44]

Graves now frantically attempted to establish his batteries on the crest to open a counterfire. From left to right, Vaught's, Anderson's, Semple's and Wright's batteries unlimbered their pieces. They did manage to disable one of Crittenden's guns, but little else went their way. They were not only clearly outgunned but also outpositioned because the Union artillery was on a higher elevation.

It was now imperative that Robertson's battery come forward on the left and attempt to neutralize the guns in the area of the Round Forrest. But Robertson could not be found. A staff officer vainly searched the field for him. Graves later reported that he never saw the captain during the entire engagement. Mistakenly thinking that the left side of the hill had not been cleared of the enemy, Robertson took it upon himself to "alter the plan." He never moved his guns beyond the woods. This was probably for the best. The additional artillery would have been of little use. Breckinridge admitted as much, saying that it would have been a "vain contest."[45]

As the Southerners streamed back in disorder up the slope

and past the artillery, the Federals reformed and launched a counterattack. "Feeling that this was one of the cases it being necessary to sacrifice one arm of the service for the safety of another, I resolved to maintain the artillery in its position," Graves commented. It was a gallant decision—probably a correct one—but it would prove to be costly.

A blistering fire poured into the Confederate artillerymen. Captain Wright fell mortally wounded and Major Graves was wounded twice. The detachment of Semple's battery was nearly wiped out; twenty of forty-five men were lost in thirty minutes. In addition, one of their Napoleon guns was captured. The Washington Artillery quickly exhausted its ammunition. While waiting for additional rounds, a detachment was sent to man one of Anderson's pieces, whose men were lying on the ground to avoid the deadly fire. Wright's gunners fired double charges of canister, but the blue onslaught could not be stopped. "It was only when the enemy was within pistol shot and all our artillery ammunition was exhausted that the order to limber to the rear was given," Graves noted. The Louisiana gunners removed their cannon when the enemy was only fifty yards distant. They lost five men and eight horses in the melee. As the cannoneers were in the process of limbering up, Graves foolishly reversed himself and ordered the crews back into position. After firing only one volley, he again ordered a "Limber to the rear!" By this time, however, the Federals were sweeping up the slope, overrunning two of Wright's guns, and killing or wounding fourteen men and ten horses.[46]

Captain Robertson, who had decided on his own initiative to sit out the assault, did at least take steps to cover the retreat. He positioned his battery in front of the woods where the assault began and was soon joined by Vaught's Washington Artillery. Other gun crews stopped as they withdrew, but all of them were out of ammunition and were ordered to continue to the rear. "So soon as our guns were unmasked, fire was opened on the enemy's line and continued until dark, with a very heavy fire of skirmishers upon the artillery," Robertson stated. He reported a loss of six men and a like number of horses and admitted that some of his men would have fled had he not leveled his revolver at them. "I am clearly of the opinion that if there had been no artillery on that field the enemy would have gone into Murfreesboro that evening," he wrote. "There was no organization that I could see or hear of until after the enemy had been checked, save in the artillery."[47] This statement was probably an exaggeration. By the time the Federals reached his artillery, the attack had sputtered to a halt and night was fast approaching. Still, the long arm did represent organized resistance in an otherwise chaotic situation.

It can perhaps be argued that Breckinridge's attack was doomed from the start. If there was any chance for success, however, it was imperative that the artillery be coordinated. This did not occur. No single hand directed operations. This rightly should have been the responsibility of the army chief of artillery, Lieutenant Colonel James Hallonquist, but evidence is lacking that he played any part in the entire episode. As a result, only half of the thirty-seven guns available on the east bank became significantly engaged.

Major Graves also found it impossible to control so many scattered guns on line. After the battle, Lieutenant John Mebane, now commanding Wright's battery, wrote, "Had our battery gone to the rear when the other batteries of the division did, we would have saved our guns; but being under the immediate supervision of the [division] chief of artillery, we did not move without orders from him."[48]

During the night of January 3–4, Bragg ordered a retreat. Polk's corps marched to Shelbyville and Hardee's to Wartrace. It was miserably cold. "My God what suffering," lamented a Mississippi artilleryman. "Wet through—cold and chilly—no sleep for four or five nights, and march through mud and water, some without any shoes, and some sick, and some with fingers and toes frozen, while behind on the bloody field were thousands moaning out the little life left them. The rain still poured down."[49]

Artillery casualties at Murfreesboro were light, especially considering that Bragg lost a third of his army. Twenty-five men were killed, 148 were wounded, and 9 were missing, a total of 182. Batteries incurring heavy losses included Robertson's (20 men and 15 horses), Semple's (20 men and 14 horses), Wright's (14 men and 10 horses), Stanford's (10 men and 7 horses), and Vaught's (9 men and 8 horses). Three guns of the gray artillery were captured and several were disabled. The blue long arm came out decidedly second best, however; it lost 374 men, a staggering 688 horses, 30 guns, 21 caissons, 4 battery wagons, and 6 traveling forges.[50]

At Murfreesboro, the Confederates had once again tried but failed to use their artillery on the tactical offensive. The terrain was simply too difficult and the maneuvers of the batteries too uncoordinated to be effective. "Our artillery could rarely be used," admitted Bragg, "while the enemy, holding defensive lines, had selected formidable positions for his batteries and this dense cover for his infantry, from both of which he had to be dislodged by our infantry alone." One historian has stated that the Confederates "attempted to use artillery on the offensive at Murfreesboro, but the terrain was unfavorable for this and artillery accomplished little."[51]

Much of it, for all practical purposes, simply sat out the first day's battle. Several batteries, such as Scott's Tennessee, literally did not fire a shot, and others were only minimally engaged. When Mebane's battery reported to General Hardee, it was "ordered to park in a field about a half mile west of Stone's River," where it sat the battle out. Marshall's battery fired only a few rounds and those were "by order of General Breckinridge, to assist in steadying our own troops, though not having a very fair shot at the enemy."[52]

As for the Union army, the case seems clear: Its powerful artillery tipped the scales in its favor. Otherwise, the Rebels might have been victorious. After the war, General Thomas Crittenden wrote: "Before this battle I had been inclined to underrate the importance of artillery in our war, but I never knew that arm to render such important service as at this point."[53]

Chapter 6

"All Hands Fixing Up the Battery"

During the early days of January 1863, Bragg committed his weary army to a defensive line along the Duck River in south central Tennessee. Polk's corps wintered at Shelbyville and Hardee's at Wartrace; the army headquarters was at Tullahoma. "The batteries of the [Polk's] Corps of the army are all encamped together," wrote Captain James Douglas, commanding a Texas battery. "We have a beautiful camp four miles west of Shelbyville. We have twelve batteries which present a very imposing appearance on drill."[1]

Casualties in the late battle had been staggering, and the ranks were now dangerously depleted. Bragg needed time to refit his thinned division, and his antagonist was more than willing to let him have it. The Army of Tennessee thus lulled away the ensuing winter and spring months. "All hands fixing up the battery. Many things out of order," wrote a Mississippian.[2]

The efficiency of the army was maintained during the winter–spring respite. A contest was held to determine the best-drilled battery, the prize being a handsome and highly coveted new banner. "All hands agree that the contest will be between my battery and Scott's," stated Captain Douglas. When it was held a few days later, however, he complained, "I rather think Scott will get the prize, as he is a pet with Bragg's army."[3]

Meanwhile, Bragg had been reshaping his army. The most pressing problem was the shortage of manpower. After Murfreesboro, the effective strength was down to 20,000 infantry and 1,500 artillery. The Army of the Cumberland was believed to consist of 60,000–70,000 troops and to be receiving periodic reinforcements. In February, General Polk expressed alarm over intelligence reports and Yankee newspaper stories that Rosecrans had 36 batteries with 216 guns, while Bragg could muster only 20 and 80.[4]

The ranks were bolstered throughout the spring by returning

stragglers and a stringent roundup of conscripts. The latter

added 9,500 names to the rolls within ten weeks. Several cavalry
brigades under Earl Van Dorn arrived from Mississippi in February. T. J. Churchill's Texas brigade, exchanged and reequipped since the capture of Arkansas Post, was transferred to
Tullahoma. By April, Bragg's army had swelled to 40,000 infantry, 15,000 cavalry, and 2,500 artillery.[5]

Replacements brought most of the artillery companies up to
strength. By March, Hardee's and Polk's batteries averaged 96
and 103 men present for duty, respectively. Pritchard's two-gun
battery was disbanded, and 19 of the men were sent to Carnes's
battery. Captain Charles Swett went back to Vicksburg to obtain fresh recruits for his company, but he returned empty-handed. He was assigned 12 infantrymen to fill his vacancies.
Some additional artillery was received, including Captain W. H.
Fowler's Alabama Battery, ordered up from Mobile. By late
April, Bragg had 129 guns, including 25 with the cavalry. Nevertheless, Rosecrans still held a two-to-one edge in cannon.[6]

The artillery horses were reported to be "above the average in
flesh and grooming." Bragg concurred that they were in "fine
condition" and reported no shortages to Richmond. In March
1863 the batteries averaged sixty-nine horses and twenty-five
mules apiece, about the same as before Murfreesboro. Inspections turned up a few minor difficulties. A poor system of tying
the animals had led to some straggling and thefts. Also, a shortage of currycombs existed. These were only irritations,
however.[7]

Actually, the favorable reports concerning the livestock were
deceptive. They failed to reveal that hard campaigning, disease,
a shortage of long forage, and strenuous overuse were beginning
to take a toll. A May 1863 report pointed out that, of the 845
horses in Polk's ten batteries, 255 (fully 1 out of 4) were unserviceable. Replacements were becoming progressively more difficult to come by as Bragg yielded more and more of middle
Tennessee, the heart of the army's horse supply.[8] He therefore
issued an order that all the available ones in Atlanta be impressed for his artillery. Guards were placed on all roads leading
out of the city to stop people who were attempting to avoid compliance. Horses were even hidden in basements and cellars.
Georgia Governor Joseph Brown issued a formal complaint. The
impressment was eventually stopped, but not before Bragg had
obtained a fresh supply of animals.[9]

Transportation was also in a state of disarray. Wagons were in short supply and, because of the destruction of several railroad bridges, they were being worn out in lengthy forage forays. When an inspector checked Douglas's Texas Battery, he reported that "the foraging arrangements of this battery are unsatisfactory. There are only three wagons for all purposes in the company. These run constantly for forage. The distance traveled for it is thirty miles and the time consumed in the trip is three days."[10]

In March 1863 the 19 batteries in Polk's and Hardee's corps possessed 94 vehicles and 424 animals. Only 4 ambulances, 2 ordnance wagons, and 1 traveling forge were included. The remaining 87 wagons were used to carry baggage, long forage, and other items. Ammunition was scarce beyond the rounds in the limber chests and caissons.[11]

Deficiencies were also discovered in ordnance stores. In February an inspection was made of Cheatham's and McCown's division artillery. Officers complained that paper fuzes were "entirely worthless." The inspector found that, almost without exception, spherical case shot were being substituted for shells to gain the advantage of the metallic Bormann fuze; the Confederate laboratories did not attach Bormanns to shells. Cheatham's battalion, except for Turner's company, was deficient in bridles and halters. Douglas's battery suffered from "general dilapidation and want of care in little things." The ammunition was badly packed and, warned the inspector, "it will lead to an explosion some day if not corrected." McTyre's battery was found to be in generally better condition, though it was short of currycombs. The harness in Douglas's and McTyre's batteries was bad. The leather was not greased well, tallow often being the only lubricant available. Stanford's battery had not received any ammunition since the battle. "This battery [Stanford's] is very effective when properly equipped," observed the inspector.[12]

Criticism concerning the quality of the fixed ammunition was heard from other quarters. Captain W. Overton Barret reported that, at Murfreesboro, his battery had fired seventy-three rounds of 6-pounder spherical case shot, nearly all of which burst prematurely. A Tennessee officer grumbled about the inferiority of the powder, which in turn affected the range performance of the projectiles. In March, Captain Henry Semple discovered that arsenal employees had prepared some of the fixed ammunition with rifle rather than cannon powder. "Rifle powder is not fit for cannon, as it is so fine and burns so rapidly, that exploding all at once, it endangers the gun and the men who serve it," he charged. Complaints were also heard about "worthless friction primers." In June a board, consisting of Lieutenant Colonel James Hallonquist and Majors Felix Robertson, Llewellyn Hoxton, and Melancthon Smith, was established to study the ammunition and to "make any suggestions in regard to changes and improvements."[13]

The army chief of ordnance, Colonel Hypolite Oladowski, defended the bureau's workmanship and thought that the problems encountered were largely attributable to the men themselves. Concerning the inferiority of paper fuzes, he concurred that those of the Bormann type were "surer to explode projectiles." He maintained, however, that the difficulty in premature bursting could be avoided by careful cutting. "It is ascertained that during engagements the men often cut them through," he commented. The ammunition was "of good quality and well prepared." Oladowski conceded that harness often broke in a short time, but blamed this on a deficiency of quality leather and lack of care by the men. Difficulties with friction primers were "more the neglect of artillery officers than their fabrication." Oladowski had toured the Atlanta Arsenal shops and was convinced that those being turned out were uniform in size and superior in quality.[14] He did complain to Colonel John W. Mallet of the Central Laboratory, at Macon, about the polygonal shells that artillerymen were using in target practice. An inspection showed that the shell fragments were of unequal thickness, he noted, which demonstrated "that the core had not been truly centered."[15]

Problems persisted. In early May an inspection of Polk's artillery revealed the deteriorating condition of several gun carriages. Smith's battery was reported to have "one gun carriage very clumsy and unsafe—bad material." A new one was also needed in Robertson's battery. All four of those in Stanford's were marked for replacement, but a frustrated gunner in the company wrote that "it will be a job to get new ones." One of the caissons in Cobb's battery was listed as "miserable."[16]

After Murfreesboro, Oladowski had dispersed twenty-one captured caissons throughout the army. Smith's battalion also received a traveling forge and battery wagon. The chief source of battery equipment for the Army of Tennessee, however, remained the Augusta Arsenal. It produced excellent gun carriages and caissons, but the carpenter shops were clearly overtaxed. Oladowski's continued pleas nonetheless brought some response. Between March 28 and May 22, Colonel G. W.

Rains, commanding at Augusta, forwarded to the depots at Tullahoma and Chattanooga twenty-one caissons, thirty-seven limbers, one battery wagon, and three traveling forges.[17]

None of the batteries were so badly equipped that they were put out of service, but numerous shortages lessened overall efficiency. In May, Cobb's battery possessed 633 rounds of ammunition but only 500 friction primers, 2 spare wheels, 24 extra horseshoes, and 3 sponge buckets.[18]

The most serious shortage remained in the supply of fixed ammunition. In addition to replenishing the large number of rounds expended at Murfreesboro, Oladowski attempted to stockpile 50 rounds per gun at the Columbus Arsenal and 100 rounds per gun at the Atlanta Arsenal.[19] It was a goal that proved to be impossible to meet. In late April 1863, a full four months after Murfreesboro, the supply of ammunition in the army was still far below the prescribed 200 rounds per gun. At that time, 18,942 rounds were on hand, 16 percent of which were short-range canister. This amounted to 163 rounds apiece for the 12-pounder Napoleons, 171 for the 6-pounders, and 130 for the howitzers. Rifled ammunition was even more scarce: only 95 rounds apiece for the 10-pounder Parrotts, 75 for the 3-inch rifles, and 66 for the 3.3-inch rifles.[20]

The armament was also a growing cause of concern. Inspections indicated that several field pieces were in a run-down condition. In February a 12-pounder howitzer in Douglas's battery was reported to be badly scarred. It was still serviceable, but a replacement was requested. Several months later, an inspector noted that two Leeds & Company 12-pounder howitzers in Waters's battery needed to be exchanged, as well as a damaged howitzer in Humphreys's battery.[21]

An even bigger problem related to the rifle guns. Bronze rifles had long proved to be troublesome. Their rifling grooves were notorious for quickly wearing down. When this occurred, the guns became useless. In January, Oladowski turned in two of them, noting that "they are partially impaired by reason that the rifle benches [lands] are worn out." In May the rifling grooves in all four bronze 3-inch rifles in Stanford's battery were reported to be "worn down near the bottom of the bore." The same situation cropped up again in the fall. At that time, two bronze 6-pounder rifles in Swett's battery needed to be exchanged because the rifling grooves were worn out between the trunnions and the breech.[22]

There was a larger and more far-reaching element in the armament deficiency. The 6-pounder and 12-pounder howitzer, standard weapons of the western Confederate field artillery, were continually being outmatched by the more powerful, long-range guns of the enemy. The smoke had barely cleared from the Murfreesboro battlefield before battery commanders began complaining of their inadequate armament. "Six-pounder guns cannot maintain a fight with long range guns," declared one officer. The 6-pounder was also considered to be too heavy for effective cavalry use.[23] The need for additional long-range artillery was pressing. At Murfreesboro, Rosecrans held a commanding three-to-one edge in rifles. Some relief came in early 1863, when Bragg was issued seven 3.8-inch bronze rifles and two 3.65-inch iron Wiard rifles, Yankee trophies that had been captured by his army in the late battle. Richmond also sent down two large 20-pounder Parrott rifles.[24]

That spring, Bragg began a program of armament modernization. The weapon selected to become the backbone of his artillery was a bronze smoothbore gun: the light 12-pounder Napoleon. It had been developed by the French in the late 1850s and named after Louis Napoleon III. Designed as a hybrid weapon, it had a range of a gun (1,680 yards for solid shot) and could also fire the explosive shell or spherical case shot of the howitzer. At distances of 300 yards or less, it could spew out canister balls like a giant, sawed-off shotgun. Also, the reliability of smoothbore ammunition stood in stark contrast to that of the unsure rifle projectiles.[25]

In March, Bragg ordered that all his old 6-pounders be gradually phased out and recast into light 12-pounders. At that time, his armament consisted of 134 pieces: forty 6-pounders, forty 12-pounder howitzers, sixteen 12-pounder Napoleons, six 10-pounder Parrott rifles, seven 3.8-inch rifles, eleven 3-inch rifles, two 3.3 inch rifles, and one Ellsworth breech-loading gun.[26]

The 12-pounder Napoleons cast at the Tredegar Iron Works in Richmond continued to be earmarked for Lee's artillery, which was undergoing a similar transition. The main supplier of Napoleons to the Army of Tennessee was the Confederate foundry at Augusta, Georgia. The guns were cast of a metal that had recently been invented by the Austrians and recommended by Confederate diplomat James Mason. It was a composition of copper, tin, wrought iron, and zinc. When completed, the guns were tested with a charge of powder and by loading them to the muzzle with bolts. Casting at Augusta began in late 1862, and by the following spring some seventy pieces had been cast. Not until some weeks later were they bored, finished, and mounted.[27]

The transition proceeded at a snail's pace, particularly because of the government's distribution policy. Not until the spring of 1863 did the Confederate foundries at Macon and Columbus, Georgia, begin to turn out light 12-pounders, and their first priority was not Bragg's army. In February, Oladowski was informed that he should not expect any Columbus Napoleons for at least six months. Meantime, some of them had been sent to the Mobile defenses. Macon completed its first two Napoleon batteries in June 1863, both of which were promptly shipped to the Army of Mississippi. Lack of governmental priority, such as was given Lee's army, severely retarded Bragg's modernization program. During the first four months of 1863, the Army of Northern Virginia received forty-nine new light 12-pounders; the Army of Tennessee, only five![28]

By late April, the armament composition had changed little. Bragg counted 129 guns: thirty-five 6-pounders, forty-one 12-pounder howitzers, twenty-one 12-pounder Napoleons, four 10-pounder Parrott rifles, two 20-pounder Parrott rifles, twelve 3-inch rifles, two 3.3 inch rifles, ten 3.8-inch rifles, and two 3.65-inch Wiard rifles.[29] In May, Polk's artillery consisted of ten batteries of forty-two guns. Robertson's Florida and Smith's Mississippi batteries had six and four 12-pounder Napoleons, respectively; Stanford's Mississippi, four bronze 3-inch rifles; and the remaining companies (Barret's Missouri, Carnes's Tennessee, Douglas's Texas, Garrity's Alabama, Humphreys's Arkansas, Swett's Mississippi, and Waters's Alabama) each two 6-pounders and two 12-pounder howitzers.[30]

Oladowski continued to press for more guns. On May 22 he wrote Colonel M. H. Wright, at the Atlanta Arsenal, that he could not send in any more 6-pounders for recasting until he had other guns to replace them. "I respectfully request you to send from your arsenal to Augusta such guns (bronze) as you may deem unfit for service and I shall send you guns which will be exchanged as soon as I will receive in their place 12-pounder light guns," he declared.[31]

An exchange pipeline was soon open. When Oladowski was informed that a battery of Augusta Napoleons was soon to be forwarded, he turned in a bronze Leeds & Company 6-pounder from Fowler's battery for recasting. In early July, six new Augusta Napoleons, complete with gun carriages and caissons, were sent by rail to Bragg. Unfortunately, the train derailed en

route. The gun tubes were uninjured, but the carriages and
caissons were smashed to pieces. The debris had to be sent back
to the arsenal shops for reworking.[32]

While Bragg continued to receive guns in driblets, Rosecrans
was modernizing his armament with lightning speed. At
Murfreesboro, the Northern commander had possessed only ten
Napoleons. During the spring of 1863, however, dozens of new
light 12-pounders arrived by rail. The weapons bore such company names as "M. Greenwood & Co., Cincinnati" and "Revere
Copper & Co., Boston." James and Wiard rifles were also being
phased out in favor of more popular guns: 3-inch rifles and 10-pounder Parrott rifles. After the Battle of Murfreesboro, General Hardee had observed that "long range cannon and improved projectiles can be made only by great mechanical skill,
heavy machinery and abundant resources."[33] The Northern industrial complex was proving his statement to be depressingly
correct.

Chapter 7

"For the Want of Field Officers"

During 1862–63 recurring disharmony permeated the officer corps of the Army of Tennessee. One writer has observed that the officers "devoted more time and almost as much energy to squabbling among themselves as they did fighting the Yankees."[1] Because the chiefs of artillery were all field grade officers, they lacked sufficient clout to exert a significant effect on the factions and power struggles among the general officers. In many respects, however, the wrangling among the artillery line officers reflected problems that the entire army faced.

On the surface, it appeared as though Bragg was successful in welding together an efficient artillery command structure. His chiefs were young, knowledgeable, and well educated. Yet, although several of them were West Point graduates who had served in the U.S. Artillery, none enjoyed any combat experience or training in the handling of groups of guns. When compared with Robert E. Lee's artillery officers, they were a rather lackluster, undistinguished group. Even more disturbing, the rank of several was related more to loyalty to Bragg than to performance.

By late 1862 the higher echelon of the Army of Tennessee had assumed a curious quality. Sensing an ever-growing hostility among numbers of his officers, Bragg increasingly began to surround himself with a cadre of hard-core supporters who had served under him in the early months of the Department of the Gulf. The list transcended every branch: Generals Jones Withers and Patton Anderson in the infantry, General Joseph Wheeler in the cavalry, and Lieutenant Colonel James H. Hallonquist and Major Felix H. Robertson in the artillery.[2]

James H. Hallonquist, a native of South Carolina, rose to the top fast—probably too fast. He was a West Point graduate who had served in the 4th U.S. Artillery, though he lacked combat experience. Much of his military service was spent in the non-glorious position of artillery instructor at Fort Monroe, Virginia. He spent the first three years of the war primarily in administrative duties positions, first as an ordnance officer at Pensacola and later as an inspector and mustering officer at Mobile. When Bragg moved his corps to Corinth, he requested the young major as his artillery chief. Shortly after Shiloh, Hallonquist was promoted to lieutenant colonel and soon appointed as chief of artillery of the Army of Tennessee. He was twenty-eight years old at the time. Little in his record suggested he was ready to handle the new responsibilities that were thrust upon him.[3]

Hallonquist never seemed to rise above the low-level tedium that had characterized his earlier career. He gave personal attention to matters that could have best been left to subordinates. While the army went into winter quarters in and around Tullahoma, Hallonquist journeyed to Atlanta to oversee personally the equipping of several batteries. He returned in March 1863 and began supervising the testing of several 6-pounders. That fall, he squabbled with ordnance officers over minor issues. In short, he was preoccupied with housekeeping details to the exclusion of administration and tactical innovation.[4] His career remained closely aligned with Bragg's and he rapidly lost status when the general later departed. Nor was he to be a success in his postwar engineering business. Heavy drinking and financial reversals led him to commit suicide in 1883 at the age of forty-nine.

Another Bragg protégé was an odd-looking young Texan by the name of Felix H. Robertson. Robertson had entered West Point in 1857 at the age of eighteen and resigned in January 1861, only three weeks before his graduation, because of what he termed as the "political action of my section." He offered his services to the Confederacy and was assigned to Charleston. There, he first met Hallonquist. How closely associated they were is not known, but on April 20 both were transferred to Bragg at Pensacola. Robertson ably commanded a Florida battery at Shiloh and Farmington, but it was his close ties with Bragg that propelled him into the position of acting chief of artillery of Polk's corps in the December 1862 reorganization. The Texan would eventually attain the rank of brigadier general, a grade also held by his father, Jerome Robertson, in Robert E. Lee's army.[5]

Robertson was a harsh disciplinarian who was intensely disliked by his men. Because of his dark complexion and slanted eyes, rumors spread that he was of Indian descent. His name around the campfire became "Comanche Robertson." A drunk artilleryman who called him "half 'Injin" one night paid dearly. The next day, the captain had him strung up by his thumbs with his feet barely touching the ground. This cruel punishment incurred so much animosity among the men that some of them expected the young Texan to be murdered.[6]

After Murfreesboro, Bragg became involved in an obsessive vendetta to purge the army of those generals whom he disliked. The artillery was not unaffected by this high-level power struggle. In an attempt to obtain evidence against General John C. Breckinridge, Bragg turned to his old crony, Captain Robertson. Because the captain's Murfreesboro report had not been particularly critical of Breckinridge, Bragg requested that he prepare a revised report to "do justice" that would skip regular channels and be sent directly to his headquarters. Robertson understood what was wanted. He now wrote a scathing denunciation of Breckinridge's conduct during the January 2 assault. Shortly thereafter, the captain was allowed a brief tour in Richmond (a payoff for his loyalty to Bragg asserts one modern writer), during which time he lobbied on Bragg's behalf. Upon his return, he was greeted with a major's commission (Bragg's attempt to obtain him a lieutenant colonelcy had been unsuccessful) and command of the newly organized artillery reserve, an organization that was to report directly to army headquarters. All of this came on the heels of Robertson's own miserable performance during the Battle of Murfreesboro.[7]

Another Bragg favorite was Captain J. R. B. Burtwell. Much to the chagrin of a crack Georgia battery, the Washington Artillery of Augusta, the general overturned the results of the company election in the summer of 1862 and appointed Burtwell as captain. In late 1862, he again pushed him up the ladder, this time as artillery chief of Withers's division.[8]

By the spring of 1863, a distressing situation had arisen in the artillery officer corps. It centered chiefly on the lack of advancement opportunities and the often capricious manner in which promotions were meted out. Several factors restricted advancement. The number of executive officers was regulated by law: a colonel for every forty guns, a lieutenant colonel for every twenty-four guns, and a major for every sixteen guns. The War Department was slow in approving nominations, however.[9] At Murfreesboro, Bragg was authorized one colonel, one lieutenant colonel, and six majors. His eight chiefs of artillery actually consisted of one lieutenant colonel, four majors, and three captains:

Chief of Artillery	*Commanding Artillery of:*
Lt. Col. James H. Hallonquist	Army of Tennessee
Major Llewellyn Hoxton	Hardee's corps
Capt. Thomas R. Hotchkiss (acting chief)	Cleburne's division
Major Rice Graves	Breckinridge's division
Major George Mathes	McCown's division
Capt. Felix H. Robertson (acting chief)	Polk's corps
Major Melancthon Smith	Cheatham's division
Capt. J. R. B. Burtwell (acting chief)	Wither's division

Hotchkiss and Graves were wounded at Murfreesboro.

Too, a high casualty rate in the infantry morbidly assured a constant turnover in officers. Not so in the artillery. By the spring of 1863, not one of its line officers had been killed in battle. Although this meant that officers of long experience were serving in the artillery, it also meant a bottleneck in the promotion system. On account of a similar situation in Robert E. Lee's artillery, many of his officers transferred to other branches for advancement.[10] This simply did not occur in the western long arm. The result was that artillery officers remained in grade for lengthy periods.[11]

The early months of 1863 brought little relief. Hallonquist still shouldered the insignia of a lieutenant colonel. Several battalion commanders in Lee's artillery at that time held higher grade. General Hardee informed the War Department in March that, though he had thirty-four guns, no officers of field rank were assigned: "Each division of my corps has an officer of artillery, acting as its chief, one of whom has been recommended as a major; the other is a captain, acting temporarily until the vacancy occasioned by the assignment of the former chief to duty elsewhere is filled." The battery commanders in Cheatham's division personally petitioned the War Department concerning a promotion for their battalion commander, Major Melancthon Smith. The request was denied. As late as June 1863, the War Department had still not approved the nominations of Captains Burtwell and Robertson to major. "Difficulties arise constantly under the general order for massing artillery for the want of proper field officers," Bragg informed Richmond.[12]

The lack of promotion opportunity was only half the problem. The selection of those to be advanced created the thornier issue. Bragg had earlier embarked upon a campaign of patronage by elevating his personal favorites, James Hallonquist, Felix Robertson, and J. R. B. Burtwell, to the highest levels of responsibility. A promotion policy seemingly based upon a "favored son" status continued to persist. Bragg even went so far as to overturn the election results of a Georgia battery to appoint his old battery sergeant from the Mexican War as lieutenant.[13]

Perhaps the most irritating aspect of this patronage system was a total disregard for seniority. The results of this policy were predictable: friction and jealousies. In December 1862, Bragg appointed eighteen-year-old Lieutenant John W. Morton as Nathan Bedford Forrest's artillery chief. The young lieutenant had served well at Fort Donelson and, impressed with Forrest's dramatic escape there, had requested service in his command. Yet, Morton's youth (he later became the youngest artillery captain in the Confederacy) and limited experience hardly merited the position to which he was being assigned. Further, he lacked the rank of the man he replaced, Captain S. F. Freeman. Forrest was enraged. "I'd like to know why in the hell Bragg sent that tallow-faced kid here to take charge of my artillery," he barked. "I'll not stand it. Captain Freeman shan't be interferred with." The assignment stood, however, and Morton later became the finest horse artilleryman in the western theater. That fact failed to alter the capricious nature of his original appointment.[14]

In January 1863, Captain John Wesley Eldridge was promoted to major upon the personal recommendation of Bragg. He was later assigned as artillery chief of A. P. Stewart's newly created division. Although Eldridge's service record was good, he lacked seniority, his battlefield experience was limited, and only a few months earlier he had lost a reelection bid to command his own Tennessee battery. Further, Bragg overrode Stewart's recommendation of Captain Thomas J. Stanford, the senior artillery officer of the division, to be his artillery chief.[15]

Perhaps no other appointment created more furor than that of Captain Thomas R. Hotchkiss of Mississippi, an ordnance officer who had been temporarily assigned as General Cleburne's artillery chief just prior to Murfreesboro. During the battle, Hotchkiss kept good control of his batteries and was twice wounded. In May 1863 he was promoted to major and permanently assigned the position.[16]

The appointment had barely been consummated before outcries filled the air. The loudest one was voiced by Cleburne's senior battery commander, Captain Henry Semple, who angrily charged that Hotchkiss had never been formally tested for the position and added: "I have the honor to represent upon my observations, that the Major is very illiterate, as his written orders in my possession amply testify. As far as I can judge, his acquaintances with the drill of Light Artillery is very imperfect, and his education has been so indifferent, that he is almost totally ignorant of the simplest hunches of mathematics." He urged that a board be appointed to examine Hotchkiss's competency.[17] The unusual request angered the army chief of artillery. "I entirely disapprove of subordinates applying for the

Lieutenant Colonel Felix H. Robertson was a controversial Bragg crony who was despised by his men. (Library of Congress)

examination of superiors," wrote Hallonquist. Cleburne, too, thought that Semple had become "unduly prejudiced." Hotchkiss retained his position, but bad blood persisted between the two men.[18]

The Hotchkiss-Semple feud pointed to the need for standardized testing as a means of evaluating officers and of avoiding the perception of favoritism. Bragg himself admitted that a "general examination of artillery officers would disclose much incompetency and improve the service." In July, Majors Hotchkiss and Eldridge were belatedly called before an examining board in Chattanooga and given oral examinations.[19]

Chapter 8

"The Assignment of Artillery . . . Will Be Rigidly Adhered To"

When forty-five-year-old General Braxton Bragg rose to command of the Army of Tennessee in June 1862, the assumption might have been made that the western artillery was destined to attain its high tide. After all, it was in this branch of the service in the regular army that he had received his experience and risen to prominence. His name had become familiar to the nation when at Buena Vista, during the Mexican War, General Zachary Taylor reportedly ordered him to "Give them a little more grape, Captain Bragg."[1] Yet, as army commander, he was to display a curious blind spot: he did not seem to know what to do with his artillery.

Bragg demonstrated this inability on both the tactical and organizational levels. Each area was influenced—and weakened—by his service as an artillery officer during the 1837–56 era. In the end, it was his strength (long artillery experience) that proved to be his biggest weakness. The artillery was undergoing a transition, something he failed to appreciate. His old army mentality prevented him from fully grasping the concept of centralized control, the tactical massing of guns, and the changing supportive role of the artillery. His approaches were tried and tested, but by the time of the Civil War they were obsolete.

Bragg's failure was first exhibited on the tactical level. To understand his mentality, a knowledge of how artillery had been used during his tenure of service in the regular army is required. The principle of massing guns, which had been established during the Napoleonic Wars, was largely ignored in the American artillery service. Indeed, at the outbreak of the Mexican War, only five batteries of field artillery were active. In battles such as Monterey and Buena Vista, in which Bragg participated, artillery companies as a rule acted independently and only rarely operated in conjunction with other batteries.[2]

This tactical method was indelibly impressed upon young Bragg's mind. As a corps commander at Shiloh, he predictably fell back upon his old army training. He seemed content to let batteries individually pound away at the Hornets' Nest, while he resorted to the shock method of the infantry assault—a favorite early nineteenth-century tactic. At the Round Forest, at Murfreesboro, he merely repeated his earlier errors.

Bragg also demonstrated his inability with the artillery on an organizational level. Once again, his early training was largely to blame. Locking himself into the old system, he lacked the flexibility to reevaluate organizational structures. Although he introduced a degree of organization in the long arm, his efforts were at best unimaginative and at worst flagrantly parochial.

Bragg reorganized the army in August 1862 and made additional modifications in December. His compact two-corps structure was basically solid and far superior to the clumsy arrangement Beauregard had used at Shiloh.[3] To provide a balance for Bragg's tactical inabilities, however, some historians have overemphasized his organizational expertise. Even though the army's structure was now improved, it was not without flaws. One writer has pointed to inadequacies in the cavalry organization.[4] That of the artillery, too, remained outdated and incomplete.

The largely ineffective performance of the western long arm through 1862 lay primarily in its fragmentation: assigning a battery to a brigade. The branch was viewed simply as an extension of the infantry and enjoyed little identity of its own. This outdated approach produced a crippling effect on the battlefield. The brigade-battery organization simply did not lend itself to the massing of guns in battle. A quick concentration of artillery might possibly have been decisive at the Hornets' Nest at Shiloh and the Round Forest at Murfreesboro. When the Confederate artillery finally did mass in these two battles, albeit belatedly, a satisfactory result was achieved. Still, apparently no correlation could be seen between effective organization and the massing of guns.

Preoccupied with infantry and cavalry reorganization, Bragg spent little time with the artillery. Division batteries were now loosely grouped together and referred to as "battalions," but the label was misleading. Actually, it represented little change from Beauregard's old system. Batteries were still assigned to and operated with individual brigades.[5]

Bragg did take time to appoint division artillery chiefs, but the position initially held such slight clout that frequently the senior battery commander of the division doubled in this capacity. Captain Charles Swett, for example, commanded his own Mississippi battery and, as senior officer, served as Cleburne's artillery chief. No orders were issued outlining administrative guidelines.

In the spring of 1863, the Army of Tennessee was again reorganized. In May the War Department ordered J. P. McCown's and John C. Breckinridge's divisions and Earl Van Dorn's cavalry division to Mississippi. Breckinridge's artillery, minus Anderson's battery, and Van Dorn's horse artillery also departed, but McCown's batteries remained and were reassigned. A hastily formed division was assembled under General A. P. Stewart, which added a fourth division to the army. All the batteries were now reduced to four guns each, except Robertson's and Slocomb's, which retained six apiece.[6]

No significant restructuring of the artillery occurred. A few of the batteries were shuffled about and nothing more. As late as April 1863, they were still assigned to brigades. While Robert E. Lee was streamlining his artillery and moving toward centralized control, Bragg clung to outdated concepts. His General Orders No. 7, issued January 17, 1863, stated that "the assignment of artillery to brigades will be rigidly adhered to."[7]

Revisions came only after prodding from above. On January 7, 1863, the War Department issued the rather poorly worded General Orders No. 7. The artillery was at long last established as a separate arm, distinct from the infantry. Based upon the model of Lee's artillery, the general orders also fixed the division as the level of operation for the long arm. The order was put into effect in the Army of Tennessee in April.[8]

The new plan provided several long-needed revisions. Division artillery chiefs received increased executive and administrative authority. Receiving orders directly from division and corps commanders, they would henceforth control the tactical maneuvers of their batteries. Battery reports would also be made directly to them. Thus, the role of the brigadier general vis-à-vis the artillery was greatly reduced. In camp, division batteries would now be parked together rather than with their respective brigades. The directive was not as far-reaching as might be hoped. The batteries were still to march with and receive rations from their brigades. Still, a long stride forward was made in liberating the artillery from the control of brigadier generals and giving it recognition as an independent arm requiring officers of its own.[9]

Bragg did bring two new dimensions to the western long arm

when he organized an artillery reserve and a horse artillery. The former soon disintegrated, and the latter would require months for fruition. The artillery reserve, as the name implies, was a group of fresh batteries that could be quickly concentrated in a contingency at a designated point for relief or for massing guns. Bragg set aside three companies for this purpose in the fall of 1862: Gibson's Georgia Battery, Baxter's Tennessee Battery, and Byrne's Kentucky Battery. The reserve was little more than a number of unattached batteries commanded by no single officer. It is difficult not to conclude that it was simply an aggregation of all the batteries left over after each brigade had received its share. No sooner had the organization been formed than it fell apart. On December 1, 1862, Gibson's battery was ordered to Chattanooga to be refitted. On the 31st, that of Baxter, which had been mustered in only a few weeks earlier in Dickson County, was detached for garrison duty at Shelbyville. This left only Byrne's battery, which served as an unattached company.[10]

In February 1863, Bragg resurrected his defunct artillery reserve. Four batteries—Massenburg's Georgia, Lumsden's Alabama, Barret's Missouri and Havis's Georgia—were set aside at Estelle Springs and specially equipped. The armament consisted of the best cannon in the army, many of which had been captured from the Union. The 12-pounder Napoleons were each issued two caissons so that a full load of 200 rounds might be carried at all times. The rifle guns were also furnished a higher than average number of rounds. On April 30 the reserve consisted of seven 12-pounder Napoleons, two 20-pounder Parrott rifles, one 10-pounder Parrott rifle, four 3.8-inch bronze rifles, two 3.65-inch Wiard rifles, one 3-inch rifle, twenty-eight caissons, two battery wagons, three traveling forges, 180 horses, 130 mules, and 174 single sets of harness. Not everyone was satisfied. General Hardee complained loudly about the loss of two of his best batteries to the new organization.[11]

Much to the chagrin of the men of the newly organized reserve, Captain Felix H. Robertson, Bragg's old protégé, was given command. The harsh disciplinary measures instituted by this bantam young captain marked him as the most unpopular officer in the artillery. The men of Havis's Georgia Battery were elated when they received news in June that they would be transferred back to Hardee's corps. As the company marched past Robertson's headquarters, some of the men shouted: "Good-bye Comanche." The battalion adjutant heard the captain mumble: "Never mind, I'll have you again." He thereupon proceeded to general headquarters, where he requested of Bragg, and was subsequently granted, the return of the battery. "It was a mournful set of men as we took the line of march back to Robertson . . . to our old camp on Duck River," a Georgian stated.[12]

Bragg also formed the nucleus of a horse artillery in the fall of 1862. These units accompanied cavalry and differed from field batteries primarily in their larger complement of horses, which made it possible for all the cannoneers to be mounted. The idea was not new. Indeed, Bragg himself had commanded such a battery years earlier in the regular army and had strongly advocated the usefulness and mobility of this type of unit. Under these circumstances, it seemed to be late in coming to the western long arm. A horse artillery had been established in the Virginia army nine months earlier.[13]

In October 1862, Captain F. F. Freeman's six-gun Tennessee Battery began operating with General Nathan Bedford Forrest's partisan brigade. The next month, J. H. Wiggins's Arkansas Battery and B. F. White's Tennessee Battery were assigned to General Joseph Wheeler's regular cavalry brigades. John H. Morgan's partisan brigade also had a section of Ellsworth rifles attached.[14]

One early advantage afforded by the horse batteries was the added punch they gave to Confederate cavalry. In December 1862, Forrest swept through west Tennessee. At Lexington, a section of guns, commanded by Lieutenant John Morton, engaged two Yankee 3-inch steel rifles. The enemy cannoneers were driven off and the pieces captured. Dubbed "bull-pups" by Forrest, they became the pride of his artillery. They were presented to Morton, and a new Tennessee battery was organized, consisting of sixty-three officers and men. At Humboldt, the newly organized company aimed the rifles at a loaded troop train. Morton wrote that the startled bluecoats "tumbled off into the swamp, running in all directions."[15] Later, the cannoneers would even engage Federal gunboats.

In the spring of 1863, just as the infant horse artillery was cranking up, it ran into trouble. On April 19, Freeman's Tennessee Battery was moving down the Lewisburg Pike near Franklin when it suddenly stumbled into the 4th U.S. Cavalry. The gunners were not even able to unlimber before they were overrun. Several officers and men were killed and thirty-one captured. Captain S. F. Freeman, who was taken prisoner, was murdered when he was unable to keep pace with the retreating Federals. The troopers abandoned the cannon after hacking up the gun carriage wheels.[16]

Bragg's horse artillery had gotten off to an impressive start in late 1862, but it was still in the formative stage. Time was needed to expand it and build leadership. These factors, coupled with the near-total destruction of Freeman's company, severely restricted the effectiveness of the horse artillery throughout the spring and summer of 1863. During that time, its counterpart in the Army of Northern Virginia reached its apex.

●

Bragg perhaps should not bear total culpability for the inept artillery organization that existed in the Army of Tennessee during the first year of his command. In the Virginia army, the design and furtherance of a highly effective structure came about largely through the army's top artillerymen: William N. Pendleton, E. P. Alexander, and Stapleton Crutchfield. These men were spurred into action by the man at the top, however: Robert E. Lee. That Bragg lacked the highly creative officers found in Lee's artillery was not entirely his fault. His failure came in not providing the impetus for change. Perhaps the greatest irony was that, in his younger days in the regular artillery, he was seen as somewhat of a visionary. As a commanding general, however, youthful vision gave way to inflexibility.

Chapter 9

"The Field Was Badly Adopted to Artillery"

Throughout the winter and spring months of 1863, the Army of Tennessee enjoyed a protracted period of inactivity along the Duck River. A major command change occurred in July, when Hardee was transferred to the Department of Mississippi. His replacement was Lieutenant General D. H. Hill, formerly of the Army of Northern Virginia. Hill's corps now comprised the divisions of Cleburne and Stewart, and Polk had those of Cheatham and Hindman. Hill brought his own chief of artillery, Major James H. Bondurant, who was soon promoted to lieutenant colonel.[1]

During June the army was abruptly shaken from its quiescence. Advancing from Murfreesboro, Rosecrans's army, during the latter part of the month, seized Hoover and Liberty gaps and Manchester. The Confederate right wing buckled. Bragg decided to abandon Tullahoma and withdraw across the Elk River. On June 27, Wheeler's cavalry was struck as it was retiring from Shelbyville. A brief fight ensued, during which 300 of his troopers were captured. J. H. Wiggins's Arkansas Battery of the horse artillery was badly cut up in the process; eight or ten men were wounded and thirty captured, including the captain. Three guns were taken.[2]

The Confederates continued to withdraw to Cowan. As they did so, Churchill's brigade and Douglas's battery supported the cavalry on the left at Allisonia bridge. The enemy soon appeared. "A heavy battery opened on my position," wrote Captain Douglas. "Major Hotchkiss ordered my cannoneers to fire, but I took the responsibility to order them to lie down until I gave the word as the enemy shells were doing us no harm and we were not in position to do them much damage." After a brief fight, the rear guard retired.[3]

By the first week in July, the Confederates had begun to enter Chattanooga. The retreat from Tullahoma had been an ordnance, as well as strategical, disaster. All along the roadside were strewn muskets, cartridge boxes, and knapsacks. Artillery losses were not so severe, but Major Melancthon Smith reported the abandonment of ten sets of harness and Major J. R. B. Burtwell twelve sets, one traveling forge, and a battery wagon.[4]

Bragg's army, 43,000 strong, encamped at Chattanooga throughout the remainder of the summer. His artillery consisted of twenty-six batteries, in which 2,645 men were present for duty. One battery was attached to each brigade, and there was a reserve battalion.[5] Lumsden's and Dent's batteries were six-gun outfits, as were those of Freeman and Morton of Forrest's cavalry. All the other companies possessed four guns, except Pritchard's two-gun section, which was phased out shortly thereafter.

The lull provided an opportunity to catch up on target practice. On August 6, Private Magee of Stanford's battery wrote: "Commenced firing at 10 o'clock with first piece—very unsatisfactory. Each gun has four shots allowed it. The second piece followed us. Neither one hit the target a distance of 1400 yards. Will not fire the 3rd and 4th pieces—are unfit." That same day, Private Grammer of Swett's battery commented: "Swett's and Douglas' batteries had target practice, distance of 1200 yards, for the purpose of trying our guns. Neither hit the target though a few good line shots were made."[6]

The next day, Magee recorded: "Resumed firing at 10 o'clock— no better success. Our battery condemned. We will get a new battery of Napoleon guns." Continuing on the 8th, he reported: "Fowler's battery fired today—very good shooting. Struck the target twice [at] 1400 yards. Smith's old battery commanded by Lt. Turner also fired. Struck the target twice [at] 1250 yards. He made very good shots. The shooting from all the batteries except Fowler's and Scott's was very bad." General Polk concluded the training session with a grand review of his corps artillery.

●

By mid-August the Union army was once again on the prowl. In a series of rapid marches reminiscent of the Tullahoma campaign, Rosecrans outmaneuvered Bragg and forced him out of Chattanooga. Union troops entered the town on September 9, a day behind the Southerners, who withdrew to Lafayette, Georgia. Rosecrans pursued. His 60,000 man Army of the Cumberland consisted of the corps of George Thomas, Alexander McCook, and Thomas L. Crittenden, plus a reserve corps under

Gordon Granger and two cavalry divisions. The powerful
Federal artillery comprised thirty-four batteries, almost all six-
gun outfits, which counted 204 pieces, half of which were rifles
and half smoothbores. Nearly three-fourths of the latter were
light 12-pounders. The batteries were in divisional groupings,
but were ineffectively assigned to brigades, similar to the Confederate organization.[7]

As the Northerners advanced, Bragg gathered reinforcements. Realizing that Simon Buckner's two divisions would be
unable to hold Knoxville against A. E. Burnside's corps, he ordered Buckner to join the Army of Tennessee. The 8,000 troops
did so about the time of the Chattanooga evacuation. Major
Samuel C. Williams's battalion (the batteries of Baxter's Tennessee, Kolb's Alabama, and McCants's Florida) and Major A.
Leyden's 9th Georgia Artillery Battalion (companies C, D, and
E and Jeffress's Nottoway Virginia Artillery attached) accompanied the east Tennessee column. The seven batteries totaled
twenty-nine field pieces. Buckner's corps chief of artillery was
Major Thomas Porter, an Annapolis graduate, who had been
severely wounded at Fort Donelson.[8]

General Joseph E. Johnston sent from his army in Mississippi
the divisions of John C. Breckinridge and W. H. T. Walker and
the brigades of John Gregg and Evander McNair, totaling
11,500 troops. Major Rice Graves's battalion (Cobb's Kentucky
Battery, Mebane's Tennessee Battery, and the Louisiana Washington Artillery) was attached to Breckinridge's division.
Walker's artillery included Ferguson's South Carolina and Martin's Georgia batteries. Gregg's and McNair's brigades were accompanied by Bledsoe's Missouri and Culpepper's South
Carolina batteries. The seven companies totaled thirty-two
guns.[9]

Johnston's troops required nearly a week to reach Chattanooga. Walker's and Breckinridge's divisions did not arrive
until August 28, well ahead of the artillery. As late as September 4, Bragg wired Walker: "Send an officer to Atlanta to
stop your artillery and take it to Kingston. If the guns and
horses are not on the same train, let the one be halted at Atlanta
until the other comes up, that both may reach Kingston and
Rome together."[10]

Bragg's largest accession was Lieutenant General James
Longstreet's corps of the Army of Northern Virginia. The 15,000
troops and Colonel E. P. Alexander's battalion of six batteries
made the grueling 900-mile journey from Orange Courthouse,

Virginia, via Petersburg, Wilmington, Augusta, and Atlanta. Men and equipment were forced to change trains on several occasions because of the varying railroad gauges. Only five brigades (about 9,000 men) and none of the artillery made it in time to participate in the imminent battle.[11]

By mid-September, Bragg's enlarged artillery corps, not including Alexander's battalion still en route, consisted of 40½ batteries (175 guns). In addition to the Army of Tennessee's 26½ batteries (114 guns), Buckner's artillery from east Tennessee furnished 7 batteries (29 guns), and that of Johnston from Mississippi provided 7 batteries (32 guns). Because Ferguson's battery of Johnston's command remained in Rome, it was not to participate in the upcoming battle.

The armament (of the reporting batteries) included twenty-three 6-pounders, thirty-one 12-pounder howitzers, two 24-pounder howitzers, forty-one 12-pounder Napoleons, twelve 3-inch rifles, eight 10-pounder Parrott rifles, three James rifles, two 6-pounder rifles, and one Blakely rifle. Most of the companies had either two or three calibers of guns, which not only lessened their efficiency for specific functions but also made ammunition supply difficult. Still, this would be one of the few occasions when the western artillery would approach numerical parity with its Federal counterpart.[12]

As Rosecrans's widely separated columns moved southward, Bragg saw the opportunity to strike a blow at his opponent. On September 10, Hindman's division and Buckner's corps (Stewart's and Preston's divisions) were ordered to attack James Negley's nearly isolated division in McLemore's Cove. The battle plan ineffectively called for division batteries to follow in the rear of their assigned brigades. Samuel Williams's reserve battalion was placed in column between Preston's and Hindman's divisions. The entire affair was bungled and Negley escaped. In the minor skirmishing that ensued, Hill's artillery chief, Lieutenant Colonel Bondurant, was wounded.[13]

Losing the opportunities to strike Thomas at McLemore's Cove and later Crittenden at Lee & Gordon's Mill, Bragg now made hurried maneuvers to concentrate his army, as did Rosecrans. During these marches, division batteries traveled in the center of brigades, thus making concentration impossible in the event of battle. The two reserve battalions (Robertson's and Williams's) were kept intact as units, but on September 18, on the eve of battle, no one could find Robertson's battalion. It was supposed to report to Hindman's division, but early that morning Polk was notified that scouts were unable to locate it. By the time it finally was found, Polk had changed orders and directed that it report to Cheatham's division, on the Long Hallow Road in the direction of Lee & Gordon's Mill. The battalion spent the entire morning floundering around on back roads. Around noon, it came upon Bushrod Johnson's division and stayed with it for the remainder of the day.[14]

By the night of September 18, both armies blindly faced each other along the banks of Chickamauga Creek, about twelve miles south of Chattanooga. Bragg's army was concentrated primarily on the west bank from Reed's bridge to Dalton's Ford. He determined to interpose troops between the Union left and Chattanooga. A clash would evidently take place soon, but, because both armies were groping around in dense wooded areas and neither knew the exact position of the other, predicting at what point it would come was difficult.

●

At 7:30 on the morning of the 19th, a Union brigade of John Brannan's division blundered into the Confederate concentration on the Reed's Bridge Road. Initially, the brigade encountered only Nathan Bedford Forrest's cavalry, supported by John Morton's and A. L. Huggin's Tennessee batteries. The guns were placed in front of the dismounted troopers—Forrest's favorite style of using artillery—and slowed the Union advance. It happened to be Morton's twenty-first birthday. He had been presented a new artillery suit that was neatly packed away in a wagon. Much to his chagrin, he later learned that an army mule had helped himself to the uniform and gnawed it terribly.[15]

After pushing Forrest aside, Brannan encountered Ector's and Wilson's brigades of S. R. Gist's division. These troops advanced with the Rebel yell, but were in turn driven back by Union reinforcements. In seesaw fashion, the Federal right flank was now hit by St. John Liddell's newly arrived division, which sent its adversaries reeling back and captured two batteries. Liddell was then checked by the counterattack of a third Union division, under Richard Johnson. Both batteries were retaken.[16]

Because of the thick forest terrain, the Rebel artillery was only minimally engaged during the morning assault. "Owing to the nature of the ground, and the rapidity with which the brigade advanced, I found it impossible to get the battery into position to render assistance," wrote Lieutenant Harvey Shannon, commanding Swett's Mississippi Battery. Captain W. H. Fowler likewise admitted that the service of his Alabama battery "was necessarily limited, because the character of the field where we operated was so badly adopted to the use of light artillery."[17]

At 11:00 Cheatham's veteran division, accompanied by Major Melancthon Smith's powerful battalion of five batteries, arrived on the field. The division moved forward, initially pushing the enemy back. Two additional Union divisions were fed to the front line, however, as the battle rolled southward. The Southerners fell back, leaving several of their batteries exposed in the process. A number of horses were killed in a crossfire directed at Scogin's Georgia Battery, which was forced to abandon one gun and a caisson. Scott's Tennessee Battery also withdrew, but not before three men were killed, thirteen wounded, and fourteen horses disabled.[18]

The most promising of the Confederate attacks came at 2:30, when Major General A. P. Stewart's "Little Giant" division burst from the woods, wrecked the Union center near the Lafayette Road, and captured twelve guns. The Rebels penetrated as far as the Glenn-Kelly Road before the attack sputtered to a halt and was driven back by two fresh Union divisions under Joseph Reynolds and J. S. Negley as well as the massed fire of fourteen guns.

As Stewart's infantry fell back, a devastating fire poured into John Humphreys's 1st Arkansas Battery. Two limbers were wrecked, twelve horses disabled, and one gun left in a no-man's-land, though it was later hauled to safety. During the entire action, the battery was unable to fire a single shot for fear of hitting its own infantry, who were "scattered in groups along our front, and in small parties coming back from the charge."[19]

W. W. Carnes's Tennessee Battery of Cheatham's division came into line on Stewart's right. It had the misfortune of being at the wrong place at the wrong time. As the guns were unlimbered, a withering fire was unleashed by the counterattacking Federals, who during the next ten minutes nearly engulfed their opponents. A limber was brought up to withdraw one of the guns, but all six horses fell dead in a heap under the blistering fire. Captain Carnes was heard to shout: "We can't save the battery; let the men leave as quick as possible." By that time, almost every horse was dead. The Yankees rushed in among the struggling, dying animals and captured all four guns, still double-shotted with canister. Nineteen of Carnes's men died; twenty were wounded, many severely; and forty-nine horses were killed in harness. The battery was destroyed.[20]

The artillery also faced pressure elsewhere along the line. When Stewart was ordered to the right, the position held by his division west of Thedford Ford was occupied by Major S. C. Williams, commanding the reserve battalion of Buckner's corps, with the batteries of Kolb's Alabama and Darden's Mississippi. At 2:00 they were subjected to severe artillery fire that downed both men and horses. Williams's guns stood silent, however, because his fuzes were "so uncertain that he would have run the risk of killing our own men by firing over their heads."[21]

It was almost dark when Pat Cleburne's division replaced that of S. R. Gist's on the Confederate right. At 6:00 Cleburne, supported by Cheatham, attacked along the Lafayette Road. The Federal right was pushed back about a mile. Semple's and Douglas's batteries followed in the rear of Wood's brigade. They "encountered a hot fire of musketry and artillery as [they] advanced across an open field," reported Lieutenant Richard Goldthwaite. Major Thomas Hotchkiss, Cleburne's artillery chief, fell wounded and was replaced by Captain Henry Semple. The two batteries unlimbered and began firing, but by now it was so dark they were "guided entirely by the flash of their guns in the darkness." The Texas battery "gained a position in 80 yards of the wall [barricade] and opened with two pieces. I took 'Sallie' [gun named for Sallie White] alone and by main strength mounted her within the fort," Captain Douglas explained to his wife.[22] Despite the fierceness of the assault, the Southerners were unable to break the enemy hold on the road. As far as Cleburne's artillery fire was concerned, most of it went too high and did little damage beyond creating havoc in the timber. The first day's battle had ended inconclusively.

During the night, both armies rearranged their dispositions. Polk was given command of the right wing (five divisions) and Longstreet, who arrived at 11:00 P.M., was assigned the left (six divisions). The attack the next morning was to be made in echelon from north to south.

●

By 9:30 A.M. on the 20th, Polk's line was at last ready to advance. Thirty minutes later, Breckinridge's division rolled forward toward the Lafayette Road. His right and middle brigades, under

Daniel Adams and Marcellus Stovall, respectively, seized the
road, then wheeled to the south and smashed the Federal left in
the area of the Kelly Field. The Louisiana Washington Artillery
advanced sixty yards behind Adams's brigade. As the Confederates penetrated deep into the Federal rear, the battery unlimbered near the Kelly house. "We drove them off, limbered to rear,
and moved across the orchard and took position beyond the ravine," reported Captain C. H. Slocomb. "The enemy here
opened a heavy artillery fire upon us, which was returned,
Adams's brigade charging them as their fire was silenced." At
this point, twenty-five-year-old Major Rice Graves, Breckinridge's artillery chief, was mortally wounded.[23]

Adams and Stovall received no help and were consequently
pushed back by Union reinforcements. Adams's men rallied on
the Washington Artillery at the Kelly orchard. The New Orleans cannoneers were subjected to a severe counterfire and
were forced to retire, after four of them were killed, sixteen
wounded, and thirteen horses disabled.[24] Cobb's battery, following in the rear of Helms's brigade, fared no better. So dense was
the terrain that the limbers could not be brought up, and the
guns had to be rolled into line by hand. According to Captain
Robert Cobb, "The enemy poured into my front a most galling
fire, his line being entirely concealed by the thickness of a small
growth of timber." The battery was forced to withdraw.[25]

Cleburne's division, on Breckinridge's left, was now thrown
into the fray. For nearly an hour, the Confederates recoiled as
repeated assaults were made on the log barricades. As Douglas's
battery moved at a gallop through the fallen timber, it was suddenly hit by a dangerous flank fire and forced back. Calvert's
Arkansas Battery unlimbered, but a howitzer was quickly disabled by Union artillery fire. Semple's battery kept up a "constant, though slow and deliberate fire," until its ammunition
was exhausted and it was ordered back, after losing ten men and
two horses.[26]

Around noon, Walker's corps (Gist's and Liddell's divisions)
replaced Breckinridge's and Cleburne's shattered commands.
The renewed attack was poorly handled. The fresh divisions
butted against the Cleburne-Breckinridge front in ineffective
brigade-size attacks. Liddell's artillery (Swett's and Fowler's
batteries) advanced, but were hardly engaged. Fowler's unit
came under a "sustained fire of small arms from a very large
infantry force," which rendered the position "totally untena-
ble." Cheatham's division was not even sent into action. By mid-

afternoon, Polk's wing had made no headway in seizing the Lafayette Road and had sustained 30 percent casualties.[27]

A lull in the battle occurred around 11 o'clock as Longstreet prepared a massive assault column to attack the Union center. The divisions of Stewart, Johnson, Hindman, Law, McClaws, and Preston, some 23,000 men, stood poised astride the Brotherton Road. The spearhead of the assault, Johnson's division, was to penetrate east of the Lafayette Road past the Brotherton farm. Just how much artillery was available is difficult to ascertain. Glenn Tucker speaks of "only forty-two guns" in the left wing. This "paucity of artillery" was attributable, he states, to the fact that Longstreet's artillery was not with him when he reached the battlefield. Tucker concluded: "Alexander was missed by Longstreet."[28] Eleven division batteries, totaling forty-six guns, were assigned to Stewart's, Preston's, Johnson's, and Hindman's divisions. Because a few pieces had been disabled by this time, Tucker's estimate of forty-two appears to be accurate. Three batteries (eleven guns) of Williams's reserve battalion were also available, however, which brought the total number to fifty-three.

That Alexander's large battalion would have been of assistance assumes that it would have been used properly. Such may not have been the case. Apparently only one (Everett's) of the fourteen batteries available even moved out with the attacking column. Sheer negligence was partially to blame. Neither of Bushrod Johnson's batteries (Bledsoe's and Culpepper's), "for reasons unknown to me," declared Johnson, followed their brigades into action. Dawson's Georgia Battery was still refitting from A. P. Stewart's abortive attack of half an hour earlier. When William Bate's brigade of that division moved out, its battery, the Eufaula Light Artillery, "remained in position," reported Captain W. J. McKenzie. Williams's battalion followed Preston, but that division was not initially committed.[29]

The rugged terrain was also a factor. The long arm was being called upon to perform an offensive mission in extremely rugged and wooded country. "Old Peter [Longstreet] did not waste much time in search for a substitute chief of artillery because his survey of the field showed it to be mainly a heavy woodland poorly adopted to the use of artillery," Tucker stated.[30]

The terrain was not the only, indeed, perhaps not even the most significant, of the shackles. Once again, the shibboleth of the western artillery—a faulty organizational structure—was at fault. Despite the implementation of the War Department's order calling for the grouping of batteries, the battalion as a tactical unit was practically ignored. All divisional batteries followed their assigned brigades—the same as at Shiloh a year and a half earlier. Significantly, the only occasion in which the artillery was to exert any measureable effect during Longstreet's assault was when Samuel Williams's reserve battalion was committed as a unit.

At 11:00 Longstreet issued the attack order. In a scene that Bushrod Johnson described as "unspeakably grand," the Confederates swarmed past the Brotherton farm and discovered a hole in the Union line that had been created by an error in the shifting of troops. Rosecrans's entire right wing collapsed under the pressure, and the bluecoats ran pell-mell toward McFarland's Gap. Numbers of guns (Johnson's division alone claimed nineteen pieces) and thousands of prisoners were captured.

By 2:00 Longstreet's troops had approached the Dry Valley Road, only a few miles from McFarland's Gap. Johnson brought up Everett's battery (E, 9th Georgia Artillery Battalion) to the vicinity of the Vittetoe house to open fire on the escaping Federals. The bursting shells created total consternation. An enemy battery attempted to unlimber and return fire, but the Georgians made quick work of them and disabled one of their guns. Southern infantry moved in and captured three guns and seven caissons.[31]

The fight now stabilized as Brennan's Union division, bent back at a right angle to Rosecrans's left, formed along a spur of Missionary Ridge known as Snodgrass Hill. Desperate, but unsuccessful, assaults were hurled against the position, but hastily constructed log and rock breastworks enabled the Yankees to hold. Longstreet still had Preston's fresh division, but, before committing it, he needed to take care of the Federal fire enfilading his right. These troops were part of Thomas's corps, which had held firm during the melee to their right. At 4:00 Major Thomas Porter, Buckner's artillery chief, placed Williams's battalion (then consisting of eleven guns) near the Poe house to take these troops in reverse.[32]

At this point, the artillery should have been committed in mass. At the very minimum, Robertson's reserve battalion ought to have supported Williams. But where was Major Robertson? As he had done at Murfreesboro and on the march to Chickamauga, he demonstrated an uncanny ability to be unavailable when he was most needed. Exactly where he was at

4:00 is impossible to determine because he apparently submitted no After Action Report. His battalion statistical table, however, shows that seven of his twenty-one guns never fired a shot. His remaining fourteen guns expended only 151 rounds during the two days of battle. Years later, a member of the battalion recalled that Robertson on the 20th took great pains "not to expose us unnecessarily," and even the men who hated the pedantic young officer remarked that day that "he takes care of us." Indications are that the battalion was little used at all, much less significantly so.[33]

At 4:00 Williams's batteries opened fire at a range of 1,000 yards and kept up the pounding for about forty-five minutes. Grose's brigade of Palmer's division was completely taken in reverse. The Yankees were hit by "the most terrific cannonading I have heard during these battles," wrote a Union officer, "and in a few minutes completely enfilading our entire rear." Major Porter boasted that Williams's guns demonstrated "great execution."[34]

In the late afternoon, Steedman's division of Granger's reserve hurried to assist their beleaguered companions on Snodgrass Hill. Moving from Rossville Gap down the Lafayette Road, Forrest's calvary, guarding Bragg's right flank, moved to intercept. He placed his artillery (Morton's, Huggins's, and Huwald's batteries) as well as a borrowed section of Napoleons from Cobb's battery on a ridge parallel to and 600 to 800 yards distant from the Lafayette Road. As the Yankees approached, the line of artillery went into action and drove the enemy off the road. Forrest's troopers advanced dismounted. "My artillery was ordered forward, but before it could reach the road and be placed in position a charge was made by the enemy," explained Forrest. The gray troopers held long enough for the batteries to hastily withdraw to their original position and open with a "destructive fire" at "short range."[35]

To avoid Forrest's artillery, Steedman's troops left the Lafayette Road. Passing through the Mullis farm, they arrived on Brannan's right, just as the Southerners were attempting to outflank the position. The Yankees checked several determined assaults. William Preston thought that the artillery was of little use in the offensive action against Snodgrass Hill. "In the attack on the [Snodgrass] hill no artillery could be used by us effectively," he declared, and added that the "struggle was alone for the infantry. Few fell who were not struck down by the rifle or the musket."[36]

At 5:30 Thomas, the ranking Federal officer on the field, began to withdraw the remaining troops. Three regiments,
consisting of about 550 men, were sacrificed, but the rest of the
Federals escaped under cover of darkness. Bragg made no effort
at pursuit.

•

The contribution of the Confederate artillery at Chickamauga
was extremely disappointing, especially because more guns
were fielded than in any previous battle. Historian Shelby Foote
concludes: "Chickamauga was by no means an artillery fight."[37]
Certainly the terrain limited mobility. This rugged, heavily
wooded area of north Georgia was simply not artillery country.
"As most of the ground over which the battle was fought was very
thickly wooded, we could not see more than 300 yards to the
front, and consequently could very seldom use artillery," explained Major Porter. In one respect, the terrain favored the
Confederates, however, because it helped to neutralize the superior range of rifled guns, of which Rosecrans possessed far more.
Captain Thomas Stanford commented that the ground "would
not permit the use of artillery, and especially a rifle battery."[38]

Other circumstances limited the role of the artillery. Once
again, the Army of Tennessee had fought a battle on the tactical
offensive. It attempted to use its long arm aggressively, several
times advancing batteries to within 100 yards of the Federal
line. The artillery was essentially a defensive arm, however,
and, as one historian observed, "the use of artillery on the offensive at Chickamauga was not so successful as the Confederates
had hoped."[39]

Nor was the artillery judiciously employed. Bushrod Johnson
instructed his batteries to "move with the infantry and come
into action whenever opportunity permitted."[40] This "make
yourself useful" policy seemed to be typical. Batteries were always committed individually and never in mass.

The artillery also lacked overall direction. This could have
been partially alleviated by placing the batteries of each wing
under a single leader. Unfortunately, the two most qualified
officers, Lieutenant Colonel James Bondurant, of Polk's wing,
and Colonel E. P. Alexander, of Longstreet's wing, were not present on the field. Glenn Tucker remarks that Longstreet "did not
waste much time in search of a substitute chief of artillery" to
replace Alexander. Yet, Longstreet later contended that, lacking

a chief artilleryman, he was forced to give orders concerning the artillery directly to the corps commanders, who were preoccupied with infantry movements.[41]

The statistics affirm the artillery's minor role. Despite the enormous casualties suffered by the Confederates (26 percent of the army), a modest 43 artillerymen were killed and 166 wounded, or an estimated 6 percent. Carnes's battery sustained the heaviest loss (only 38 of the men escaped unharmed), and 11 were killed and 22 wounded in the Washington Artillery. Scott's and Dents's batteries had moderate losses of 16 each and the Eufaula Artillery 14. Casualties in the other batteries, however, were very light.[42]

Later speaking of the unusually heavy loss of artillery horses, Bragg estimated that a third of them were killed or disabled. This was one of the reasons he advanced for not vigorously pursuing the enemy. The statistics simply do not support this. The batteries reported losses of only 231 horses. Rosecrans's, on the other hand, claimed a figure of nearly 600.[43]

The paltry expenditure of ammunition was yet another indication of the limited participation of the artillery. The field batteries reported a total of 4,568 rounds fired, or an average of only 38 per gun. This compares with Rosecrans's expenditure of 7,325 rounds and Robert E. Lee's expenditure at Gettysburg of 22,000 rounds, or an average of 150 per gun.[44]

One fact that did not escape the notice of Confederate officials was that much of their ordnance simply failed to work under combat conditions. A howitzer in Scott's battery was placed out of service when the cap square broke. No less than four gun carriage trails (one each in Havis's and Lumsden's batteries and two in Peeples's) broke down as the cannon recoiled during firing. A howitzer in Everett's company was disabled when the axle tree broke, and two guns in Martin's battery were placed out of commission when the limber poles snapped. Major Williams reported that three-fourths of the shells fired by his battalion failed to explode. The artillery officers in Breckinridge's division complained about friction primers that were "perfectly worthless and unreliable."[45]

Despite the poor use of the artillery, or more notably its limited use, Chickamauga was still a Confederate victory and, as such, the spoils went to Bragg. Included were thirty-nine field pieces (six 6-pounders, six 12-pounder howitzers, four 12-pounder Napoleons, one 12-pounder mountain howitzer, six 3-inch rifles, seven 10-pounder Parrott rifles, and nine 3.8-inch

James rifles), twenty limbers, thirty caissons, one battery wagon, 156 single sets of artillery harness, and about 2,100 rounds of ammunition. It was the most significant artillery cache of the war for the Army of Tennessee. A few batteries exchanged captured pieces for disabled ones on the field, but most of them were shipped by rail to the Atlanta Arsenal.[46] No one suspected that within two months many of them would be shipped back to Bragg, this time to replace a large number that the Union had captured.

Chapter 10

"Limber to the Rear"

Lieutenant Andrew Neal of McCants's Florida Battery was jubilant that the Southerners had "whipped the Yankees badly" on the banks of Chickamauga Creek. "We have only to press them to reap the victory," he exclaimed. Forrest's cavalry had pushed to the outskirts of Chattanooga, and Morton's horse battery was shelling one of the Union forts. In command headquarters, however, Bragg remained unconvinced he had won a victory. Dawdling for two days, he made limited reconnaissances, gleaned the battlefield for small arms, and counted his surviving artillery horses. Not until the morning of September 23 was the army put in motion and the sound of Confederate artillery rattling over the twelve-mile road to Chattanooga heard. Meantime, Rosecrans's battered army had beefed up old Rebel fortifications and thrown up a strong defensive line around the southern side of town.[1]

During the last week in September, Bragg established his army in a six-mile semicircle southeast of the town stretching from Lookout Mountain eastward across the valley below Missionary Ridge to the Tennessee River. Longstreet commanded the left, Hill the center, and Walker the right. The encirclement was not total, but it was effective.

Bragg decided to invest the town and starve the beleaguered Federals into submission. Rosecrans's army could be supplied by water, rail, and road. His primary supply routes—the Tennessee River, the Nashville & Chattanooga Railroad, and the south bank wagon road—all merged together at the base of Lookout Mountain. Bragg recognized that, if a row of cannon could be established across its summit, the supply routes around Moccasin Bend could be effectively blocked. Thus, the mission of the artillery: cut the Union jugular.

Longstreet, commanding the Lookout Mountain sector, assigned the task to the recently arrived battalion of Colonel E. P.

Alexander of the Army of Northern Virginia, which had rolled into Ringgold Station during the early morning hours of September 25 after a grueling seven-and-a-half day journey from Virginia. It consisted of one Louisiana and five Virginia batteries, a total of twenty-three guns. The horses had been left behind in Virginia, and others would now need to be furnished.[2] Alexander was not impressed with the Army of Tennessee. "This army is far inferior to the Army of Northern Virginia in organization and spirit, and I regret very much that I ever left the latter," he complained. Concerning the western long arm, he found the organization imperfect, the fixed ammunition of poor quality, and the guns of inferior caliber.[3]

The battalion soon began its assigned task. Hauling guns up the small trail leading to the summit was difficult. Mules and skids were used for the heaviest ones. Nighttime work was required because the trail was commanded at several points by Federal batteries on Moccasin Point. All the cannon were carefully placed behind huge boulders to protect the crews from Union crossfire. Twenty long-range pieces and a few howitzers were eventually placed in position. The carriage trails of the latter were sunk deep in the ground so that they might be used as mortars.[4]

From atop the 1,500-foot lofty eminence, Rebel gunners were afforded a sweeping panoramic view of the bend in the Tennessee River and the Federal camps in Lookout Valley. Scanning the vast scene with his field glasses, Alexander carefully selected his targets. Then, at 1:00 P.M. on September 29 his batteries opened fire, which drew an immediate response.[5]

Daily, Alexander's guns vainly lobbed shells into the Federal encampments, the sound reverberating throughout the valley. Although the muzzles were depressed to the utmost, the range was simply too far and the angle too steep. Alexander later recalled firing every day at a "vicious little battery" in Moccasin Bend, almost directly below the mountain. "This battery had nearly buried itself in the ground under high parapets, and fired at us like a man shooting a squirrel in a tree," he commented. "We propped our trails up in the air to depress the muzzles, and tried to smash our opponents into the earth with solid shot and percussion shells; but we never hurt them much, and when we left the mountain they were still as lively as ever."[6]

Other difficulties were experienced. One of Bragg's best rifled pieces, a 20-pounder Parrott in Massenburg's Georgia Battery, burst at the muzzle on the second day of the siege and wounded two artillerymen. Another area of concern was poor rifle shells, which often failed to explode upon impact. If that was not enough, before the siege was over, Alexander's three 20-pounders had exhausted their supply of shells. A single 24-pounder siege gun, which had been brought up by rail from Atlanta and placed on the right flank of the army, sent shells crashing into the Federal camps in that sector, but with little effect. "They are too well posted to be shelled and this business is all foolishness," complained a disgusted artilleryman.[7]

Major Felix Robertson accomplished a dangerous sortie one evening. By night, two batteries of the reserve were quietly moved down to the riverbank and placed directly across from an enemy camp. They were carefully camouflaged. At dawn, when the Union bugler sounded "Reveille," Robertson shouted: "Battalion! Ready! Fire!" The two batteries burst out in a thunderous salvo that lasted for six to eight minutes, until the Federal batteries responded. The major yelled: "Limber to the rear! To the right, march! Gallop!" The guns whirled off into the woods. An Illinois artilleryman later confessed that "They made things lively for a time."[8]

Despite such harassing tactics, the Confederate long arm inflicted little damage during the month-long siege. Ranges would need to shorten before that could occur. Still, the strategic presence of artillery crowning the mountain heights, coupled with menacing cavalry raids in the rear, reduced the flow over Rosecrans's supply routes. This was all Bragg needed. Rainy weather in mid-October made it nearly impossible for the Federals to haul supplies over the sixty-mile trail leading from the railhead at Stevenson, Alabama, across Walden's Ridge to the north bank of the Tennessee River opposite Chattanooga. As the days ticked away, the Union army became desperate for provisions and by the third week it was placed on quarter rations. The animals did not fare so well. An estimated ten thousand horses and mules died of starvation, which immobilized the artillery.

Meanwhile, Bragg had been encountering his own supply problems. During October, his army experienced a severe shortage of corn and long forage. A lieutenant in Darden's Mississippi Battery warned that "for the want of forage my horses are rapidly falling off." Captain J. T. Humphreys, commanding an Arkansas battery, informed his division artillery chief that "during the past five days I have received twelve sacks of corn for sixty-nine horses." Between October 14 and 18, Douglas's Texas

Battery received seventy-nine bushels of corn and no hay to feed seventy-five horses and twenty-five mules. During October, half the army's artillery horses had to be moved to the rear to feed on grass.[9]

Bragg's grip on the Union bread line was fleeting. During the early morning hours of October 27, a Federal expedition brushed aside token resistance and secured Brown's Ferry, an upriver position out of Rebel artillery range. A new supply route to Bridgeport, Alabama, was thus opened. Bragg considered attacking the two Union corps in Lookout Valley, but the road leading down to the valley was too steep for cannon to traverse safely. Longstreet's batteries would need to make a detour of fifty miles, a move considered to be impractical. No new plan was forthcoming.[10]

•

Meanwhile, Bragg, in early November, had undertaken a wholesale reorganization of his army—partially for efficiency but primarily to disperse the anti-Bragg element. Three corps were created under Longstreet; Breckinridge, who replaced D. H. Hill; and Hardee, who took over from Polk. Liddell's small division was phased out, which left ten infantry divisions.

The long arm did not escape the shake-up. By the time numerous batteries were shifted about, several battalions only faintly resembled their former organization. Major Melancthon Smith retained only two of his original five batteries. Major Williams's reorganized battalion was assigned to Buckner's division and Leyden's battalion to McClaws's division of Longstreet's corps. The reserve battalion, under Bragg's protégé Felix Robertson, remained intact. Lieutenant Neal expressed the sentiments of many of the men when he stated: "I do not care to leave this [Williams's] battalion, as we have fought together and I know them to be good and excellent troops."[11]

Carter Stevenson's division, which had been paroled and exchanged since the surrender of Vicksburg, arrived with two Georgia batteries: John Rowan's and Max Van den Corput's. Both were temporarily armed with Yankee cannon that had been captured at Chickamauga. Twenty-seven infantrymen were assigned to Rowan's company as drivers.[12] Carnes's Tennessee Battery, which had been badly damaged at Chickamauga, was also reequipped in early November. It was issued four light 12-pounders, and some additional men from Scott's

Tennessee Battery were assigned. But, because a shortage of cannoneers remained, the battery remainded out of service.[13]

Several new faces emerged on the field staffs. Captain Charles Slocomb temporarily replaced the deceased Rice Graves as Breckinridge's artillery chief. Captain Robert Cobb was appointed as acting chief of Stevenson's newly arrived batteries. Captain Henry Semple served as A. P. Stewart's top artilleryman during the brief absence of Major J. W. Eldridge.

Bragg's reorganized long arm totaled forty-six batteries, consisting of 3,636 officers and men. The armament, minus the horse batteries, included 145 guns: twenty-two 6-pounders, twenty-eight 12-pounder howitzers, four 24-pounder howitzers, forty-eight 12-pounder Napoleons, twelve 10-pounder Parrott rifles, four 20-pounder Parrott rifles, nineteen 3-inch rifles, seven James rifles, and one Blakely rifle. The guns averaged 156 rounds apiece.[14]

Chief of Ordnance Hypolite Oladowski continued to push for better cannon. In early November, he estimated that twenty-two 12-pounder Napoleons were still required to replace the 6-pounders then in service. Later that month, he informed Colonel M. H. Wright, at the Atlanta Arsenal, that all the 6-pounders that had been used at Chickamauga were "repulsed by 12-pounder light guns." One battery of 6-pounders and 12-pounder howitzers, he noted, was "entirely smashed and taken by the enemy." On November 12 four new government Napoleons arrived and they were immediately issued to Bledsoe's Missouri Battery. A week later, Bragg dispatched a special messenger to speed delivery of a battery of Macon Arsenal light 12-pounders.[15]

•

By early November, it had become apparent that the Union army was undergoing a massive buildup. Bragg had known for some weeks that corps from General William T. Sherman's Army of the Tennessee were hastening from Mississippi, that three divisions under Joseph Hooker had arrived from Virginia, and that the reorganized Army of the Cumberland was now commanded by George H. Thomas. Further, an intercepted dispatch revealed that Major General Ulysses S. Grant was arriving to take overall command of the corps now massing. Reports of 90,000 Federals in Chattanooga were not exaggerated.

In the light of this information, Bragg foolishly proceeded to do the opposite. On November 4 he dispatched Longstreet's two divisions, 12,000 men, and 5,000 cavalry under Wheeler on a hapless venture to wipe out Ambrose Burnside's isolated corps at Knoxville. On November 23, Buckner's small 3,000-man division entrained for east Tennessee. Longstreet's artillery included Alexander's and Leyden's battalions, some thirty-five guns. In addition, Wheeler took with him three of his four batteries. Still not satisfied, Longstreet argued that Wheeler's guns should be exchanged for "three good batteries of long range pieces." Buckner's artillery, Major S. C. Williams's battalion, was later recalled to the army and assigned to the artillery reserve as a second battalion.[16]

Bragg had miscalculated. Grant did not reinforce Burnside as anticipated. Instead of relieving Union pressure on the Chattanooga line, Bragg now found himself with less than 30,000 troops confronting a far superior Federal force. According to one historian, he "attempted to defend an impossible line, weak both in men and geographical advantages."[17] Now that Longstreet was gone, Bragg's left flank on Lookout Mountain was defended by Carter Stevenson's division. A section of Howell's Georgia Battery was placed at the Craven house on the plateau below the craggy summit. Because the plateau was commanded by Federal artillery in Moccasin Bend, Howell's horses had to be left at the base of the mountain. In the event of a sudden reversal, removing the pieces would be impossible.

The cannon on the summit of Lookout Mountain were now silent. Alexander's guns were gone. Stevenson assigned Garrity's lone Parrott battery to man Lookout Point. At 1:00 A.M. on November 24, it was relieved by a section of Napoleon guns from Van den Corput's battery. There was one glaring problem. In the event of an attack, the guns could not be depressed enough to reach the base of the mountain. Brigadier General John Jackson's counsel to sink their wheels and elevate the carriage trails so as to sweep the slope went unheeded.[18]

The morning of November 24 was marked by a cold rain and heavy fog. At 10:00 some 10,000 troops under Hooker smashed into Stevenson's line. Forty guns of the Army of the Cumberland, brought up by Sherman's artillery horses, had been concentrated on Moccasin Point to give coverage. They now opened a thunderous barrage. Van den Corput's section responded, but the heavy fog shrouded the movement of the enemy, and very little could be accomplished. By noon the shattered Confederate force had been pushed back past the Cra-

ven house and Howell's two 6-pounders captured. Using the
signal corps as forward artillery observers, Van den Corput's
gunners continued to shell in the direction of the farm. By 2:30
the engagement was clearly over, and Bragg ordered his troops
off the mountain.[19]

In a night meeting with his corps commanders, Bragg decided
to make a stand on Missionary Ridge. Hardee would command
the right, where it was known that Sherman had crossed the
Tennessee River and was massing troops in the vicinity of Tunnel Hill. Bragg committed heavily to Hardee's front. Cheatham's
and Stevenson's divisions were moved over to the right that
night. Thus, massed in Hardee's compact area were the divisions
of Pat Cleburne, Carter Stevenson, W. H. T. Walker, and Benjamin Cheatham. This left Breckinridge holding the center and
left of the ridge, nearly four miles in length, with the divisions of
Patton Anderson, William Bate, and A. P. Stewart. Rossville
Gap was protected by only two regiments and a battery.[20]

For the first time, the western artillery was to be employed on
the tactical defensive. At Shiloh, Murfreesboro, and Chickamauga, an attempt had been made to use it offensively, but the
effectiveness was limited. It was on the defensive, however, that
Civil War artillery performed at its peak efficiency. But, despite
Bragg's lengthy artillery experience, this was the first time he
had been called upon to deploy large numbers of guns defensively. To his unaccustomed eyes, Missionary Ridge appeared to
be perfectly suited for large-scale artillery operations. In the
valley below, any attack on the center would have to be made
across a 1,200-yard wide open plain. It was presumed that artillery crowning the heights above could thoroughly sweep the
field. Bragg therefore placed nearly all his cannon, some ninety-
six of them, on the crest of the ridge.[21]

Actually, Missionary Ridge presented serious engineering,
geographical, and tactical planning problems for the artillery.
The battery emplacements on the crest were prepared too close
to the edge. Consequently, the gun barrels could not be depressed enough to sweep the slope. This in effect created an
obtuse angle: A represented the pieces on the crest, B the foot of
the ridge, and C a point about two hundred yards in front of the
ridge base. The artillery would thus be delivering what General
Bate termed a "plunging fire" between points A and C, thus
creating a blind spot.[22] To remedy this, some howitzers (which
were designed to lob shells) could have been placed on the reverse slope. Indirect fire such as this was rare during the Civil

War, but Van den Corput's battery had tried it rather successfully the day before at Lookout Mountain.

The terrain also complicated matters. Although the ridge was crisscrossed with small roads, hauling the guns to the top proved to be no easy task. Young Lieutenant René Beauregard, the son of General P. G. T. Beauregard, who was commanding a South Carolina battery, reported that his horses were so feeble that they could barely draw the pieces up the slope. But, by assigning a company of infantry to each of them and using ropes and pulleys, they were slowly drawn to the top.[23] Once they were on the narrow crest, maneuvering them was difficult. In the event of a reversal, the only escape for some batteries would be to go careening down the reverse slope. The open plain over which the Yankees would need to advance was also deceptive. Those moving on the double-quick could be out of the artillery fire zone within ten minutes. Precious little time would be available for the batteries to do their work.

The guns were also maldistributed. Bragg sprinkled them over the whole length of his overstretched line. Batteries were divided into sections and even single gun crews and placed on commanding rises, often separated by hundreds of yards. Although Anderson's division, for example, covered a front of nearly a mile, only ten widely scattered guns were on line. The Federals were massing a 6,000-man division in that sector alone.[24]

To complete the list of errors, by the morning of November 25, much of the Southern artillery had still not taken position. Cleburne, anticipating a retreat the night before, had prematurely sent his artillery train across Chickamauga Creek. When word was received at midnight that a stand would be made, it had to be hurriedly recalled. During the early morning hours of the 25th, it began retracing its steps.[25] Stevenson's artillery was also late in coming up. The division did not start its journey from Chattanooga Valley until late on the night of the 24th. Because the long arm brought up the rear of the column, it probably did not depart until after midnight. The batteries did not actually get into position on the ridge until noon of the 25th.[26]

A similar situation occurred in the center. Not until 3:30 on the afternoon of the 25th did the Washington Artillery move up on the ridge from the valley via Rossville. Dawson's Georgia Battery did not establish its position until 3:45 P.M. A number of batteries consequently lacked protective earthworks. Despite the army's presence at Chattanooga for two months, it soon

became evident that much of the artillery's defense would be a
hurried, last-minute affair.[27]

On the morning of November 25, Bragg's fears of an attack on
his right were realized. At 11:00 Sherman hurled his Vicksburg
veterans against Cleburne's division. The Rebel artillery was in
position, albeit belatedly: Swett's Mississippi Battery on Tunnel
Hill, Douglas' Texas Battery on line with Govan's brigade, and
Calvert's Arkansas Battery over the tunnel.[28] The assault soon
focused on Tunnel Hill, where Swett's four Napoleon guns
crowned the summit. Three times the Yankees charged up to
their very muzzles, only to be driven back. Lieutenant Harvey
Shannon, the thirty-two-year-old former Vicksburg surgeon
who temporarily commanded Swett's company, was struck by a
shell fragment that broke his collar bone, punctured a lung, and
came out near the backbone. So many officers and sergeants in
the battery were killed or wounded that a corporal was eventually forced to take command. Seven infantrymen were hurriedly detailed to assist in manning the guns.[29]

Toward noon came a lull in the battle. Cleburne ordered two of
Swett's Napoleons over to Govan's brigade because "Douglas'
guns were too light in their present position." Calvert's battery
was sent to replace Swett's detached section. The respite was
brief. At 1:00 the hill was again fiercely assaulted. The cannoneers spun the wheels of elevating screws until the barrels
were depressed to the utmost. Lethal blasts of canister tore gaping holes in the surging blue ranks. A countercharge routed the
Federals and sent them reeling back down the hill.[30]

A good opportunity was missed by not opening on the attackers with an enfilading fire from Stevenson's artillery to the
left of Cleburne. When the assault began, however, these batteries were still not in position. Meantime, Barret's Missouri
Battery of the reserve had been placed on a hill to the south of
the tunnel and had opened on the Federal right. Sherman's attacks were almost over by the time three of Stevenson's four
batteries were positioned. Because of insufficient room, Marshall's battery was left at the base of the ridge. Only one more
attack was made, and it was easily broken up by Stevenson's
cannon.[31]

Events now began unfolding on the left. By early afternoon,
Hooker's three divisions had driven the Confederates out of
Rossville Gap and were pushing them back up Missionary Ridge
toward Bragg's headquarters. By 3:30 the Rebel left was collaps-

ing. At the same time, it became obvious that something major was about to happen in the center. The Army of the Cumberland was engaged in heavy activity in the valley below. At 3:40 six shots boomed from a Federal battery on Orchard Knob. At once, eleven brigades, some 20,000 men, moved out of their fortifications and began a one-mile drive toward Missionary Ridge. From the crest, they looked like two solid lines of glittering bayonets stretching for two miles.

The spotlight now focused on the gray artillery. Even as the Yankee infantry advanced through the wooded area, bursting shells began to pepper the air. As the bluecoats cleared the woods and moved out onto the open plain, the artillery fire intensified. To one Union officer, the crest "came alive with the roar and flame of artillery." To another, the fire was "terrific beyond conception." Guns thundered and leaped back in recoil; they were quickly sponged down and fresh rounds rammed home. Union troops quickened their pace and then broke into a run. Federal siege guns in Chattanooga roared above the din of the field pieces. Gunners on Orchard Knob made a direct hit on a Confederate caisson on Missionary, which caused a huge explosion.[32]

Despite Bragg's later claim that "our batteries opened with fine effect," the barrage did little to blunt or even delay the attackers. Many of the shells burst harmlessly in the air, and others burrowed in the ground without exploding at all. One Union officer noted that fatigue took a far heavier toll among his men than the artillery fire.[33] Almost before anyone realized what was happening, Breckinridge's defense line at the base of the ridge was overrun. As the Southerners scurried up the mountain, waves of Thomas's Cumberlanders pressed onward behind them while the gray artillery stood helplessly mute. Cannoneers lit short fuzes and hurled projectiles by hand at the attackers. Panic broke out as caissons dashed along the crest.[34]

The initial breakthrough came at Zachariah Deas's brigade of Anderson's division. The Southern line simply melted as the troops ran down the south side of the slope. Anderson had Major Alfred R. Courtney's four batteries on line: Garrity's Alabama, Dent's Confederate, Waters's Alabama, and Scott's Tennessee. The frightened gunners began limbering up. As a fleeing gun crew rumbled along the crest road, the drivers furiously lashing their horses, it was suddenly encircled by blue infantry. Garrity was able to save three guns but lost one Napoleon as well as a wagon and suffered twelve casualties. Dent's battery, set up

along a line around the Shallow Ford Road, was wiped out; the
losses included five of six Napoleons, two caissons, twenty-eight
men, and thirty-five horses. Waters's two 6-pounders and two 12-
pounder howitzers were overrun, along with two caissons. Scott
managed to remove only one of his four guns. The battalion, for
all practical purposes, was annihilated.[35]

Cheatham's division was posted to the right of Anderson.
When the attack spilled over into that sector, Cheatham rearranged his line facing southward across the ridge. In the confusion, several of his batteries were hit hard. Captain William B.
Turner was heard to shout: "Number four, solid!" and then
"Limber to the rear!" McCants's Florida Battery was also caught
in the melee. "Finding our support gone and that it was impossible to drive back the immense column, I determined to retire
firing," explained Lieutenant Neal, "but the mountain range
was too rough to manage the pieces by hand and I could not get
the horses up to the guns." The battery lost two 6-pounders and
a limber.[36]

The victorious Federals fanned out in all directions down the
slope and along the crest. Dent's captured guns were trained left
on Bate's right flank. When two limbers in the Washington Artillery were struck, horses and men were mangled and a deafening explosion seemed to shake the entire mountain. The
Louisiana gunners hastily limbered up four of their six cannon
and galloped down the reverse slope. The guns become mired
down at the bottom of the ridge, however, and the crews were
forced to abandon them. Four limbers and sixty horses were
salvaged, but as a fighting unit the battery was destroyed.[37]

Havis's Georgia, Barret's Missouri, and Massenburg's Georgia
batteries of Robertson's 1st Battalion Artillery Reserve and a
section of Kolb's Alabama Battery from Williams's 2d Battalion
were scattered along the line. Havis lost one 12-pounder
Napoleon and one 3.8-inch James rifle, and Barret was forced to
abandon a 20-pounder Parrott caisson when a wheel axle broke.
Massenburg received the severest blow, however. His Georgians
were overrun and all four of their 10-pounder Parrott rifles captured. The only equipment salvaged were two limbers.[38]

In the center of Bate's line, Mebane's Tennessee Battery was
nearly surrounded. It had expended some 543 rounds of ammunition and the limber chests were now nearly empty. The
cannoneers hitched up their four 12-pounder howitzers and
withdrew to a second line east of their position. Remarkably,
only three men and two horses were lost.[39]

Cobb's Kentucky Battery, set up near Bragg's headquarters, was not so fortunate. It was a hard-fighting but ill-fated outfit that enjoyed the dubious honor of having sustained more casualties to date than any battery in the army. Prior to Missionary Ridge, it had lost a staggering 91 men and 112 horses. During the Union attack, the Kentuckians fired off shots from their guns "Lady Breckinridge" and "Lady Buckner," one round exploding dangerously close to General Phil Sheridan. "I shall take those guns for that," he blurted. Making good his vow, his men later swarmed over all four guns and caissons. Cobb's casualties included eleven men and three horses. Another battery was gone.[40]

A. P. Stewart's line, to the left of Bate, was hit from the front, rear, and both flanks. The entire division was routed. Incredibly, much of the artillery escaped. Dawson's Georgia and Stanford's Mississippi batteries lost only a few men and horses; Oliver's Alabama battery, one gun but all the horses.[41]

Two of Bate's brigades fell back a thousand yards and established a defense line to cover the retreat. They held tenaciously for more than an hour as Bragg's disoriented soldiers continued their flight toward Chickamauga Creek. Although a number of batteries were now without horses and equipment, efforts were made to keep the men together as units. Hardee managed to rally his own and Breckinridge's troops in the valley below.

The surviving batteries were now desperate to reach the Chickamauga Creek bridge before it was destroyed. To be stranded on the north bank meant certain capture. Lieutenant Beauregard was so concerned he would lose his four 12-pounder Napoleon guns, Yankee pieces captured at Chickamauga, that he shed tears. He was unaware of any road off the ridge, and his horses were so feeble they could barely draw their guns. Somehow, the troops managed to move the cannon down the south slope, only to encounter a boggy creek. The first gun became stuck deep, and after one or two pulls the horses simply laid down—despite the profanities and beatings of the drivers. About ninety infantrymen from the 66th Georgia plunged into the cold water and "put their shoulders to the wheels." In this manner, one gun was crossed at a time.[42]

Perhaps no battery experienced more frustrating delays than did Rowan's Georgia. The afternoon had now faded into dusk, and the drivers, unable to see, kept running the cannon off the road. Encountering stumps and deep ruts, the crews had to unlimber them and pull them out. The bridge over Chickamauga

Creek had already been set to the torch by the retreating South-erners as John Rowan's last crew arrived. The cannon were raced across as flames leaped up around them. Again, near the rail-road, a cannon got stuck in a bog, and the horses refused to pull it. Around daylight of the 26th, a mule team was sent to assist, and the piece was removed. But the horses now refused to haul the traveling forge. All the tools were discarded to lighten the load, but to no avail. More mules were called for. By the time the additional teams arrived, the infantry rear guard was passing and warned the artillerymen to fall back because enemy skir-mishers were in close pursuit. A lieutenant rapidly hitched up the mules and pulled the forge away.[43]

•

During the early morning hours of November 26, Bragg began pulling his disorganized army out of Chickamauga Station, and it trudged southward toward Dalton, Georgia. So grave did he consider the crisis, he believed that all his remaining artillery might be lost in the retreat. Cleburne's division was handed the task of stalling the Federals until the army made good its es-cape. He positioned his troops on Taylor's Ridge, a mountain overlooking Ringgold Gap.

By 8:00 A.M. on the 27th the enemy began to appear. Two

Confederate Artillery captured at Missionary Ridge

12-pounder Napoleon guns that were captured by the Fed-erals at Missionary Ridge. Sten-ciled on the carriage trails is: "Macon Arse-nal 1863." (Library of Congress)

Napoleon guns from Semple's battery, commanded by Lieutenant Richard W. Goldthwaite, were masked with brush on the
skirmish line. The spearhead of the Federal advance fell into the
trap. When the Yankees were barely fifty yards away, Cleburne
clapped his knee and shouted: "NOW, Lieutenant, give it to 'em,
NOW!" Lanyards were jerked, and the guns belched out blasts of
canister. When the smoke cleared, an Arkansas infantryman
saw "patches of men scattered all over the field" and the rest of
the bluecoats were running "as fast as their legs could carry
them." After skirmishing for five hours, Cleburne pulled his
troops back. The Federals did not pursue.[44]

Back in his mountain stronghold at Dalton, Bragg began to
tally his losses. The infantry, as always, had suffered the most
casualties, in excess of 6,500. In comparison, the artillery reported a modest 6 percent loss: 16 killed, 59 wounded, and 87
missing, a total of 162, a third of whom were in Courtney's
battalion.[45]

The artillery's light casualties did not give a true indication of
its wrecked condition. The battle had been an ordnance disaster.
Officials at Richmond had been led to expect the worst, but even
they were stunned. When the truth was finally known, Bragg
had lost a staggering one-third of his artillery, including thirty-
nine field pieces (nineteen 12-pounder Napoleons, nine 6-
pounders, three 12-pounder howitzers, three 3.8-inch James
rifles, one 3-inch rifle, and four 10-pounder Parrott rifles), two
24-pounder siege guns, twenty-eight caissons, twenty-five limbers, four battery wagons, one traveling forge, 2,336 rounds of
fixed ammunition, and a good deal of harness.[46]

Chief of Ordnance Hypolite Oladowski immediately went
about restocking. Some of the Union guns captured at Chickamauga and earmarked for recasting into Napoleons were
called up from Atlanta to fill the void temporarily. Because of
the loss of so many Napoleons and Parrotts, however, the armament modernization program had received a serious setback.
The most difficult problem confronting Oladowski was in the
supply of fixed ammunition. The ninety-six guns on Missionary
Ridge had expended 1,033 solid shot, 2,742 spherical case shot
and 2,642 shell, a total of 6,417 projectiles, or 65 rounds per gun.
Inasmuch as the arsenals at Atlanta and Augusta could produce
only 125–150 rounds of artillery ammunition per day, the equivalent of one month's total combined output of both of them would
be required to replace the ammunition expended and captured
in the battle.[47]

It was perhaps ironic that Bragg's last battle resulted in an artillery disaster. In a real sense, this would always be his branch. In it, he had received his experience and risen to prominence. In many respects, however, the long arm was now different. Tactics, armament, and organization had all measurably changed since the Mexican War. Bragg's failing was that he did not adjust to these changes. In a larger sense, this was one of his major shortcomings as a commanding general. On November 30 his formal resignation was accepted by the Richmond government. Two days later, the "old artilleryman" left Dalton without fanfare.

Chapter 11

"This Neglected Branch of the Service"

The battles around Chattanooga had exhausted the Army of Tennessee. Rest and recuperation were sorely needed. Fortunately for the temporary commander, Lieutenant General William J. Hardee, the Federals did not launch a December offensive as they had the year before at Murfreesboro. His troops thus settled in for the winter—the third for many of them.

Artillerymen were required to labor three to four days on shelters for the animals before they could begin construction of their own winter quarters. In the typical battery camp, small cabins were arranged on either side of a wide street about a hundred yards in length. The officers' cabin was at the head of the street. Guns and caissons were assembled in a park near the camp. One of the largest artillery encampments, three miles southwest of Dalton, included the companies of Carnes, Gracey, Rowan, Van den Corput, Smith, Turner, and Baxter.[1]

Life was closely regulated. At daylight, the men were awakened by the company bugler sounding "Reveille." Fifteen minutes later came the "Stables" call, signaling the grooming, feeding, and watering of the horses. Breakfast was served at sunrise, and at 10:00 the animals were inspected. The company was assembled for roll call at noon, followed shortly by dinner. Several times a week, company inspection was conducted at 2:30. The afternoon "Stables" came at 4:00. At sunset, the company was called out for dress parade, followed by supper. The men were in their quarters at 8:00, and "Taps" was sounded an hour later.[2]

Daily, a few men from each battery were allowed to go on foraging expeditions. Purchases of chickens, eggs, milk, and butter brought a welcome relief from the routine of salt beef and cornmeal. Nor were the men above occasional stealing. A Mississippian recounted that his battalion camp was searched for seven hundred pounds of bacon stolen from a local farmer.[3]

Sunday was customarily a day of rest. The men attended worship with the infantry because the batteries lacked chaplains of their own. In a wave of revivalism that swept the army at Dalton, perhaps the most noted artillery convert was the new army chief of artillery, Brigadier General Francis A. Shoup, who arrived in March 1864. This decision was to lead him to a postwar occupation similar to that of his counterpart in Lee's army, Brigadier General William Pendleton, an Episcopalian minister.[4]

Life was not all drill and regimentation. On Christmas Day in Key's Arkansas Battery, the men danced "happily to the tune of an old fiddle." Henry Semple's battery celebrated with a meal of turkey, sausages, and eggnog. Still, no one could escape the reality that another wartime Yuletide had passed, and one man candidly wrote that it was "a poor Christmas."[5] A late winter snow prompted several large snowball fights. "Just after stable call Major Hoxton sent me word to bring my company out as he wanted to storm Major Palmer's battalion," wrote Lieutenant Neal of McCants's battery. "We captured their camp with a yell and whipped them off the ground. Everything was taken in good fun but it was rough play. The ground was speckled with blood from bruised noses."[6]

Hardee soon set about the task of rebuilding the wreckage in his army. Initial reports dwelt upon the "infinite trouble" he was having in supplying and reequipping the men. Morale was at a low ebb. Stragglers continued to trickle in, but by December 8 the troops numbered only 39,000, including 2,500 artillerymen.[7] The badly crippled artillery was depleted of guns, ammunition, and horses. The situation received Hardee's early attention. On December 6 five of the hardest-hit batteries— Scogin's Georgia, Massenburg's Georgia, Rivers's Arkansas, Waters's Alabama, and Baxter's Tennessee—were stripped of their remaining guns and horses and assigned to garrison duty in Atlanta. Scott's Tennessee Battery was discontinued, forty-two of the men being transferred to Swett's company. Dawson's Georgia Battery was ordered back to the Army of Mississippi. The battalions were realigned so that each consisted of three batteries. The reorganization provided a more efficient and compact structure.[8]

Hardee was soon informing the Richmond government and the army's new commander-in-waiting, General Joseph E. Johnston, that the troops were rapidly recovering. On December 17, Hardee even suggested an offensive. Taking pride in replacing many of the captured cannon, he noted that the artillery was once again "serviceable." At best, these reports were exaggerated half-truths. At worst, they created a false impression in Richmond of the Dalton situation.[9]

The artillery was certainly far from recovered. On December 14 only ninety-five pieces were assigned to the infantry, including eighteen old 6-pounders. A number of batteries possessed only two or three guns, and two companies, Bledsoe's Missouri and Anderson's Georgia, had none. The artillery ammunition of the two corps and the reserve averaged only 120, 137, and 146 rounds per gun, respectively. Shortages also existed in ordnance stores. Mebane's Tennessee Battery, for example, needed twenty-four saddle blankets, six bridles, eight halters, three saddles, and fifty horse brushes.[10]

Nor was the artillery exempt from the manpower shortage that the army was experiencing. The batteries averaged only eighty-one effectives each. Howell's Georgia Battery had ninety-six men, ten of whom were in the hospital. Captain Howell complained that "another thirty men [were] absent from sickness or pretending. None gone less than three months, some eleven months."[11]

●

General Johnston arrived at Dalton on December 27. For the next few weeks, he inspected his new command. "I had every man turn out with his brush broom to clean the battery for inspection," explained Captain Thomas Key. "General Johnston reviewed General Cleburne's command and after he passed through the battery I was honored with an introduction to him by General [Lucius] Polk. . . . General Johnston is about fifty years of age, is quite gray, and has a spare form, an intelligent face, and expressive blue eye. He was very polite, raising his cap to me after the introduction."[12]

Discrepancies with earlier optimistic evaluations soon became apparent. Johnston found that morale was low, desertions high, and discipline lax. Some 6,000 men lacked muskets; and, as many, shoes. Beef rations were of poor quality. The logistics involved in undertaking an offensive were nearly insurmountable. Crossing the Tennessee River into Alabama would require 150 wagons to haul pontoons. Johnston immediately recognized that the artillery was one of his principal problems. The organization was poor, and the gun crews were deficient in training, especially in firing. Field grade officers were scarce. The armament modernization program, which Bragg had started ten months earlier, was far from complete. The batteries were nearly immobile because of the run down condition of the horses.[13]

All the troops in the army were started on a rigorous training program. The artillery battalions were reviewed and inspected each Saturday. Gun crews practiced on targets ten feet square at ranges of 600–1,000 yards. Sham battles were conducted at corps level, while the bands played "Bonnie Blue Flag" and "Yankee Doodle" to add realism. One observer wrote that "the lines were formed skirmishers advanced and the whole corps moved forward in double line of battle. . . . The artillery when the advance began was thrown forward on the flanks of the line and shelled away very vigorously with blank cartridges." One man, whose battery was dubbed to be "captured," grumbled that he could "see no fun nor sense in it."[14]

As part of his attempt to mold the army into a cohesive fighting unit, Johnston adopted a uniform "stars and bars" battle flag. Battery standards, measuring 2½ by 3¼ feet, were somewhat smaller than the regimental. Lieutenant Neal sent his battery's old flag home to his father for safekeeping. "It was a handsome banner when new but three years exposure has soiled it considerably," he explained.[15]

Not all the banners conformed. The batteries in Hotchkiss's battalion, as in all of Cleburne's division, retained their distinctive blue battle flags with white "silver moon." The name of the battery and a crossed-cannon insignia (denoting artillery) was inscribed on the disc. Various battle honors were painted on the blue field. The flag of Swett's battery, for example, proudly bore the names of "Shiloh," "Murfreesboro," "Chickamauga," and "Tunnel Hill." In early 1864 the Louisiana units in Gibson's brigade were issued unique flags. The Washington Artillery thus carried a white standard, the "stars and bars" being located in the upper left-hand corner. Inscribed on the white field was a red crossed-cannon insignia and the name "5TH CO. W.A." The flag also bore the names of six battles.[16]

Confidence in Johnston and improved morale brought about mass reenlistments of the three-year men. Captain James P. Douglas's Texas Battery unanimously reenlisted, and other companies followed the example. About 85 percent of the artillerymen in Hardee's corps, some 1,026 men, signed for the duration of the war.[17] Some additional artillery was received. In December, Captain Charles Fenner's Louisiana Battery arrived

from garrison duty in Mobile. The next month, Major James
Waddell's battalion of two Alabama batteries—W. D. Emery's
and R. H. Bellamy's—arrived at Dalton. They had been exchanged since the surrender of Vicksburg, but needed horses
and field guns. By late January, the artillery had swelled to 33
batteries, which possessed 117 guns.[18]

Despite the mass reenlistments and fresh batteries, the artillery, along with the army as a whole, still faced a serious manpower shortage. A few Georgia batteries received some recruits,
but most of the companies, especially those from states now far
away, had no source from which to draw. Requests for infantry
transfers to fill existing vacancies were denied. Johnston remarked that "all his army would go into cavalry and batteries if
it were allowed" and that he "would not transfer a soldier drilled
in infantry to make a bad cannoneer."[19]

•

The most urgent of the artillery's problems related to the horses,
none of which were combat-ready. Their feeble condition was
attributable primarily to a shortage of forage. In December and
January, no long forage and only half-rations of corn were issued. Captain John Rowan, commanding a Georgia battery, reported that his starving animals had gnawed completely
through their bridles. An artillery battalion commander complained that this horses had received only thirteen pounds of
corn over a three-day period. The corn that was issued, which
had been stored in open-air bins for long periods of time, was
often mildewed and weevil-eaten. In January, Johnston directed
that almost half the artillery horses, most of those in the cavalry,
and all the mules not needed for camp service be sent to the
valley of the Etowah, near Kingston, where pasturing was better
and a supply of grain nearer.[20]

Near the end of January, the trains began to run again on a
regular basis, and the supply of corn increased. Soon full rations
of corn were being issued, but little or no long forage. Major John
Johnston complained that his artillery horses went four days
without it and then received only five pounds to the ration. A
frustrated Captain Rowan commented: "Corn alone will not
keep the animals in condition; they will not eat rations of corn if
no long forage is furnished. Horses fed on corn alone are more
liable to disease."[21]

In early January, an alarmed Johnston informed President

Davis that the horses were not improving and were so feeble that the guns could not be maneuvered or saved in the event of battle. After the review of a corps in February, it was discovered that the teams of the Napoleon guns were unable to draw them up a small hill. At that time, sixty-four pieces were at Dalton, and forty-eight were with the pasturing teams at Kingston.[22]

Disease spread among the stock. Rowan lost eighteen horses in three weeks, and ten of his remaining forty-eight were listed as unserviceable. Captain R. W. Anderson lost nearly all his animals in January. A Tennessee gunner, lamenting the condition of the stock, noted that the men "thought as much of their horses as of their fellow soldiers."[23] Little could be done for the animals. Home remedies were used for minor afflictions, but no cure was available for distemper or the highly contagious glanders. A veterinary surgeon was requested for the army. Also, a large horse infirmary was established in Laurens County south of Macon. But difficulties persisted.[24]

Appeals went out for help. On February 8, Johnston wrote President Davis that the artillery was deficient 400 horses. About a week later, the army quartermaster requested 500. Two weeks after that, the quartermaster-general in Richmond was informed that 600 were needed. When pressure continued for an offensive, Johnston informed the government that to make the artillery effective "at least 1000 fresh horses are required."[25] The Richmond government, armed with the exaggerated Hardee appraisals of December, remained dubious of Johnston's claims. The ambiguity of his reports widened the credibility gap. In the short span of a month, he had raised the number of required horses from 400 to 1,000. Future reports failed to substantiate these needs, and, from the beginning, official requisitions were placed for only 500 horses. One historian has suggested that Johnston simply used this issue as an excuse to justify his inaction against the Federals.[26]

Even if the case was overstated, the situation was severe. In late February, an inspector found that many of the guns were drawn by four or five horses, rather than the required six. Mules were used in some of the teams. A number of the late arrivals were diseased and useless before they were even placed in service. When Captain Key was issued five new animals for his battery, he described them as "among the poorest specimens I have seen since the beginning of the revolution."[27]

The shrinking boundaries of the Confederacy forced Johnston to compete with other departments for the dwindling supply of animals. Since as early as the fall of 1862, Robert E. Lee had been drawing horses from Georgia for his artillery. Little reliance could be placed upon the districts of Mississippi and Alabama because of their previous commitments to other departments. In desperation, agents scoured the Georgia countryside carrying orders to impress "everything not needed for the plow."[28]

The Richmond government remained unimpressed with Johnston's continued insistence that the artillery needed more horses. In March, Lee's artillery chief, Brigadier General Pendleton, was dispatched to Dalton to inspect the batteries. He was one of a series of envoys sent by Richmond to ascertain whether or not Johnston's reasons for not taking the offensive were valid. Convinced that the main Union offensive would come in Virginia, the Richmond government seemed unable to comprehend that the Federals now possessed the power to wage a two-front war.

The problem of insufficient and run-down artillery horses was not totally unfamiliar to Pendleton. A similar situation had long existed in the Army of Northern Virginia. A study revealed that the life span of an artillery horse in that army was only seven and a half months. Further, the mortality rate among animals in that branch was much higher than in the transportation service.[29]

Pendleton arrived at Dalton at daybreak on March 11, and, despite his exhausting journey, immediately began to inspect the artillery reserve. Accompanied by Major W. C. Preston, the army's artillery inspector general, he reviewed the three assembled battalions. The next day, similar inspections were made of Hardee's and Hood's battalions. During the next few days, written inquiries were submitted to battalion commanders and an impressive array of data gathered. By the 16th, the work had been completed.[30]

Pendleton noted that the horses were "certainly thin," a condition "not uncommon in our artillery service." He added, however, that "this state of things did not strike me to a greater extent . . . than in other commands" and that the animals were "nearly, if not quite, up to the average seen at this season in most of our artillery animals." Fresh horses were continuing to come in, and Pendleton concluded that "no serious anxiety need be felt, I believe, respecting them."[31]

Despite these words of assurance, the situation was far from resolved. On April 1 some 1,900 horses were on hand, or an average of 63 per battery. Ten percent of them were in an unserviceable condition. An additional 445 were estimated to be required.[32]

In April another inspector, Colonel A. H. Cole, was sent to Dalton to study Johnston's "frequent calls for horses . . . varying in numbers at different times." Cole was startled to discover that, of the 525 fresh artillery horses that had been received, about 100 had been diverted for use by wagon masters, clerks, and officers. The army quartermaster had not turned in broken-down stock for rehabilitation, which resulted in the loss of 2,500 animals between January and April. One writer has concluded that Johnston's frequent correspondence on this subject was "exaggerated and careless at best; wrong and misleading at worst. Even more damaging to the general's credibility was the fact that much of the problem . . . was of Johnston's own making."[33]

•

Johnston pushed ahead on the armament modernization program, but his efforts were frustrated by a shortage of raw materials. The casting of 12-pounder Napoleons was predicated on the availability of copper because each gun required more than a thousand pounds. The Ducktown copper mines, outside Chattanooga, which had been the source of 90 percent of the Confederacy's copper supply, were now in Union hands. Casting of bronze Napoleons continued for the time being at government foundries, but at a curtailed level. This was accomplished by utilizing stockpiled supplies and by melting down obsolete cannon.[34]

The Army of Tennessee continued to compete with Mobile and the Army of Mississippi for light 12-pounders. In February 1864, Colonel G. W. Rains, at the Augusta Arsenal, informed Oladowski that a battery of Napoleons had just been completed for him, but that it had instead been ordered to Demopolis, Alabama. Another battery was nearly ready, however, and Rains assured him it would be sent as soon as possible.[35]

Faults continued to be found with ordnance. In February an Augusta Napoleon in Swett's battery needed to be returned to the arsenal on account of flaws. Shortly thereafter, tests were performed on a new battery of Macon Arsenal 10-pounder Parrott rifles. Oladowski found the results "so much unsatisfactory that I really do not understand its cause." Subsequent inspections revealed that the grooves in the rifling varied in depth and that one gun was larger in diameter than the others. A Tredegar 3-inch rifle in Oliver's battery was marked for replacement because the rifling grooves had entirely worn away.[36]

When Pendleton inspected the armament in March, he found fifteen 6-pounders still in use, which he described as "nearly useless." The twenty-seven 12-pounder howitzers were "scarcely more valuable." Pendleton did see the need for a few howitzer batteries for use in broken and wooded country, but felt that the number on hand was far too large. He recommended that all the 6-pounders be turned in and exchanged for 12-pounder Napoleons and that some of the howitzers be swapped for rifled guns.[37]

Fresh consignments of Napoleons continued to be rushed to Dalton. In March a battery of Columbus Napoleons was received, followed by a battery of Macon Napoleons in April and five Augusta Napoleons in early May. By early April all the 6-pounders had been phased out. A few rifled guns were also received. Bellamy's battery obtained two Tredegar-made 3-inch rifles and two 3.2-inch Blakely rifles. On April 30 the armament consisted of sixty-four 12-pounder Napoleons, thirty-eight 12-pounder howitzers, six 3-inch rifles, ten 10-pounder Parrott rifles, and two Blakely rifles:[38]

Battalion	Napoleons	Howitzers	Rifles
Hoxton	8	4	—
Hotchkiss	8	4	—
Martin	6	6	—
Cobb	8	4	—
Courtney	4	4	4
Eldridge	6	2	4
Johnston	12	—	—
Palmer	8	—	4
Waddell	—	10	2
Williams	4	4	4

Many rifled shells continued to be deficient. In February, Rains sent Oladowski the first shipment of new shells for his 10-pounder Parrotts. Instead of being in the standard 10-pounder Parrott pattern, they were actually designed for the 3-inch rifle. They fit Parrott guns perfectly, however, and Rains assured Oladowski that "I have but little doubt you will find them superior to the Parrott shell." To remedy the premature explosions that were occurring with the Blakely shells, Rains recommended that the prescribed powder charge be reduced to 1½ pounds.[39] Pendleton's March inspection uncovered several other minor ordnance-related problems. A few defective 10-pounder Parrott shells still remained in Lumsden's battery. Fowler's and Semple's batteries required new friction primers and Gracey's some additional fuzes. Garrity needed two and Douglas four new gun carriages.[40]

Leather articles of all kinds remained in great demand. Despite Colonel Moses Wright's pledge to turn out a hundred single sets of artillery harness per month in his Atlanta Arsenal shops, a shortage remained. The leather often broke in a short time and needed to be replaced. Emery's and Bellamy's batteries had to be totally reequipped with harness. Swett's battery was still using the same harness it had been issued back in '61, which was in better condition than recent government issues. Key's battery received forty-eight sets in early April, the first it had obtained in three years. Jeffress's battery possessed the best harness in the army; it had been captured at Chickamauga.[41]

The multiplicity of items required by the artillery was demonstrated by a single day's issuance to Robert Cobb's battalion. On March 25 it received, among other items, 211 rounds of ammunition, 6 dozen buckles, 15 pounds of axle grease, 2 prolonges, 32 curry combs, 4 sponge buckets, 125 pounds of rope, 5 trail hand spikes, 2 sponges and rammers, 12 priming wires, and 3 fuze mallets.[42]

Plagued by shortages, the men often resorted to their own craftsmanship. An artificer in Turner's battery constructed new trails for the gun carriages in his company. Several of Darden's men fabricated drivers' saddles that were considered to be superior to the government product. Gracey's men contrived excellent horse brushes.[43]

Transportation continued to present few problems. Each battery was allowed one baggage wagon, two forage wagons, and an ambulance. Besides the rounds in the caissons, three ammunition wagons were authorized per Napoleon battery and two per howitzer battery. Typical of the battalions was Courtney's, whose train in February 1864 consisted of nineteen vehicles: one headquarters wagon, one traveling forge, three baggage wagons, three ambulances, six forage wagons, and five ammunition wagons. Traveling forges were later removed from the battalions, and repair work was left to small portable forges. Officers complained that they often could not produce sufficient heat to weld broken parts, tire rims, horseshoes, and other items. Battery wagons were also discontinued during this time and regular wagons substituted for them.[44]

•

By mid-March, Johnston had penned the outline of a new army organization. The Tennessee regiments, much to their delight, were once again grouped together under Benjamin Cheatham. The trans-Mississippi troops formed a division under Pat Cleburne and the Georgians one under W. H. T. Walker. The seven divisions of the army were divided into two corps, under Hardee and the newly arrived John Bell Hood. The long arm, too, was reorganized. For some time a quasi-battalion structure had been in effect in the western artillery, but it was Johnston who solidified it. Each battalion was to consist of three four-gun batteries. Johnston assigned one battalion to each division, but kept three back as a general reserve. Field staffs were to consist of a major commanding, a quartermaster, a commissary, and as adjutant a detached officer from one of the batteries. Surgeons were moved up from companies to battalions, to which at least two and sometimes three were assigned.[45]

Centralization of the batteries into battalions brought grumblings from lower-grade officers who saw their powers increasingly diminished. A battery officer complained that "a captain under this battalion management is a perfect automaton." Another artilleryman described the battalion as "anything but satisfactory to the captains and lieutenants, because in such large bodies requisitions were never so well filled, nor ground so advantageous for action or camp chosen." For the most part, Pendleton was pleased with Johnston's structure, though he personally preferred battalions of four batteries commanded by two field officers. He did suggest a "system of administration."[46]

Johnston next grouped the battalions into three "regiments," one for each of the two corps and the reserve. Hardee's regiment (Hoxton's, Hotchkiss's, Martin's, and Cobb's battalions) totaled 12 batteries, 48 guns, 742 horses, and 1,243 men. Hood's regiment (Courtney's, Eldridge's and Johnston's battalions) mustered 9 batteries, 36 guns, 582 horses, and 1,078 men. The reserve (Palmer's, Williams's and Waddell's battalions) comprised 9 batteries, 36 guns, 566 horses, and 1,016 men. The horse artillery was formed into a battalion of 5 batteries, 22 guns, about 335 horses, and 420 men.[47]

Officer reaction to the reorganization was mixed. Lieutenant Neal felt it was cumbersome. He complained that his regiment (Hardee's) would never be able to find ground for an encampment and would take up two miles of the road on a march. Major Melancthon Smith, on the other hand, reasoned that the regimental structure would facilitate the massing of guns in battle. The organization, he wrote, would add "much to the morale, esprit de corps and entire efficiency of this neglected branch of the service."[48]

How did Johnston's artillery organization stack up against that of the Army of Northern Virginia? Actually, many of the reforms initiated by Johnston had been in effect in Lee's long arm for a year. Lee's artillery corps groupings were termed "divisions" rather than "regiments" and his battalions usually consisted of four batteries, but the structure was basically similar.

One major break with Lee's organization was in retaining the artillery reserve on an army level. In the spring of 1863, Lee had sent his reserve battalions down to the corps level. This largely alleviated situations where a large single body of batteries would remain inactive during an emergency. The Union armies, too, were altering the reserve concept. In the spring of 1864, the Army of the Potomac's artillery reserve was broken up. In the upcoming Atlanta campaign, that of General William T. Sherman's was to be left in Chattanooga and Nashville and used solely to replace field losses. Johnston thus enlarged his reserve at a time when other major armies, both North and South, were dispensing with it.[49]

Johnston's thirty-six gun, army-level reserve turned out to be more theoretical than actual. During the early weeks of the Atlanta campaign, the reserve battalions were never to function together as a tactical unit. Both on the march and in battle, they were to operate on a corps level. In July 1864 the structure was abandoned, and the battalions were assigned to the corps as a reserve—exactly as in Lee's artillery.

At the heart of Johnston's new artillery organization was an attempt to remedy the evils caused by decentralization, not the least of which was dispersed firepower. But Johnston's new structure, improvement though it was, was flawed. In camp and on the march, the artillery battalions were to operate on a corps level and report directly to their regimental superiors. In combat, however, they were to report to their assigned division commanders. The result was ambiguity and confusion. In too many situations, it was not understood who exercised authority over the battalions: infantry or artillery officers.

A case in point occurred in May. The Atlanta campaign had been in progress barely two weeks before difficulties arose. General Cleburne fired off an angry letter detailing them:

> I was officially informed through your [Hardee's] Headquarters that Major Hotchkiss, with his battalion, would report to me. I find he is from time to time receiving orders through his immediate regimental superior, which withdraws him from my control. Last night I was prevented in this way from directing Major Hotchkiss how and when to withdraw from his position on the creek near Calhoun, and the consequence was that his artillery disarranged to some degree the progress of the whole corps. The pieces in position near Calhoun were withdrawn without my knowledge; and at Reseca, in executing a most delicate movement, I was required to look after the safe transit of that artillery to this side of the Oostanaula when it was in position at a point removed from the ground I occupied and immediately under the eye of General Bate. I desire my authority on this mattter be clearly defined; if it is not, I fear some disaster may occur.[50]

The Union artillery was also undergoing a transition during this time. Initially in the Atlanta campaign, the batteries of the Army of the Cumberland, many of which had been reduced to four guns, operated on a division level. Thus, tactically speaking, little difference existed between Johnston's organization and that of the enemy. In late July, however, Union divisional batteries were formed into "brigades." They were composed of six or seven batteries and commanded by a corps chief of artillery who held the rank of major. This was not only an improvement in supply and administration, but more importantly also in tactics. It elevated the operational control of the artillery to the corps level. Thus, the Union artillery stole an organizational march on its Confederate counterpart.[51]

•

Johnston had accomplished much for the artillery. Even though he may have merely capitalized on its weakened condition to avoid launching an offensive, his efforts resulted in advancements in command, organization and armament. Except for the number of horses per battery, the artillery reached its peak efficiency at Dalton. Whether or not these improvements would permit it to contend on an equal footing with the Federal long arm, which had long dominated in number of guns, weight of metal, mobility, ammunition supply, and skill, remained to be seen.

Chapter 12

"Complaints Have Been Heard from Your Artillery Officers"

The artillery organization initiated by Johnston in the spring of 1864 called for a full complement of field grade officers to command it. The artillery reserve and horse artillery were each to be headed by a lieutenant colonel and each of the two corps regiments by a colonel. Johnston informed Bragg—now in an advisory capacity in Richmond—that "there is not means of ascertaining if it [the artillery] has officers fit for colonels or lieutenant colonels. Both of these grades should be filled."[1] The restructuring raised the possibility of long-overdue promotions. Several majors were in line for them, and rumors floated freely as to who would be chosen. Melancthon Smith enjoyed seniority and held a West Point diploma. Felix Robertson, through hardly revered by his men, remained in Bragg's esteem. Llewellyn Hoxton was also considered to be a strong contender.[2]

Promotions had long been a thorny issue in the western long arm, but the brooding came to a head under Johnston. Lieutenant Colonel James Hallonquist, Bragg's handpicked army chief of artillery, was politely shelved and given nominal command of the artillery reserve. Hardee suggested that none of his artillery officers were competent for higher grade. Johnston conceded that he had not been impressed with the little he had seen of those in the February skirmishing before Dalton. "They exhibited a childish eagerness to discharge their pieces," he complained. Further, none had ever commanded more than twelve guns. On March 12, Johnston wrote Bragg: "The defects in the organization of the artillery cannot be remedied without superior officers, for whom we must depend upon the government."[3]

Johnston passed over the obvious selections—Hallonquist, Smith, and Robertson—and looked to their peers in the Army of Northern Virginia. This created deep resentment. Four field officers had already migrated from the Virginia front. Major Samuel Williams, a West Point graduate, had transferred in the

summer of 1862, followed the year after by Major Alfred R.
Courtney. When General D. H. Hill arrived in the Army of Tennessee in the summer of 1863, he brought with him his own
artillery officer, Major J. W. Bondurant. Since that time, Bondurant had been promoted to lieutenant colonel and was now
junior only to Hallonquist. Hill was later transferred, but Bondurant remained with the army. When General John Bell Hood
arrived at Dalton, he likewise brought his own artillery head,
thirty-four-year-old Colonel Robert F. Beckham, a West Point
graduate. Prior to Beckham's promotion and transfer, he had
been a major commanding Lee's horse artillery. All these officers were men of proven skill and ability, but every transfer
blocked a run of appointments from within the Army of Tennessee. Whether or not Johnston was justified in his Virginia
search, it was bound to augment the perception that the western
long arm was merely the stepchild of Lee's artillery.[4]

Now that Hallonquist was deposed, Johnston actively sought
a candidate for army chief of artillery. In February he applied for
Colonel E. P. Alexander, but Lee refused to relinquish his top
tactical artilleryman. Additional pleas proved to be fruitless,
though the colonel desired the position. Bragg's counterproposal
of Brigadier General William Pendleton failed to receive
Johnston's endorsement. Perhaps the ever-suspicious Johnston
perceived Pendleton as "Richmond's man."[5]

Bragg ran several more names by the commanding general,
including the former defender of New Orleans, Major General
Mansfield Lovell. Bragg described Lovell as "one of the best
artillery officers in the old service, a good judge and fond of good
horses, which is a qualification Alexander is deficient in."
Johnston was receptive to the Lovell suggestion. "You speak of
Major General Lovell in connection with this," he wrote. "Might
not he be assigned to it? It is no more inadequate to the grade of
major general than are most of the divisions of infantry." Even
though Lovell had been exonerated of all charges stemming
from the New Orleans defeat, he nonetheless remained in the
poor graces of the Davis administration. Bragg was thus unable
to deliver on his own suggestion.[6]

While inspecting Johnston's batteries, Pendleton, apparently
unaware that he himself was under consideration, began lobby-
ing for the promotion and transfer of two of his officers in the
Virginia army. He sought to have Colonel Thomas Carter be
promoted to brigadier general and assigned as Johnston's army
chief of artillery and Lieutenant Colonel Robert Dearing ad-

vanced to colonel to command Hardee's batteries. Pendleton recognized that many of his fellow officers in Lee's artillery enjoyed little opportunity for deserved promotion. What he failed to realize was that an even worse situation existed in the western long arm. Although the states of Alabama, Georgia, Mississippi, and Tennessee furnished two-thirds of the batteries in the Army of Tennessee, they claimed only a third of the field officers. This was precisely the type of disproportionate arrangement that Pendleton bent over backward to avoid in his own artillery.[7]

When the recommendation of Carter and Dearing received Johnston's endorsement, smoldering resentments were transformed into verbal criticism. "Recently some complaints I learn privately have been heard from your artillery officers that they were being sloughted by their juniors in the Army of Northern Virginia," Bragg informed Johnston in March. "Lieutenant Colonel Dearing was junior, for instance, to all the field officers with you until recently promoted in the organization of General Lee's artillery." Bragg acknowledged the leadership gap in the western long arm, but feared the morale effect of continued transfers.[8]

Johnston responded that he knew of only one complaint and that had come from "an officer of the Virginia army, who, after his arrival here, had been promoted to lieutenant colonelcy over several senior officers. Lieutenant General Hood having brought with him a colonel of artillery, this officer thought himself ill used." The reference was obviously to Lieutenant Colonel James Bondurant. It would have, indeed, been ironic if the officer who finally spoke out on this issue had himself been a part of the problem. Shortly thereafter, he was transferred to Mobile.[9]

The War Department ended the speculation by appointing a compromise candidate as army chief of artillery: Brigadier General Francis A. Shoup, a thirty-year-old West Point graduate and an artillery officer in the regular army. He ably commanded Hardee's batteries at Shiloh and was later promoted to brigadier general and led a Louisiana brigade at Vicksburg. Upon the surrender there, he was sent to Mobile. After his prisoner exchange was formalized and he recovered from sickness, he requested duty with the Army of Tennessee. Everything in his record suggested he could fill his new office with distinction. He enjoyed seniority in rank as well as ability. He was described by Bragg as "an educated and disciplined soldier," and even Pendleton conceded that "he is said to be an excellent officer."[10]

Shoup arrived in Dalton in late March. Throughout April, he sought to ensure that the artillery obtained its share of incoming recruits, schooled his officers in tactical command, and performed his administrative duties. He gave every indication of supplying what the western long arm had sorely lacked: strong leadership at the top. Yet, although nominally in charge of all the batteries, as the army chief he could not exercise as much tactical authority as his subordinates. The position was actually one of a glorified staff officer and general troubleshooter.[11]

The two remaining appointments came as no surprise. At the last minute, Hardee gave, with Johnston's concurrence, a belated endorsement of Major Melancthon Smith's promotion to

Brigadier General Francis A. Shoup briefly served as army chief of artillery during the Atlanta campaign. (Library of Congress)

colonel and command of Hardee's artillery. Smith had temporarily commanded the regiment since its formation in February. Whether or not he was prepared for tactical as well as administrative leadership on the corps level was uncertain.

Command of the horse artillery and a lieutenant colonel's commission went to Bragg's old ally Felix Robertson. While at Dalton the twenty-five-year-old Texan had continued to correspond directly with Bragg. When Johnston argued against a spring offensive, in part because of the artillery's weakened condition, Robertson was telling his former commander what he wanted to hear: it was "ready to do good service."[12]

The promotion of Robertson left a battalion vacancy. A number of company-level officers had been recommended for promotion. Thomas Stanford had seniority as well as an excellent service record. Charles Lumsden was a graduate of the Virginia Military Institute. Young Hiram Bledsoe was a capable officer, but was said frequently to leave important tasks to subordinates. Charles Slocomb had temporarily commanded a battalion and enjoyed the added advantage of leading the army's most prestigious battery: the Washington Artillery.[13]

In February the decision came down. Captain Henry Semple, the opinionated forty-three-year-old Alabama battery commander and former Montgomery lawyer, was notified that he had been promoted to major and assigned an artillery battalion in Hardee's corps. The appointment came at a time when Semple's hands were full. Once again, he was at loggerheads with his battalion commander, Major Thomas Hotchkiss. The ever-quarrelsome Hotchkiss had been busy at Dalton. By March he had preferred various charges against five of his officers. In February, he had Semple arrested for the trivial charge of failing to file a quarterly ordnance return—nothing more than a retaliation for their feud the previous spring. A trial was held in which Semple was exonerated of all charges. The court concluded: "The whole testimony of the prosecutor shows a bias against the accused and he admits that he is unfriendly towards him." Semple accepted his new commission but requested—and subsequently received—a transfer to the Department of the Gulf.[14]

Semple's departure left a battalion vacancy remaining. Once again, a promotion was made from outside the army. In March a twenty-five-year-old former lawyer, Captain John W. Johnston, was promoted to major and assigned an artillery battalion in Hood's corps. Johnston had commanded a Virginia battery in John Pemberton's old Vicksburg army and since his prisoner exchange had been in search of a new command.[15]

The spring round of appointments was thus complete and all vacancies were filled. As of April 1, 1864, the following field officers were assigned (listed in order of seniority):

Brigadier general: Francis A. Shoup

Colonels: Robert F. Beckham, Melancthon Smith

Lieutenant colonels: James H. Hallonquist, Felix H. Robertson

Majors: W. C. Preston (Inspector), Alfred R. Courtney, Joseph Palmer, John W. Eldridge, Samuel C. Williams, James P. Waddell, Llewellyn Hoxton, Thomas R.

Captain Henry Semple, the opinionated Alabama Battery commander, reflected the disharmony that was prevalent among the officers of the western artillery. (Alabama Department of Archives and History)

Hotchkiss, John Rawle (horse artillery), Robert Martin, John W. Johnston [Captain Robert Cobb, commanding a battalion in Hardee's corps artillery, did not receive his major's commission until May 1864.]

For the first time, the western artillery was fully staffed with a complement of field grade officers. The transfer of three officers (Shoup, Beckham, and Johnston), however, had effectively blocked a number of anticipated intraarmy moves. In the end, not one of the eight captains and only one of the four majors who had been recommended for advancement by their superiors were promoted.[16]

The jockeying for field grade positions nearly overshadowed command changes on the company level. Several of these occurred. In late December 1863, the fiery thirty-three-year-old Lieutenant Thomas Key, a former newspaper editor, received a captain's commission to command the Helena (Arkansas) Light Artillery. He had previously demonstrated his ability by leading his company at Tunnel Hill and on the retreat to Dalton. Captain Henry Semple's transfer passed the command of that Alabama battery into the capable hands of twenty-five-year-old Lieutenant Richard W. Goldthwaite. The War Department removed Captain T. B. Ferguson from command of his South Carolina battery for unstated reasons. His replacement was young Lieutenant René Beauregard, son of the famed Louisiana general.[17]

The most dramatic turnover took place in McCants's Florida Battery. In March the lieutenants had Captain Robert P. McCants arrested for habitual drunkenness. Rather than face the humiliation of a trial, he resigned and was removed from the army. "I do not think there is a better artillery officer in the army than McCants," commented Lieutenant Neal, "but he cannot command the respect of his men or his officers." Lieutenant Thomas J. Perry succeeded him.[18]

Although the artillery was still short a few captains, the supply of company-level officers was adequate. By April, twenty-six captains, forty-seven first lieutenants, and fifty-six second lieutenants were assigned. This averaged out to one officer per twenty effectives.[19]

Difficulties had plagued the Army of Tennessee's artillery officers since the fall of 1862. Bragg initiated a patronage policy that disregarded seniority and elevated his personal favorites. This led to jealousies and bickering among the officers. When Johnston reorganized the long arm in the spring of 1864, the time for a number of long overdue promotions seemed at hand. These hopes were dashed when he looked to the Army of Northern Virginia for his future leadership. The Richmond government intervened to work out a compromise. When all was through, however, only 4 of the army's 141 artillery officers had been promoted.

Chapter 13

"Boots and Saddles"

The ground was covered with a mild frost on the unpleasantly crisp spring morning of May 2, 1864. In the camp of Hotchkiss's battalion, a bugler sounded "Boots and Saddles" as the men began stirring about and harnessing their animals. As the battalion rattled slowly toward the drill ground for morning maneuvers, a courier suddenly galloped up and ordered it back to camp. The distant booming of cannon could now be distinctly heard in the direction of Ringgold. The Union army was on the move.[1]

Johnston placed all his troops on full alert. The artillery battalions that had wintered at Kingston had already been mobilized and returned to Dalton. They were now ordered to their respective divisions. Felix Robertson's battalion of horse artillery, which was still in the rear grazing horses, was directed to proceed immediately to Rome to bolster the defense of that place.[2]

Once again, the Army of Tennessee faced a formidable array of men and equipment. Major General William T. Sherman commanded an army of 110,000 seasoned troops, divided into the Army of the Cumberland, under George Thomas, and the smaller Army of the Tennessee, led by James B. McPherson, and the Army of the Ohio, headed by John M. Schofield. Sherman readily admitted that his cavalry was inferior to that of the Confederates, but his artillery was solid. He began the campaign with 41 batteries of about 207 guns and 4,459 officers and men. In addition, an artillery pool of 18 batteries at Nashville and Chattanooga would provide replacements for field losses.[3]

In opposition, Johnston's reborn Army of Tennessee mustered about 55,000 troops, divided into 27 infantry and 8 cavalry brigades. The long arm, now overhauled and reorganized, consisted of 35 batteries with 138 guns, 3,757 men, and about 2,225 horses.[4] The ammunition level was relatively stable, but the rounds, as always, would need to be carefully husbanded.

As a major advance became imminent, Johnston urgently appealed to Richmond for additional forces. Troops were accordingly stripped from some coastal garrisons and rushed by rail to Dalton. Included were H. W. Mercer's brigade from Savannah and James Cantey's division and two batteries from Mobile. General Leonidas Polk hastened from Mississippi with the infantry divisions of W. W. Loring and Samuel French and W. H. ("Red") Jackson's cavalry division—in all some 14,000 troops and 8 batteries of 32 guns. Johnston would have a third corps.

Sherman's campaign strategy stressed outflanking rather than overwhelming force. Instead of confronting Johnston directly by converging from the west down the Chattanooga-Dalton highway and the north on the Cleveland Road, he planned a more complicated route. While Thomas and Schofield kept the Confederates preoccupied on the Dalton front, McPherson's army of 25,000 would make a wide flanking movement through Snake Creek Gap, eighteen miles to the south.

At daylight on May 9, Union artillery opened with a resounding crash on Rocky Face Ridge, west of Dalton. A man in Fenner's Louisiana Battery later recalled that a comrade was lying quietly on the ground reading a newspaper when he received a direct hit from an incoming shell. The sight of the remains was so horrible, explained the survivor, that he "could not eat for four days."[5]

Sherman pressed Johnston's line at three points during the day: Mill Creek Gap, the right angle connecting Cheatham's and Stevenson's divisions, and to the north on the Cleveland Road. The Union artillery was also active. Three batteries were anchored on a small ridge between Tunnel Hill and Rocky Face and exchanged shots with Rebel guns. The Federals also succeeded in planting a section of guns on the southern crest of Rocky Face and opened with an enfilading fire. An attempt to place a battery on the railroad in Mill Creek Gap was foiled when young Richard Goldthwaite's Alabama gunners obtained the range. The first shot burst squarely in the midst of a Yankee gun crew and felled five of them. The piece was temporarily abandoned.[6]

While heavy skirmishing continued around Dalton, McPherson's army emerged from Snake Creek Gap and began probing the Reseca defenses. It was met by Cantey's division, recently brought up from Mobile. Rebel artillery support included the eight Napoleon guns of John J. Ward's and Joseph Selden's Alabama batteries. Learning from prisoners that the Southerners were in at least division strength and fearing that Johnston might pounce upon him from the north, McPherson cautiously withdrew into the gap and waited.[7]

Loring's division rolled into Reseca on May 10–12. The infantry was accompanied by Major J. D. Myrick's battalion of three batteries: Captain R. L. Barry's Lookout (Tennesee) Artillery, Captain Alcide Bouanchaud's Pointe Coupe (Louisiana) Artillery, and Captain J. J. Cowan's Mississippi Battery. The battalion mustered 308 officers and men, 209 horses, and twelve 12-pounder Napoleons. Only a few months earlier, the battalion had passed in review at Demopolis, Alabama. An officer in a Mississippi regiment was impressed with the well-dressed cannoneers and thought that they made "a much finer [appearance] than the infantry did." The horses were in good condition, but he noted that "they have been lately impressed and I am very much afraid they will soon become to look as artillery horses usually do."[8]

On March 13, Johnston belatedly moved his army to Reseca. He deployed his troops behind previously prepared earthworks in a fishhook shaped battle line west of town. Polk's corps (Loring's and Cantey's divisions) was on the left, Hardee's corps (minus Walker's division in reserve) in the center, and Hood's corps on the right, its right flank bent back on the Connasauga River.[9] No general engagement took place at Reseca, though several attacks were made and heavy cannonading occurred. A series of hills and ridges that extended beyond the Confederate line were dotted with Union rifled cannon. These guns inflicted casualties and jeopardized the safety of the Oostanaula bridges. Johnston's smoothbores could do little to silence them.[10]

Hotchkiss's battalion occupied a crucial knoll between Hardee's and Hood's connecting position. On May 14 the battalion, along with Walthall's brigade of Hindman's division, came under a murderous enfilade fire from an estimated thirty Union guns posted on a commanding ridge. Goldthwaite's battery lost twelve men and eight horses in the fierce barrage and had two Napoleon guns temporarily disabled. One amazed onlooker was convinced that, had the guns not been pulled back to safety beyond the crest, "not a splinter of them would be left."[11]

S. H. Dent's battery was on a ridge to the left of the Dalton Road, about a hundred yards from the Hardee-Hood obtuse angle. The guns were positioned so as to deliver a direct frontal fire. John Rowan's Georgia Battery constructed its works at a right angle to Dent to cover the Dalton Road. The men were strengthening their position when the skirmish line was quickly driven in. Dent's battery suddenly came under a blazing fire and "the men were shot down as fast as they took position beside their guns." The company was hastily withdrawn, which left Rowan exposed to fire from the left. The Georgians were shaken by a lethal enfilade. Within minutes, eight of eleven men in the far right gun crew were killed and wounded. Before the bloodletting was over, the company had lost eighteen men and nine horses. The spokes of one of the guns were so shattered by minié balls that false ones had to be rigged to remove it.[12]

Sherman's infantry continued to assault the Confederate left throughout the evening. "Yesterday evening the enemy attempted under cover of night to assault our works," wrote Lieutenant Neal of Perry's battery. "We fired a large building and lit up the field and opened on them with a dozen pieces of artillery, repulsing their attack."[13]

On the morning of May 15, Max Van den Corput's Georgia Battery was advanced to a small lunette eighty yards in front of Stevenson's division. Hood had placed the guns there in order to enfilade any Federal line advancing against Hindman. At 11:30 Joseph Hooker's XX Corps came storming through the thickets and soon converged on and quickly overwhelmed the unfinished lunette. Many of the men in the badly mauled company were taken prisoner. The attack was repulsed by the main line, but not before the Federals effected a lodgment in front of the abandoned guns, which were thus left in a no-man's-land. Later that night, Union troops dug away the front of the tiny fort and pulled them away with ropes.[14]

Confirmed reports of a Federal crossing south of the Oostanaula, coupled with the knowledge that Union rifled cannon could now reach the bridges, made the Confederate position tenuous. Johnston ordered a retreat. Green cornstalks were spread over the bridges to muffle the sound of the wagons and gun carriages. Although the movement was made under cover of darkness, the man feared that at any moment the Federals would discover it and shell the trestles. The retreat, however, came off without incident. A rifled battery, abandoned on the road the next day, would have been lost had not Wheeler's troopers, acting as a rear guard, pulled the guns to safety.[15] Johnston's artillery had come off decidedly second best at Reseca. It could not match its opponent's rapid rate of fire or superior ordnance. The battle would prove to be a harbinger.

The long arm suffered heavy casualties. Incomplete returns indicate that Van den Corput lost twenty-two, Rowan eighteen, Swett sixteen, Goldthwaite twelve, Marshall twelve, and Slocomb ten. Major John W. Johnston, the young lawyer-turned-soldier, was wounded on the 15th. Operational control of the battalion was turned over to Van den Corput for the remainder of the summer. On a battery level, Captains John Phelan and L. G. Marshall were wounded. The latter was standing too close to one of his guns and was temporarily blinded by the flash of a discharged blast. The greatest loss, however, was Captain Thomas J. Stanford, who was shot in the head and killed during the abortive assault by A. P. Stewart's division on the 15th. Stanford had led his Mississippi battery through virtually every major battle of the army and had been recommended by his superiors for promotion on several occasions.[16]

•

Unlike the mountainous and heavily wooded terrain north of the Oostanaula, the area to its south consisted of gently rolling hills that were lightly covered with trees. Sherman would thus have more room for maneuvering his corps. Searching for favorable ground, Johnston led his army past Calhoun and Adairsville. At the latter, he was joined by Jackson's cavalry division and Captain John Waties's battalion of horse artillery. Waties's command consisted of Captain Ed Croft's Georgia Battery, Captain R. B. Waddell's South Carolina Battery, and Captain Houston King's Missouri Battery—in all some 324 officers and men, 333 horses, and twelve guns, including six 3-inch rifles. Samuel French's two batteries—Captain J. A. Hoskin's Brookhaven (Mississippi) Artillery and Captain Henry Guibor's Missouri Battery—also arrived at Adairsville, though his infantry joined farther south at Cassville.

The guns, caissons, and men had been sent by rail and the horses by road, but, because of the jammed rail system, the horses arrived first. On account of the shortage of grain and long forage, their condition was far from satisfactory. Rain was falling in a deluge when the cannoneers finally arrived, but they immediately rolled their guns off the cars, hitched up the undernourished teams, and reported for duty. Ward's battery from Mobile was later united with Hoskin and Guibor to form a battalion under the command of Major George S. Storrs.[17]

A plan to ambush Sherman at Cassville by maneuvering to

pounce on his left was thwarted when Union cavalry stumbled into Hood's flank. In the melee that followed, Captain J. A. Hoskin's Brookhaven (Mississippi) Light Artillery was hard hit. The battery unlimbered its three guns (one gun was in the rear being repaired) in the front yard of an old lady's house. She came running out and loudly protested that "things had come to a pretty pass when soldiers had to fetch their horses and cannons right up into a body's front yard for a fight." Only when the guns opened fire did she abruptly cut short her one-way conversation and run back inside.

The Mississippians were initially successful in repelling a Federal cavalry regiment. Being hard pressed, however, they limbered up and retired to a fixed fortification south of the Canton Road, where they received the counterfire of the 18th Indiana Light Artillery. Shrieking shells came crashing in among the gunners. One shot made a direct hit, exploding a caisson, dismounting a gun, and killing four horses. Another shell took off Lieutenant A. J. Stewart's leg, but incredibly this did not prove to be fatal. Several gunners were captured.[18]

That afternoon, the Confederate line was withdrawn to a ridge east and south of Cassville. Hardee occupied the left, Polk the center, and Hood the right. The new position seemed to be promising. When Chief of Artillery Shoup inspected it, however, he warned Johnston that a section of Polk's and Hood's line could be enfiladed by Union rifled guns on a commanding ridge a mile distant to the right. Later that day, Sherman's guns, as predicted, opened a heavy crossfire. French's division, on the right of Polk's line, was battered. In two of French's batteries, while coming in line and before the guns could even be unlimbered, one to two horses at each piece were killed. Later that night, after consultation with Polk and Hood, Johnston abandoned the line and ordered a retreat south of the Etowah.[19] If the terrain to its north favored Sherman's army, that to its south was better suited for Johnston's smaller force. In the hilly, heavily wooded area, one of the wildest parts of north Georgia, the added range of Sherman's rifles would be of little use.

The primary role of the horse artillery during Johnston's retrograde movements was that of a delaying action. Batteries were frequently placed on the skirmish line, which caused enemy troops to slow their pursuit and deploy. After crossing the Etowah, cavalry under General Edward McCook spearheaded the Union advance, but moved only three miles before encountering Rebel cavalry supported by artillery (probably R. B.

Waddell's South Carolina Battery) outside Stilesboro. The 18th Indiana Light Artillery was immediately ordered up. For the next two hours, the Federals were stalled while opposing horse artilleries dueled.[20]

By the evening of May 24, the Southerners held a line east of Dallas running southwest to northeast. The head of Hood's column reached the crossroads at the New Hope Methodist Church on the morning of the 25th. Information was soon received that a Union corps was nearby and moving up fast. Hood quickly deployed his troops in a line facing northwest; Stewart's division was at the church. Old logs were quickly piled up for protection while John Wesley Eldridge's battalion wheeled into line.

At 4:00, as dark clouds began rolling across the skies, a vicious barrage was opened on Stewart's troops. The enemy soon appeared, an entire corps, in ranks so deep that its front did not extend beyond Stewart's. For the next three hours, in the midst of a blinding rainstorm, repeated assaults were checked. The massed fire blasted the Federal brigades apart. Lumsden's Alabama Battery of the reserve was ordered up for support. In the confusion, one man fell underneath a moving wheel and was crushed. The company was not needed, however, and remained in park at the rear of the battle. Stewart refused Johnston's offer of additional reinforcements.[21]

Eldridge's guns ripped the tightly packed Union ranks. The enemy advanced to within fifty yards of Charles Fenner's Louisiana Battery before being driven back. Three brothers handled one gun. Two were shot and the third replaced them as rammer. One man suddenly noticed blood gushing from his ears, caused by the deafening roar of the guns. Colonel Robert Beckham, Hood's artillery chief, arrived on the scene and personally took command. Eldridge's losses were high (forty-three men and forty-four horses killed or wounded), but the effectiveness of the battalion structure when applied as a tactical unit was at last yielding dividends.[22]

Additional reinforcements were received at New Hope Church, which swelled Johnston's army to 75,000. William Quarles's brigade and two batteries, J. R. Yates's Mississippi and E. Tarrent's Alabama, arrived from Mobile. These companies were united with Selden's battery to form Major W. C. Preston's battalion, attached to Cantey's division.[23] Johnston now had the largest aggregation of field artillery ever assembled by the Confederates in the western theater. The 15 battalions, which consisted of 187 guns and 4,600 officers and men, were arranged as follows:[24]

Hardee's corps	4 Battalions	12 Batteries	47 Guns	**149**
Hood's corps	3 "	9 "	36 "	*Boots and*
Polk's corps	3 "	9 "	36 "	*Saddles*
Reserve artillery	3 "	9 "	36 "	
Horse artillery	2 "	8 "	32 "	

The armament, minus the horse batteries, included 84 Napoleons, 36 howitzers, and 22 rifles.

Sherman's army was also reinforced during this time. In early June, the XVII Corps, 10,000 strong, arrived from Huntsville. The artillery now numbered 50 batteries and 254 guns. The number of six-gun and four-gun batteries was about equal. The armament consisted almost entirely of light 12-pounders and rifled guns. Included in the latter were at least 14 large 20-pounder Parrott rifles.[25]

On May 27, Sherman once again attempted to turn the Confederate right flank, and Johnston shifted accordingly. Cleburne's division was transferred to Pickett's Mill as an extension of Hood's corps. Lucius Polk's brigade was posted to the right of Hindman's division. Hotchkiss's battalion was anchored on Polk's right, to the right of which Govan's brigade provided support. When Cleburne inspected Hotchkiss's works he was not satisfied and ordered additional trenches constructed in order to secure an oblique fire to the right.[26]

At 5:00 Sherman launched his IV Corps. From atop a formidable natural ridge, Rebel infantry poured a withering fire into the enemy ranks. Goldthwaite's Napoleon battery was sent to the right to deliver an enfilade fire, but, because of the tangled thickets and deep ravines, it was unable to find a place to unlimber. Two of Key's howitzers were run up by hand to the flank trench and were used with "deadly effect" on several lines of blue infantry advancing up a depression on Granbury's brigade. Key expended some 187 rounds of spherical case shot and canister within two hours. One eyewitness observed: "Never did artillerymen do their duty more nobly."[27] Meanwhile, Key's other section and Swett's four 10-pounder Parrott rifles had enfiladed the enemy's reserves, which were massing behind a hill. "I regretted that I did not have more guns for this service," lamented Cleburne. Night ended the fighting. It was the second undisputed victory in which a division had hurled back an entire corps.

Elsewhere along the line some sharp battery duels took place.

"Phelan [Alabama battery] and Perry [Florida battery] were with Cheatham," explained Colonel Melancthon Smith, Hardee's artillery chief. "Turner [Mississppi battery] had been with Cheatham for several days, but at this place was sent to Polk at his (Polk's) particular request and having been put in a position on Featherston's brigade to endeavor to silence two of the enemies' batteries had one piece disabled and six or eight men badly wounded. Two afterwards died. About this time Capt. [J. W.] Mebane was killed."[28]

On the evening of May 27, Colonel Beckham called up Courtney's and Van den Corput's battalions to support Cleburne's division. A fierce exchange ensued between Beckham's guns and those of the IV Corps. Garrity's Alabama Battery succeeded in silencing a company of 20-pounder Parrott rifles in a contest that lasted more than an hour.[29] On the morning of the 28th, Johnston sent William Bate's division forward in a reconnaissance-in-force on the Union right. What resulted was a poorly conceived headlong assault against Union earthworks at Dallas. In the brief but fierce struggle, one of the Napoleons of the Washington Artillery was disabled. Bate, suffering heavy casualties, withdrew.[30]

Because of the nature of the campaign—heavy skirmishing and limited engagements—overall artillery casualties during May were not heavy. By May 20, in Cobb's battalion, three had been killed and twelve wounded. From May 7 to 24, in Robert Beckham's regiment, five were killed and eighty-seven wounded—almost all of whom were in Johnston's battalion at Reseca and Eldridge's at New Hope Church. By mid-June, Polk's artillery had lost only sixteen men and twenty-seven horses. Four of Polk's batteries had not even fired a shot. Only one man in Robertson's horse batteries was wounded during the month.[31]

●

June brought rains and more misery. During the first three weeks, it rained almost every day, which slowed Sherman's momentum. Fields and woods became soaked, roads turned into quagmires, and trenches became pools of water. Exhausted troops labored to move their guns and caissons over nearly impassable roads. Winds from the east turned from chilly to cold. To add to the bleakness, on June 14 a group of officers, including Johnston, Hardee, and Polk, disregarded the warnings of Rebel artillerymen and climbed to the summit of Pine Mountain to make an observation. A Federal Parrott battery suddenly opened up. Polk was struck in the chest and died instantly. Loring was temporarily assigned command of the corps.

Heavy skirmishing continued, and the artillery of both sides was used to batter down the enemy. On June 18, while occupying a dangerous salient between Lost Mountain and the Marietta Road, Major George Storrs's battalion became heavily engaged. Enemy skirmishers advanced to within two hundred yards and opened a brisk fire, while two Yankee batteries kept up an incessant pounding. A driving rain soon filled Storrs's shallow trenches with water and the recoil of the guns sank their wheels deep in the mud. Working its pieces for ten hours, Captain Henry Guibor's battery expended 418 rounds of ammunition. Most of the men had been sent to cover in the rear. Of the thirty gunners who remained at Guibor's cannon, sixteen became casualties. Late that evening, General French sadly wrote in his diary: "Capt. Guibor has lost more men than he did during the entire siege of Vicksburg."[32]

Johnston attempted to hold a new line that ran from Bush Mountain and then turned southward. Its salient was enfiladed by Thomas's artillery, however, and the Confederates were forced to withdraw on the night of June 18–19. As at Reseca and Cassville, the powerful Union artillery had once again influenced a retreat decision. Johnston moved his line closer to Marietta. The key to this new position was Kennesaw Mountain. Hardee held the left to its south, Loring occupied the crest in the center, and Hood was posted on the right extending to the railroad. The whole line bristled with abatis and breastworks.

Because of the steep incline of Kennesaw, engineers advised against planting artillery on the crest. But Major Storrs, commanding French's cannon, was not convinced of the impossibility of the task. Finding a spur in the rear of Little Kennesaw, he obtained permission to cut a roadway through the brush up the mountainside. Pulled upward by a hundred men tugging on ropes, the first gun reached the summit within thirty minutes. The ammunition chests were dismounted and carried up empty, along with the fixed ammunition. Several batteries were moved to the top in this manner.[33]

During the days that followed, deafening duels raged between the lines. On June 19, Perry's battery was between Walker's and French's divisions. Unlike the other artillery companies, the Floridians kept their flag defiantly, though foolishly, waving in the breeze. It made a tempting target for Sherman's gunners.

"Their line burst out a steady flame of fire all the day, but it did no harm except keeping us close in the muddy trenches," explained Lieutenant Neal. "The artillery fire was bad as the Yankee batteries could not see me or the smoke of my guns as the rain poured down all day."[34]

The next afternoon, Lumsden's Alabama Battery, occupying a position on the southern crest of Little Kennesaw, was ordered to open fire on a suspected enemy position to "see what they had over there." Within minutes, an estimated twenty-four Union guns blasted a thunderous reply. A shell came directly through an embrasure, instantly killed a gunner, and crashed into a caisson, which caused a column of smoke and flame to shoot high into the air. A resounding cheer arose from the opposition. "We found out what the enemy had over there and we did not stir up that hornets' nest again," commented one of Lumsden's men.[35]

Sporadic cannonading continued over the crackling of musketry. Perhaps the most incredible exchange of cannon fire in the campaign occurred. A Union gun fired a single shot and made a direct hit on a Rebel caisson on Little Kennesaw. Not to be outdone, a Confederate gun crew boomed a shot in response and destroyed a Yankee caisson. A cheer went up from both armies.[36]

Time and time again, Sherman's flanking movements had forced Johnston out of strongly fortified positions. Already Hood's corps had been shifted to beef up the left and Loring's extended to the railroad. Sherman now deviated from his former strategy and planned a direct assault on three points along Johnston's line. The attack came on the morning of the 27th. Sherman planned to soften up Cheatham's line with a massive preparatory artillery barrage. By this stage of the war, however, many officers were beginning to question the effectiveness of such a tactic. General O. O. Howard would later write that "it may occupy the enemy's artillery and keep it from effective work on our advancing men but it prevents anything like a surprise."[37]

At 8:00 A.M. Sherman unleashed his cannoneers. For fifteen minutes, the artillery of two corps blasted out a deafening barrage. Cheatham's men were unprepared; many had gone to the rear to wash and others were relaxing. They were suddenly jolted out of their tranquillity. As predicted by some, however, the barrage did little damage and fully alerted the Confederates to the impending danger. When the attack came, they were ready.

Shortly after 9:00, Thomas's Cumberlanders emerged and ad-

vanced on Cheatham's position. The Southerners' withering fire
literally swept away the leading ranks. The Yankees also
walked into an artillery trap. At Maney's salient, the batteries of
Phelan and Perry were positioned on the right and crossed fire
with two of Wright's guns on the left. Colonel Melancthon Smith
had ordered these masked batteries to hold their fire during the
barrage. When the assault began, the full fury of all ten guns
was felt and, according to Smith, "contributed no little to the
repulse." A section of Turner's battery was on line between
Cheatham and Cleburne. At this point, the enemy emerged to
within forty yards before being driven back by vicious blasts of
canister.[38]

Southern artillerymen haul a field piece to the summit of Kennesaw Mountain during the Atlanta campaign. (*Mountain Campaigns in Georgia*)

To the north, Morgan Smith's division of the XV Corps, reinforced with troops from another division, surged toward the juncture of French's and Walker's divisions. From atop the northwest summit of Kennesaw, French's cannon opened a fierce enfilade fire. The guns of Guibor's, Ward's, Hoskin's, Bellamy's and Lumsden's batteries, coupled with the fire of sharpshooters, raked the Union lines and caused them to reel back in confusion. This took place, according to Major Storrs, "before the guns got very hot."[39]

At 10:00 an assault was hurled against Loring's right wing. The brunt of the attack fell on Scott's brigade of W. S. Featherston's (Loring's old) division. Rolling forward in three waves, Federal troops advanced to within three hundred yards of the Rebel trenches. At that point, Scott's infantry, supported by the flanking fire of Cowan's, Bouanchaud's, Havis's and one of Robertson's horse batteries, erupted in a wall of flame. The advancing line staggered to a halt. Unable to advance or retreat under the massed firepower, the troops remained huddled behind rocks and crevices for almost an hour until they finally withdrew under a shower of shot and shell.[40]

By noon, the battle had sputtered to a close. Sherman had suffered terrible casualties: some 3,000 as against Johnston's 750. Confederate artillery losses were negligible. In Storrs's battalion, only two men were wounded, both in Guibor's battery. For several days, the Yankee dead lay on the battlefield. Colonel Smith wrote that "some of them were lying against our works and presented a most revolting appearance, as black as negroes—enormously swollen, fly blown, remitting an intolerable stench."

After his assault on Kennesaw failed miserably, Sherman once again resumed long-range shelling. On July 1–2, an estimated fifty-one Union guns pounded Little Kennesaw in an attempt to knock out some of French's cannon, particularly Guibor's annoying battery. Because of the angle of fire, they met with no success.[41] Rebel batteries were only partially able to respond to such barrages. Ammunition was now at a premium and most of the rounds needed to be saved to fend off a direct assault. Such comments as those of an Illinois battery captain were not uncommon: "July 1, fired sixteen rounds without getting any reply from the enemy. July 2, fired forty-one rounds; enemy did not reply." At that time, Johnston's reserve ammunition supply amounted to a mere 2,164 rounds—half in Atlanta and half on railroad cars at Vinings, Georgia. The supply included only 460 rounds of 10-pounder Parrott shells.[42]

Once again, Sherman resorted to a turning movement.
Johnston was now forced to abandon his Marietta defenses. On
the night of July 2, the Southerners filed out of their trenches.
By the 5th they had taken up a strongly fortified line on the
north bank of the Chattahoochee. In one of the missed opportunities of the war, Johnston allowed Sherman to trickle his
divisions over to Roswell, some sixteen miles upriver from his
position. During the night of July 9–10, the Confederates
retreated across the river and formed a line on the south bank of
Peachtree Creek, only a few miles from Atlanta. On the 17th
came the fateful message from Richmond ordering Johnston's
removal. The command of the Army and responsibility for saving Atlanta now passed into the hands of General John B. Hood.

●

The artillery adopted well to Johnston's defensive tactics. His
armament, consisting of 80 percent Napoleons and howitzers,
was best suited for close-range work. New Hope Church, Pickett's Mill, and Kennesaw Mountain demonstrated the potent
defensive capability of his artillery. In a pitched battle in open
country, his smoothbores would undoubtedly have been badly
outgunned by Sherman's long-range pieces.

The Southern artillery took its knocks. Johnston's statement
that no guns were lost except for "the four field pieces exposed
and abandoned at Reseca by General Hood" was a half-truth. At
least five guns were disabled. In addition, fourteen cannon
(seven heavy and seven field guns) in fixed fortifications at Reseca and Rome were abandoned when the army retreated south
of the Oostanaula and Etowah.[43]

During the campaign, it became obvious that the sheer shock
effect of artillery was much less of a battlefield factor than it had
been. This was attributable to the extensive use of entrenchments and the combat experience of the troops. "Artillery is
more valuable with new and inexperienced troops than with
veterans," explained Sherman. "In the early stages of the war
the field guns often bore the proportion of six to a thousand men;
but toward the close of the war one gun, or at most two to a
thousand men, was deemed enough."[44]

One thing was certain. Now that Hood was in command, the
nature of the campaign, and in turn the role of the artillery, was
to change drastically.

Chapter 14

"Those Brave Cannoneers"

Artillerists as well as the army as a whole viewed the removal of Johnston with mixed reactions. Captain Key wrote that "every man looked sad and disheartened," and a private in Guibor's Missouri Battery later remembered that "the soldiers were very much depressed." Lieutenant Neal, however, confided that "I cannot regard it as a calamity." "One thing for certain," declared Captain Douglas, "Gen'l Hood will fight the enemy, and I believe he can whip them."[1] Hood inherited an army of ten infantry and four cavalry divisions, totaling 42,000 infantry, 12,000 cavalry, and 3,600 artillery—some 57,600 troops—plus G. W. Smith's division of Georgia militia. Anderson's Georgia Battery was loaned to Smith inasmuch as he lacked mobile artillery of his own.[2]

Atlanta, Hood's base of supplies, was strongly fortified. It was encircled by ten miles of entrenchments: nineteen redoubts on the main line, each intended for five cannon; five exterior batteries not connected with rifle pits; and several interior batteries. A swath nine hundred to a thousand yards in width was cut in front of the works to clear a field of fire. Everything in the pathway—houses, barns, orchards—was demolished.[3] In March 1864 the city's armament consisted of seven 6-pounders, seven 12-pounder howitzers, two Wiard rifles, and two 24-pounder rifles. The number of field guns was soon increased to twenty-eight, mostly old cannon rejected by the army. Because no horses or harness were available, the weapons could only be used defensively. To give some added punch to the line, General D. H. Maury, at Mobile, transported fourteen heavy cannon to Atlanta, nine of which were eventually mounted on the northern section of the defenses. The city was thus permanently defended by thirty-seven guns.[4]

The artillery force in Atlanta was not an impressive one. In December 1863 five depleted batteries from the Army of Tennessee had been transferred to garrison duty in the city. Pritchard's understrength battery was already there. These six companies were eventually merged into four—Scogin's, Baxter's, Rivers's, and Massenburg's—and placed under the command of the Georgia militia. Together they mustered only 135 artillerists, who were thinly spread among ten of the main redoubts. They were supported by a skeleton force of mechanics and artisans, including J. H. Hudson's 100-man artillery company, composed of arsenal employees.[5]

On July 20, 22, and 28 Hood attacked and was repulsed in the battles of Peachtree Creek, Atlanta, and Ezra Church. In each instance, the artillery was used on the tactical offensive over rugged terrain in the characteristic manner of the western army: following in the rear of center of brigades. The results were predictable: limited and ineffectual participation.

At Peachtree Creek, Hood planned to overwhelm Thomas's Army of the Cumberland as it moved across the creek, before reinforcements could arrive from Schofield's and McPherson's armies, which were already east of the city. Toward that end, Cheatham (temporarily commanding Hood's old corps) was ordered to mass his artillery on his left so as to sweep the gap that had developed between Schofield's right and the creek. Sherman's forces would thus be divided.[6] Although the long arm was assigned a role in Hood's overall planning, it was only minimally utilized in the execution of those plans.

The main difficulty, as always, was the terrain. Union General Jacob D. Cox thought that the artillery provided little assistance to the Confederate attackers at Peachtree Creek. "The dense forrests made the artillery of little effect in demolishing the works or weakening the morale of the defenders," he explained, "and it was essentially an infantry attack upon entrenched infantry at close range."[7]

Operating on the tactical offensive, Confederate artillerymen were forced to man their guns with minimal terrain cover. Selden's Alabama Battery of Major W. C. Preston's battalion supported the assault of Walthall's division. The cannoneers unlimbered their pieces on an open field slope of a hill to the left of the Paces Ferry Road. Within minutes, they were raked by artillery fire from several directions and were forced to change front constantly. "We could only tell where the Yankee battery was by the smoke when they fired," explained one of Selden's men. While Major Preston (the brother of General Hood's fiancée) was directing the movements, he was killed by an incoming shell. At 4:00 Selden's men, their limbers empty, withdrew and were replaced by Barry's Tennessee Battery. The cannoneers found themselves being hit by a "galling fire" from artillery and "within easy range of sharpshooters." They lost fifteen men and three horses before retiring at sunset.[8]

Even at this late date in the war, some officers were not beyond attempting obsolete maneuvers. Captain Thomas Key proposed to his battalion commander, Major Hotchkiss, that he "run up one gun at a time and load them with canister so as to mow down the Yankee lines when our troops charged." Hotchkiss consented, but Hardee revoked the suicidal tactic.[9]

In the July 22 assault, the terrain was once again a factor. Hardee's corps was to attack McPherson's southern flank. As Bate's and Walker's divisions deployed and moved forward, however, they became entangled in undergrowth and briar thickets. The Louisiana Washington Artillery was the only battery to even advance with Bate's division, and it was soon forced to halt on account of the rugged terrain.[10] Cleburne's division attacked at 1:00, and for a while it seemed as though the enemy line might collapse. Several Yankee batteries were overrun. Goldthwaite's Alabama Battery supported the attack astride the Flat Shoals Road. Some of his men rushed up to the abandoned Union guns to turn them on the retreating enemy. As one piece was wheeled around, however, the Yankees "poured such a volley of musketry upon those brave cannoneers that they were compelled to abandon the gun."[11]

Captain Thomas Key, who the day before had replaced the wounded Major Hotchkiss as battalion commander, once again envisioned an outdated Napoleonic tactic. He ordered a section of Turner's Mississippi Battery forward to within 200 yards of the enemy's works to open with canister. The lieutenant commanding the section initially refused to carry out the dangerous maneuver. Only after some arguing were his guns brought up. Key did not mention the incident in his official report, but in his diary he wrote that the order was "very tardily done."[12] Confederate artillery support continued to be limited and uncoordinated. Hoxton's battalion, initially with Maney's division, had no sooner unlimbered and begun firing before it was ordered to disengage and report to another part of the line. Lieutenant Neal stated that his battery "left before much was accomplished."[13]

Hardee's attack had lost most of its punch before Hood belatedly launched Cheatham's corps. Captain Douglas described the scene:

On yesterday, about four o'clock, Hindman's Division advanced from our works and attacked the enemy. My battery and Dent's advanced with the attacking column. We swept across the field and through the woods for three-fourths of a mile driving their advance line from their works and pressing upon their main line of works. Here the battle grew grand . . . Dent and myself got into position 400 yards from their works and opened with vigor on the enemy . . . while our batteries in our main line of works opened on the enemy at long range.[14]

The offensive role of the artillery, never particularly effective, was made even more difficult by the extensive use of entrenchments. Eldridge's battalion moved up in support of the attack and opened with a long-range shelling. The results of the barrage could not be seen, but the Federals were well dug in and the effect was apparently minimal.[15]

Cheatham's attack fell on M. L. Smith's division of the XV Corps. The four 20-pounder Parrott rifles of Battery H, 1st Illinois Light Artillery, were overrun and a hole punched in the Federal line. As the Southerners advanced, however, Schofield's artillery opened a flank fire. The 3-inch rifles of Battery D, 1st Ohio, were loaded with double charges of canister. A Union counterattack swept the Confederates pell-mell from the field and recaptured the Parrott guns in the process.[16]

The limited role of the long arm in the Battle of Atlanta was reflected in the casualty list. Cleburne's division sustained al-

Key's Arkansas Battery moving up Peachtree Road during the Battle of Peachtree Creek on July 20, 1864. (Mrs. Wilbur G. Kurtz, Sr.)

most half of Hardee's 3,200 casualties. Yet, in Cleburne's artillery, only two men were wounded and nine horses disabled. The embattled Southerners were at least able to haul off a dozen Yankee Napoleon guns as they withdrew. One of these replaced an old howitzer in Key's battery, and two others were swapped with Confederate light 12-pounders in Swett's battery. Douglas's battery was also issued four of the Yankee Napoleons. "I have now much the finest battery I have ever had and perhaps the finest in our army. . . . My boys got almost the entire baggage of the battery [A, 1st Illinois Light] we captured," explained Douglas.[17]

Hood's long arm did precious little fighting in the battles around Atlanta. Attempts were made to use it aggressively, but the rugged terrain and extensive use of entrenchments limited its offensive effectiveness. The Union artillery on the other hand, operating on the tactical defensive, made a significant contribution. At Peachtree Creek, Thomas's batteries near the Buckhead Road smashed Walker's division. In the Battle of Atlanta, the Federals were able to marshal thirteen batteries with eighty-six guns to oppose the Confederate attack. At Ezra Church, O. O. Howard used twenty-six guns to cover the threatened right flank of the XV Corps. Once again the western Confederate artillery found itself in an all too familiar dilemma. It was essentially a defensive arm called upon to perform an offensive mission.[18]

●

After the Battle of Atlanta, a quick reorganization was effected. Lieutenant General S. D. Lee arrived to command Hood's old corps. Walker's division was broken up on account of heavy casualties and the brigades sent to other divisions. The artillery reserve was phased out on an army level and the battalions sent down to the corps—a move Robert E. Lee had made in his army a year earlier. Joseph Palmer's battalion was assigned to Hardee's Corps, Samuel Williams's to Lee's, and James Waddell's to Stewart's.

A significant number of changes also occurred in artillery personnel. The army's top man in this branch, Brigadier General Shoup, was moved to chief of staff to replace the retiring W. W. Mackall. Shoup's replacement came as no surprise. Hood appointed his former corps artillery chief, Colonel Robert F. Beckham, but his attempt to obtain the Virginian a brigadier general's commission was unsuccessful. Because the artillery reserve had been dissolved on an army level, Lieutenant Colonel James Hallonquist was now free for reassignment. He thus replaced Beckham as commander of Lee's batteries. Major S. C. Williams was promoted to lieutenant colonel and assigned to A. P. Stewart's corps artillery. Lieutenant Colonel Felix Robertson left the horse artillery to become brigadier general of cavalry.[19]

On August 8, Sherman changed his flanking tactics and undertook formal siege operations. Eight large 30-pounder Parrott rifles were brought down by rail from Chattanooga. Added to the score or so of 20-pounder Parrotts already in use, they provided

Colonel Robert F. Beckham was one of several high-ranking artillery officers who transferred from the Army of Northern Virginia. *(The Long Arm of Lee)*

powerful siege armament. For twenty-eight days, Union batteries rained shot and shell on the city. The Chattanooga siege guns pounded away at twenty-minute intervals. The persistent hammering started fires, smashed buildings, and killed soldiers and civilians indiscriminately.

Lieutenant Neal had a front-line view of the action. "Almost all of the shells they threw into the city came screaming just above our heads," he explained. "Generally they commence on this fort and throw around it shells and then elevate their guns and send the balance into the city. For a while we exchanged shots with them, but where our batteries are as well protected as ours and the Yankees before us, about as much is made of artillery duels as the sledge hammer makes out of the anvil."[20]

On some days, the artillery fire was sporadic, but on others, such as August 9, it reached a deafening crescendo. On that day, Union gunners sent more than 5,000 shells crashing into the city, though two-thirds of them failed to explode. The duel, between eleven Federal and ten Rebel batteries, lasted all day. Many of the cannoneers fell at their posts from sheer exhaustion.[21]

As Sherman maneuvered his troops into various positions, the Confederate artillery shifted accordingly. As Captain Key stated on August 18, "This morning orders were received to be ready to move at a moment's notice, General Hood thinking that the Yanks were massing on our right in front of Atlanta. By noon, however, the enemy made their appearance on the extreme left." He continued: "I ordered the batteries to throw shell in a thick woods in front of the position where the enemy had concentrated. The officers on picket duty reported that almost every shell would kill or wound a Yank, for they could hear the pitiful cries and friends calling for litter bearers. I kept up the artillery fire almost all night."[22]

Throughout the evening, the Northerners inched their works closer and in the morning opened their batteries from a new position. Key ordered up a section of Parrott rifles from Garrity's battery to "try my luck upon them." After firing only a few rounds, the Alabama gunners made a direct hit on an enemy caisson a mile and a half distant, "igniting the hundreds of pounds of powder and filling the air with ammunition chests, carriage wheels, and other objects too distant to be known."[23]

The soldiers soon became accustomed to the incessant pounding. A gunner in Marshall's Tennessee Battery said that at night the men "slept as in a mill, undisturbed by the noise." On August 7, General French explained that "as soon as the fog rose this morning the artillery of the enemy opened and continued for seven hours without intermission; but from all this we sustain little damage." The noise, he added, "annoys the soldiers a little."[24] Artillery alone would be insufficient to bring about Atlanta's submission.

Interestingly, Hood's artillery during this time was nearly the numerical equal of Sherman's. On August 15 the Union commander counted 216 guns. Even though three batteries were absent with Wheeler on a raid, Hood still had forty-four batteries with 172 pieces. In addition, four batteries of the Georgia militia manned sixteen field guns. Also, the seven 32-pounder rifles mounted on the line were far larger than anything in the Union armament. General French reported that the destructive fire of these monster cannon disabled several Union guns.[25]

The principal problem for the gray artillery was supply. This campaign would be won as much by logistics and administration as by fighting. For example, although the numerical difference between the opposing artilleries was not all that great, the Confederates were forced to limit their rate of fire because of the shortage of ammunition. On August 18, Hood's artillery averaged only 125 rounds to the gun. In comparison, the Union artillery rarely averaged less than 400 rounds at any time.

Other shortages in the Rebel long arm at that time included 156 saddles, 316 bridles, 691 halters, 298 saddle blankets, 548 curry combs, 541 horse brushes, and 17 sets of harness.[26] The men were pitifully short of clothing and equipment. The August 18 report listed a dearth of 1,935 coats, 1,974 blankets, 1,651 pairs of shoes, 4,564 pairs of socks, 1,710 haversacks, and 1,288 canteens. The inspecting officers reported that "on very few occasions have I seen articles of clothing issued to the artillery with the proper (red) trimmings for that branch of the service. In nearly ever instance it has been the uniform of the infantry, although occasionally I have seen jackets with artillery trimmings in the infantry."

The condition of the stock was becoming so critical that the mobility of the artillery was threatened. On August 18 some 2,156 horses were on hand, of which 164 were unserviceable. The batteries thus averaged only 51 horses each. A shortage of long forage had always existed, though the supply of corn had been adequate. By this time, however, a Yankee cavalry raid on the Montgomery & West Point Railroad had knocked out twenty miles of track, which left both commodities in short supply.[27]

The logistics picture went from bad to worse as the military situation rapidly deteriorated. On August 25, Sherman's guns fell silent and his armies went on the move once again. In a series of events that left the Confederate high command bewildered, Sherman, by August 30, had shifted almost all his strength to the south of Atlanta, between the West Point and Macon railroads. On the afternoon of September 1, the Federals attacked Hardee's isolated corps at Jonesboro. Fortunately for him, it was not an all-out assault or his heavily outnumbered corps would certainly have been annihilated. Even so, Govan's and Lewis's brigades were swept away, and Key's Arkansas and Swett's Mississippi batteries were overrun.

One of the Mississippi artillerymen recalled the scene years later: "It was a grand and fearful sight to see that great army coming like a monster wave to engulf us," wrote Joseph Erwin. "They were several lines deep in our immediate front in an open field. . . . We poured grape and canister into them cutting great gaps in their lines; but they closed them up with fresh men, and came on to the very muzzles of our guns."[28] The batteries lost two 10-pounder Parrott rifles and six 12-pounder Napoleons, as well as both of the battery's prized battle flags. All but a dozen or so of the Arkansans were captured and the Mississippians suffered similarly. Swett's company was disbanded shortly thereafter and the survivors formed into a small scouting troop.[29]

Hardee made good his escape, but, because the railroads were cut, Atlanta was doomed. Hurried last-minute efforts were made to salvage as much as possible. Colonel Melancthon Smith was charged with removing not only the cannon of Hardee's corps, but also those of the Georgia militia. Included were twenty-eight guns, but no horses or harness. He was promised additional animals, but, as the hours ticked away, none arrived. He, therefore, "attached these pieces to those of my regular command, many teams having two guns, and thus got off about twelve at night."[30]

That night was devoid of other good news, for a staggering amount of ordnance was either abandoned or destroyed. Hood's reserve ordnance train, stranded when the Macon Railroad was cut, was blown up. The explosions could be heard thirty miles away, and bright flashes lit up the darkened sky. Several weeks were required to tally the losses. Ordnance officials were stunned at the findings: ten field pieces, fourteen siege guns,

thirty-three caissons, thirty-nine limbers, three traveling
forges, twenty-five single sets of harness, and twelve artillery
saddles. Even worse, almost the entire supply of reserve artillery ammunition, some 14,000 rounds, had gone up in smoke.[31]

For the next several days, Hood's discouraged army trudged southward. Lieutenant Colonel Hallonquist was ordered to take the three reserve battalions and the batteries of the Georgia militia (eventually reduced to two companies of four howitzers each) to Macon for the defense of that place. Eleven batteries of forty-two guns thus departed from the army.[32]

•

The lifeblood of the army had been shed in the defense of At- lanta. One source estimates that the campaign cost the Confed- erates more than 50,000 men.[33] Everywhere lay the grim signs of suffering. High losses had often managed to elude the artil- lery, but not this time. On April 1 the 27 batteries totaled 2,861 men present for duty, or an average of 106 per company. On August 31 these same batteries numbered 2,395, or 89 per com- pany. This represented a net loss of 16 percent. From a June 10 high of 4,619 men, the Southern long arm dropped to 4,123 by August 31.[34]

The artillery was also beginning to suffer in leadership. On August 31, 199 officers were assigned, a net loss of 52 since June 10. By the end of the campaign, the casualty list read like a "Who's Who" among artillery officers. Major W. C. Preston and Captains Thomas Stanford, J. W. Mebane, John Ward, and McDonald Oliver were dead. The wounded included Majors John W. Johnston and Thomas Hotchkiss as well as Captains L. G. Marshall, James Garrity, Max Van den Corput, Frank Gracey, and Henry Guibor. Sickness had removed from service Major James Waddell in addition to Captains Joseph Selden, J. B. Rowan, and William Jeffress. On August 17, Major Robert Martin was listed as "absent without leave." Half the battalions experienced some turnover in command during the campaign.[35]

The loss of Atlanta was also a logistical catastrophe for the artillery. The task of supplying the army now fell upon the already overtaxed arsenals at Columbus, Macon, Augusta, and Selma. On September 5 officials at Macon wired Chief of Ord- nance Josiah Gorgas, in Richmond, asking if any rifled shells of 3-inch, 10-pounder Parrott, and 2½-inch Blakely caliber could be obtained north of Augusta. Colonel James Kennard, Hood's

new chief ordnance officer, frantically searched for artillery saddles and harness. On September 23, Gorgas came to his aid by
sending him saddles from the Mount Vernon, Alabama, Arsenal
and 1,000 sets of harness from Richmond. In late September the
Augusta Arsenal was called upon for, among other items, 4,000
rounds of fixed ammunition, mostly for 12-pounder Napoleons.
Colonel Rains wrote Kennard that he could ship them at the rate
of about 1,200 rounds per week.[36]

More belt-tightening lay ahead. On September 15 an inspector penned an endorsement, ironically on the back of Captain
W. C. Duxbury's glowing report of the previous April: "Artillery
not now in as good condition." The supply of ammunition was
down to a scant 106 rounds per gun. The need for horse brushes
was so serious that the men were reduced to fabricating
makeshift brushes from horsehair.[37]

The loss in cannon, though heavy, was not crippling. Since
May at least five of the army's guns had been permanently disabled and twelve captured. These losses were offset by the capture of a dozen light 12-pounders and 3-inch rifles. The
Confederates abandoned eighteen field and twenty-two siege
guns, mostly in the fixed fortifications at Reseca, Rome, and
Atlanta. These weapons were independent of the army, however,
and did not impair the efficiency of Hood's artillery.[38]

Actually, the Southern commander had more guns now than
he could logistically support. When the reserve artillery was
assigned to garrison duty in Macon, the horses were redistributed among the remaining battalions. Even then there
was a dearth. By September 20, Hood's 9 battalions counted
1,213 horses, or an average of only 44 per battery. All the guns
and caissons were reduced to 4 animals each. More drastic measures had to be taken. Two caissons from each company were
ordered to be turned in and replaced with mule wagons.[39]

In short, the Atlanta campaign had permanently crippled the
Southern long arm. In command, organization, number of
horses and guns, equipment, manpower, and ammunition supply it was left a hulk of the structure that Johnston had molded
five months earlier. Never again would it be able to compete
with its powerful Northern counterpart on anything like an
equal footing.

Chapter 15

"Hood Did Not Know How to Use Artillery"

On September 19, 1864, Hood moved the battered Army of Tennessee to Palmetto Station on the Macon Railroad. Never had the situation seemed so bleak. Shortages of food, shoes, wagons, and ammunition intensified. The total effective force of infantry, cavalry, and artillery had dwindled to slightly more than 39,000. And dissatisfaction with Hood's leadership was prevalent. Captain Key expressed the sentiments of many when he wrote: "Something must be done in the way of generalship, for we have not the force to meet them."[1]

Recruitment in the artillery had almost come to a standstill. On September 20, Hood's 32 batteries mustered 2,695 men, an average of only 84 effectives per company. Key's battery was fortunate in receiving 18 Arkansans from Swett's now defunct company. Marshall's Tennessee Battery obtained 26 conscripts from east Tennessee, only to have 24 of them desert within days.[2]

Several artillery companies were phased out of the army. Swett's outfit was dissolved, and Barry's Tennessee Battery was ordered to turn over its guns, equipment, and horses to Darden's company and report to Macon. Anderson's Georgia Battery was retained for service by the Georgia militia, and Gracey's Kentucky Battery was detached for service with the Kentucky brigade. Three batteries of the horse artillery were also absent with Wheeler.[3]

On September 20, Hood's reorganized artillery consisted of a compact nine battalions, each of which consisted of three four-gun batteries. In addition, two reduced battalions of horse artillery manned sixteen guns. The armament totaled 124 pieces, including ninety 12-pounder Napoleons, twelve 12-pounder howitzers, and twenty-two rifles, mostly of the 10-pounder Parrott and 3-inch rifle type:

Battalion	Napoleons	Howitzers	Rifles
Hoxton	12	—	—
Bledsoe	12	—	—
Cobb	8	4	—
Trueheart	8	4	—
Storrs	10	—	2
Myrick	12	—	—
Johnston	12	—	—
Eldridge	8	—	4
Courtney	8	—	4
Calloway (horse)	—	4	4
Waties (horse)	—	—	8

There were now five guns per thousand effective infantry, as compared with Lee's nine per thousand at that time.[4]

A significant change in structure occurred. On November 14, Special Orders No. 34 abandoned the regimental artillery organization and reverted to the old division-level structure. Under this setup, each battalion was assigned to and operated with a particular division in battle and on the march. This necessarily diluted the executive authority of the corps artillery chiefs, though the order was not "intended to bring in conflict with the division commanders any authority or interest in the artillery heretofore vested in the chiefs of artillery of the corps, but to secure a hearty co-operation in everything that tends to promote the strength and efficiency of the artillery arm of the service."[5]

A major command change was made in the army in the latter part of September, when President Davis transferred the disenchanted Hardee to command of the Department of South Carolina, Georgia, and Florida. Benjamin Cheatham was advanced to corps command. Hood's three corps were now headed by Cheatham, S. D. Lee, and A. P. Stewart.

A command shake-up in the artillery also took place. Colonel Robert Beckham had been in charge of Hood's artillery ever since Francis Shoup had been advanced to chief of staff in July. On September 8, however, Major General Arnold Elzy was assigned as chief of artillery. He was a West Pointer who had served in the U.S. Artillery. Still, it was certainly unique to appoint such a high-ranking officer to the artillery. For some months, Bragg and Lee had toyed with the idea that the artillery corps of the Army of Northern Virginia was equivalent to a corps of infantry and should merit a major general. Indeed, during the spring of 1863, Lee had even considered Elzy as his artillery chieftain, "if his health and habits do not interfere." His poor health was attributed to a bad skull wound he had received at Gaines Mill. Elzy was instead appointed to the quiescent Department of Richmond, where he spent much of his time organizing Virginia reserves and local defense troops.[6]

Special circumstances may have been involved in his western appointment. Lieutenant General Dick Ewell had not served well in corps command in the Army of Northern Virginia. To politely shelve him, Elzy was bumped and Ewell was given com-

Major General Arnold Elzy led the artillery during the ill-fated Tennessee campaign. (Library of Congress)

mand of the Department of Richmond.[7] Elzy's reassignment to
the western artillery may have been viewed as the only significant option available to him at the time. At any rate, once more a
Virginia transfer abruptly stepped into a top position in the
Western long arm.

•

Hood now made a sudden thrust against Sherman's supply line
by striking north of the Chattahoochee against the railroad.
The garrisons at Ackworth and Big Shanty were quickly overwhelmed, though French's division failed to capture Allatoona.
Union troops in the nearby blockhouse at the railroad bridge
surrendered, however, when Kolb's Alabama Battery opened a
sustained shelling. At this juncture, Hood abandoned the
Georgia front and planned a bold offensive. The army would
cross the Tennessee River into north Alabama, move into middle
Tennessee to capture Nashville, and then invade Kentucky.

Hood later contended that his invasion plans included "a
heavy reserve of artillery to accompany the army in order to
overcome any serious opposition by the Federal gunboats [in
crossing the Tennessee River]."[8] Actually, evidence is lacking
that he made any such plans. None of the battalions were called
up from Macon. Far from having a heavy reserve, Hood's artillery was now weaker by a third.

By October 11 the army had crossed the Coosa River and
marched toward familiar ground around Reseca and Dalton.
Only one battery, with a traveling forge and two forage wagons,
accompanied each division. Major General Elzy took the bulk of
the artillery on to Jacksonville, Alabama, Hood's new base of
supplies. After destroying the railroad from Reseca to above
Dalton, the Confederates, on October 14, marched toward
Gadsden, Alabama, and arrived there on the 20th. At that place,
the artillery reunited with the army.[9]

If the Southern offensive were to enjoy any chance for success,
the army had to move with speed and strike the scattered Union
contingents before they could unite. Almost from the beginning,
however, obstacles were encountered. The most maddening of
these occurred at Tuscumbia. Heavy rains made the roads almost impassable. The Tennessee River became swollen, partially submerging the pontoon bridge. Supplies that had been
promised had not yet arrived, and the railroad to Corinth was
still not repaired. At last on November 20, while the rain still

fell and the wheels sank up to the hubs in mud, the column snaked forward.[10]

If the truth be known, even if the weather had cooperated, the army was simply in no condition to make a rapid offensive so far north.[11] The problems encountered by the artillery are illustrative. On November 4, Major E. H. Ewing, inspector of field transportation for the Army of Tennessee, stated that "360 artillery horses would be required to supply the places of those broken down and that could not move. No horses being in reserve, they have put 240 mules received from Paxton in the gun carriages in place of horses; the remainder will, I suppose, be taken from the different wagon trains unless it is determined to leave some of the artillery at this point. Many of the horses not condemned are so poor and weak that I fear 'unless the weather and roads are very favorable' we will have to leave some of our guns in Tennessee."[12]

Forrest's cavalry, which was to replace Wheeler's and operate on Hood's left flank, was painfully slow in coming up. Forrest's artillery had become mired down in heavy mud. On one exhausting day, Morton's Tennessee Battery covered only two and a half miles. "The artillery horses were unequal to the task of pulling the heavy guns for any great distance, and they were supplied from the lead horses of the officers and those of the servants," explained Captain Morton. "These in turn being hitched sixteen to one cannon—oxen replaced horses eight to a gun. The animals were impressed from citizens along the route."[13]

Nor could Hood gather up enough artillery to protect his railhead at Corinth. On November 15 three batteries from the reserve artillery at Macon were requested as a garrison force, but none could be spared. On the 18th, Hood promised to send two batteries from the army. Major J. W. Eldridge was dispatched, but without artillery. By the end of November, only Captain Thrall's battery from Forrest's cavalry had arrived. Eldridge contended that at least sixteen guns were required as a minimum. Even then, only half the emplacements would be occupied.[14]

●

As Hood advanced, General John M. Schofield's two corps, some 25,000 strong, moved to Columbia to delay the Confederates and prevent them from reaching Nashville before Union reinforcements arrived. Rebel infantry reached Columbia on November

24, only to find the Yankees well entrenched in a line south of town. Hood now devised an elaborate plan in which he hoped to entrap Schofield. S. D. Lee, with two divisions and nearly all the army's batteries, would remain on the south bank of the Duck River and occupy Schofield with artillery demonstrations. Hood, leading Forrest's cavalry and the rest of the infantry, would cross a pontoon bridge upstream to reach the Federal rear at Spring Hill. The flanking column was to move "in light marching order with only a battery to the corps." The two batteries selected were the Washington Artillery and Guibor's Missouri Battery. Both were ordered to choose only the best horses for the march and to bring only one ordnance wagon and no caissons.[15]

In addition, Daniel Trueheart's battalion was ordered to leave at Columbia its guns and caissons, horses, and drivers and one officer from each company, while the remaining officers, sergeants, and cannoneers would go with the column. This was done in order to "man any batteries that might be captured from the enemy in this move against his rear."[16] Thus, while the cavalry and most of the infantry embarked on a crucial flanking movement, the bulk of the artillerymen settled in for the far less glorious, though no less important, task of holding the Federal divisions in place at Columbia. They were largely successful, though Schofield detected Hood's move and detached one division and his reserve artillery to Spring Hill.

Throughout November 29, Rebel batteries pounded away at the Union defenses, but not without taking losses of their own. General S. D. Lee was dangerously close to a caisson that "exploded . . . [and] hurled fragments of iron and wood high into the air, killing every man and horse immediately about it and throwing up a mountain of dirt and smoke." The most serious loss of the day was Lee's top artilleryman, Colonel Robert F. Beckham. A shell struck a large boulder and hurled a fragment of rock into his temple that mortally wounded him. "He was one of the truest and best officers of the service," Lee stated. Hood characterized him as "one of the most promising officers of his rank."[17]

Meanwhile, the artillery accompanying the flanking column had been facing difficulties of its own. A wheel on one of the guns in Guibor's battery was shattered when it struck a boulder. The cannoneers drew the spare wheel from the ordnance wagon, but much to their chagrin it did not fit. A wheel was appropriated from a nearby farmer's wagon. It was a makeshift arrangement, but the company was able to continue.[18] Yet to no avail. After sparring with the Union division at Spring Hill, Hood, on account of coming darkness on the short November day, bivouacked his troops short of the crucial road. Schofield, now thoroughly alerted to his perilous situation, withdrew all his troops that night through Spring Hill to Franklin.

An angry Hood pursued the next morning with the corps of Cheatham and Stewart. Despite the strength of the Federal position at Franklin, Hood decided to attack. The precise role of his artillery in the ensuing battle has long been disputed. The popular notion is that he attacked before waiting for the bulk of it to come up from Columbia.[19] The few batteries present were, according to him, instructed "to take no part in the engagement, on account of the danger to which women and children in the village would be exposed."[20]

Evidence points to the contrary, however. Union General Jacob D. Cox claimed that, during the assault, he personally observed Confederate artillery "in the intervals galloping forward, unlimbering and firing as soon as they were within range." Captain Douglas confirms this, stating that his battalion (Courtney's) and one battery from Hotchkiss's battalion were engaged. Courtney's battalion even reported three killed and seventeen wounded. General Bate reported that "a battery under the conduct of Colonel Pressman, participated most gallantly in the fight." Morton's battery fired a few rounds into the Federal position on Figuers Hill, but did not shoot toward the town. This was not in response to any order from Hood, however, but occurred because the young captain's mother happened to be visiting in the town![21]

Contrary to his later recollections, Hood apparently did use some artillery at Franklin. At best, however, he did not maximize its full potential. Historian Thomas R. Hay points out that the "Federal positions were comparatively crowded and all positions were subject to an enfilade fire." He concludes that Hood "either did not know how to use his artillery" or did not think of that arm "as necessary to his success. He seemed to depend almost entirely on the shock effect of his veteran infantry."[22]

At 4:00 the Rebel infantry advanced, but the results were predictably disastrous. Some 16,000 troops were hurled over a comparatively level plain offering little cover. More than 6,200 fell under murderous artillery and small-arms fire. A few hundred of Cheatham's men breached the line and overran Federal batteries on either side of the road, but were quickly driven back by a Union counterattack.[23]

Interestingly, Hood's expressed sensitivity for the town did not prevent him from bringing up and positioning his batteries that night. He ordered that a hundred rounds to the gun be fired into the Federal works the next morning. During the night, however, Schofield pulled his army back to Nashville.[24]

The devastating loss of infantry officers at Franklin has long been noted. What has not been recognized is that the artillery, despite its minimal use in the campaign to date, was also undergoing a leadership crisis. Upon the death of Colonel Robert Beckham, the ranking officer in S. D. Lee's corps was Major Alfred H. Courtney. He was on furlough, however, and would not return until the campaign's conclusion. The second-ranking officer was Major John W. Eldridge, but he was on detached duty at Corinth. Command of Lee's corps artillery fell to the only remaining field officer, twenty-five-year-old Major John W. Johnston. This meant that all three battalions were now commanded by a captain and two-thirds of the batteries by lieutenants. Some relief was obviously needed. The grade of simply too many officers was too low for the position they held. On December 10, Major Llewellyn Hoxton was promoted to lieutenant colonel and transferred from Cheatham's corps to the command of Lee's artillery.[25]

•

Hood now considered several alternatives. Clearly, his army had been shattered in the murderous assault at Franklin. In early December his effective force was listed as 23,000, a net loss of more than 7,500 since Florence. The effective artillery in Stewart's and Lee's corps was 740 and 635 respectively, for an average of only 76 per battery. Nor would the situation improve. From the time Hood entered Tennessee until the Battle of Nashville, the army received some 164 recruits. Of that number, only 1 was sent to the artillery.[26]

Perhaps unaware of the massive Union strength (70,000) that lay in wait at Nashville, Hood decided on perhaps the least attractive of his options. He would move his army up to the hills south of Nashville, form an entrenched line, and wait for the Union commander, General George Thomas, to make the next move. Before advancing, Hood ordered General S. D. Lee to leave behind as a garrison force at Columbia any batteries "whose animals you consider too weak to continue on this expedition." Marshall's Tennessee Battery made strenuous efforts to obtain fresh ones, "but none could be had, either by force or persuasion." Thus, the company stayed in place.[27]

Only with major difficulty was the Southern long arm able to continue the journey to Nashville. "The ground is so soft that my carriages mire up to the hubs and my horses are so jaded that we have had to abandon two on the roadside," lamented Captain Key on December 1.[28] As the battered Army of Tennessee reached the outskirts of Nashville, Hood deployed what remained of his troops. "We moved on the pike for that city and when in two miles we could see the Yankee forts and their flags waving from the lofty hills around the city," noted Captain Key. "Their heavy artillery opened upon my battery and threw some close shots as we passed in full view. I sought an eminence and with my opera glasses drew close to me the costly marble capital of Tennessee on which waved the stars and stripes."[29]

In sharp contrast to the twenty miles of extensive breastworks and half a dozen powerful forts on commanding elevations that protected Nashville, the Confederates hastily threw up four miles of trenches. Lee's corps held the center astride the Franklin Pike, Stewart's the left, and Cheatham's the right. Orders vaguely stated that "artillery will be placed in all favorable positions."[30] On December 8 the mercury plunged, and a mixture of sleet and rain fell during the night. By the next day, the ground was covered with a sheet of ice and snow. The temperature dropped to a bitter ten degrees. "Our artillery carriages are frozen in the ground, and ice half an inch thick coats my brass guns," explained Captain Key.[31]

•

On the morning of December 15, Thomas finally struck. By 8 o'clock the sun was beginning to burn off a dense morning fog. At that time, Federal troops in division strength attacked Cheatham's far right near the Nolensville Pike. "Being in command of four batteries, I sought our Captain Goldthwaite, who was nearest the enemy, and in a few minutes a brisk fire was going on in our front," Captain Key stated. "When a colored brigade, led by white officers, was within 200 yards of our line, our batteries opened on them and they were routed in ten minutes, leaving quite a number of the fuliginous skins lifeless and vimless on the cold ground." By noon, Cheatham's men had beaten off the attack.[32]

The Federal assault on the right proved to be only a feint. By

9:00 A.M. a massive Union wheeling movement was moving against the Rebel left. "In this almost perfectly coordinated maneuver," observed one historian," the most serious flaw was that Thomas did not particularly well utilize his artillery."[33] Stewart's corps was hit from the north and west. All the artillery in the five redoubts along the Hillsboro Pike was overrun. Lumsden's Alabama Battery was in Redoubt No. 4. Later, one of the gunners graphically recalled the panic:

> I ran towards Captain Lumsden's section, where Sergeant Jim Jones had turned No. 2 to fire canister at the Federals who were near gun No. 4. He called to me "Look out, Jim!" I dropped on hands and knees whilst he fired that canister right over my head. I took my place between his gun and the embrassure, helping handle the gun, and he gave the double charge canister again. Captain Lumsden was standing with another charge of canister in his hands. The command had been given to fire, but the man with the friction primers had run. I called out, "Captain, he's gone with the friction primers." Says Captain Lumsden "Take care of yourselves boys."[34]

By 4:30 Stewart's line had completely collapsed, and the Confederates were streaming back in disorder toward Granny White Pike. An early nightfall ended the fighting. The Federals claimed the capture of sixteen guns. Major Daniel Trueheart's battalion of three Alabama batteries was virtually wiped out except for one section of Tarrent's battery.[35]

That evening, Hood pulled his army back two miles to the south. Working throughout the night, his men were able to throw together a continuous line of hastily built trenches. Lee's corps now held the right astride the Franklin Pike. Stewart formed the center. Cheatham's troops were on the left, his line forming a salient at Shy's Hill and bending back to the south. Hood's new position was at best precarious. Only 15,000 infantry were available to man a line some three and a half miles in length. The artillery was also spread dangerously thin. S. D. Lee had twenty-eight guns, Stewart eighteen, and Cheatham thirty-four, a total of only eighty pieces. Worse yet, because of the darkness and the cultivated fields that were now solid mud, some of the batteries could not even be rolled into line.[36]

On the morning of December 16, Thomas unleashed his powerful long arm. The entire Confederate line was hit, but the barrage was particularly severe on the salient positions of Shy's

Hill on the left and Peach Orchard Hill on the right. Shy's Hill
was blasted by a crossfire from several directions. The batteries
of the XXIII Corps south of the hill took William Bate's left
brigade in reverse. Other companies pounded the hill from the
north and from the west, on the ridge across Sugartree Creek.
The batteries directly opposite Stewart's Corps also enfiladed
Cheatham's position from the east.[37]

The Rebel artillery in the Shy's Hill vicinity offered only a
feeble response. Early that morning, a section of howitzers under Captain René Beauregard was placed on the eastern slope of
the hill. Major Trueheart brought up four guns and positioned
them next to Beauregard's section. Still later, Turner's Mississippi Battery was brought up on the crest of the hill in the
salient. These ten smoothbores were clearly outgunned by the
torrent of Federal fire that blasted the hill. "The superiority of
the National artillery was such that the Confederate gunners
were forced to reload their pieces by drawing them aside with
the prolonge, to the protection of the parapet," explained General Jacob Cox.[38]

On the Confederate right, Lee's corps also came under a murderous barrage from the batteries of Wood's, Steedman's, and
Smith's corps. The Federals "opened a terrible artillery fire on
my line, principally on the Franklin Pike. This lasted about two
hours," commented General Lee. The corps artillery chief, Lieutenant Colonel Llewellyn Hoxton, noted that "during the whole
day the batteries were subjected to a terrible artillery fire,
which destroyed a large number of horses in the best cover I
could obtain, and exploded two limber chests." Hoxton's gunners
did score some hits on Company B, Independent Pennsylvania
Battery, and disabled two guns, but little else went their way.[39]

The three batteries of Kenner Garrand's division of Smith's
corps hit Edward Johnson's division in reverse. "It has never
been my fortune to witness so accurate and effective artillery
firing as was exhibited by our batteries from this point," explained a Federal battery commander. "The enemy had four
batteries, with an aggregate of seventeen guns, bearing upon
our three batteries and yet so terribly effective was our fire that
the rebel cannoneers could not be induced to work their guns,
and three of the four batteries remained silent most of the day."
General Johnson observed that the Union artillery fire was "the
most scientific" he had ever witnessed. A captured Rebel artillery sergeant claimed that his battery lost twenty-seven men
and twenty-three horses during the barrage.[40]

General Carter Stevenson described the bombardment as "an artillery fire which I have never seen surpassed for heaviness, continuance and accuracy." Rowan's Georgia Battery was on Stevenson's line. A lieutenant later recalled that "the nature of the ground was such that the horses could not be effectively sheltered from the enemy's battery on the right, and they were falling rapidly. The drivers were being wounded, and trees cut down, while the air was resonant with the howl of passing shells." At 12:30 a shell fragment struck and instantly killed twenty-nine-year-old Captain John Rowan. His body was left on the field in the hands of the enemy.[41]

Several demonstrations were made upon Lee's flank on Peach Orchard Hill during the morning. The real action of the day, however, occurred at 4:00 when Thomas launched a massive assault on Hood's left. The XXIII Corps swarmed across Sugartree Creek from the west, the XVI Corps attacked from the north, and Wilson's cavalry, some 10,000 strong, moved up from the south. Within minutes, Cheatham's corps literally disintegrated.[42]

"On the hillside facing east, in rear of the position held by Bate, was Major Trueheart with a section of artillery, all that remained of his battalion, in command of his gunners, cool and deliberate, directing the fire of his guns into the advancing and victorious enemy, until he was surrounded and captured and his guns turned on the retreating Confederates," declared a major. "Trueheart and his brave gunners, facing the enemy and intently serving his guns, his battalion colors flying while surrounded and captured, was the heroic figure on that historic field, so disastrous to Confederate arms."[43]

Cheatham's men panicked, abandoned their artillery, and streamed toward the Franklin Pike. Stewart's corps also collapsed, and the rout on the left and center became general. Lee pulled his troops back to the Overton Hills, but the retreat came so quickly that he lost sixteen guns and a number of caissons.

For Alfred Courtney's battalion, it was a repeat of Missionary Ridge. Dent's battery was overrun and all four guns captured. Garrity's Alabama Battery lost two of its pieces. Douglas's Texas Battery abandoned one cannon. One of his men described the scene:

> Closer and closer they came. We began to give them
> double-shotted loads of canister direct in their faces,
> and our infantry turned loose its fire . . . Just then
> somebody shouted, "Look to the west!" and, turning in
> that direction, we saw that the old fields far to the

southwest were covered with a mass of Confederate soldiers fleeing diagonally across our rear, in the direction of the Franklin Pike, the only way open to retreat. With lightning celerity under orders from Captain Douglas, our battery horses were brought forward, and we succeeded in escaping with the loss of two [one] of our artillery pieces.[44]

Major John W. Johnston had Rowan's and Van den Corput's batteries on line. Rowan's men stayed at their pieces to the last and poured "a heavy fire of canister at the solid masses approaching in front." It proved to be a vain contest. The victorious Federals swept over the muddy trenches and planted the Stars and Stripes on gun No. 2. The battery lost all four guns, as well as four killed, eight wounded, and sixteen captured. A cannon in Van den Corput's battery was disabled when it was driven at full speed against a tree and the carriage smashed.[45]

Stanford's Mississippi Battery of Eldridge's battalion was also overrun. "Stanford's guns were run out of the works but in the mad rush the horses were stampeded and only enough were secured to carry off one caisson," stated Captain Charles Fenner, commanding the battalion. Brigadier General J. T. Holtzclaw wrote that Stanford's battery was "so badly crippled as to be immovable, scarce a whole wheel remaining in its carriages, sustaining, without works, a fire from eighteen of the enemies guns for seven hours." The company lost all four guns and twelve men killed and wounded.[46]

Lee made a frantic effort to form a patchwork line of artillery. He rode up to Captain Fenner and asked: "Captain, have you a serviceable battery?" Fenner had just observed the Eufaula Light Artillery moving to the rear and pointed it out. "Bring that battery here at once," shouted Lee. Twelve guns were eventually assembled and, according to Lieutenant Colonel Hoxton, "were immediately placed in position and used with good effect in protecting the retreat of the army." Lee's artillery on the Franklin Pike, backed by infantry support, held long enough for the remnants of the army to escape.[47]

●

The defeated Southerners continued southward, drudgingly retracing their steps toward Columbia. The debris strewn along the roadside told the story: broken-down wagons, abandoned horses, small arms, and baggage. Even before the army reached Columbia, the gunners of Marshall's Tennessee Battery, stationed at that place, expected the worst. "Whole droves of artillery horses—ready harnessed, but starving and covered with mud—traversed the roads," observed one of the gunners. "Marshall's battery was at once furnished with eight or ten horses to each piece and caisson."[48]

The next ten days were marked by constant fighting and falling back. More artillery was lost. On December 17 a Yankee cavalry dash captured the three remaining guns of Douglas's battery. "They destroyed the harness and had to cut down the guns, and when we recaptured them we could not carry them off and were compelled to abandon them," explained Hoxton. Three guns of Fenner's Louisiana Battery were subsequently abandoned at Murfreesboro and two pieces of McKenzie's Alabama Battery were left at the Duck River because the pontoon bridge had already been removed.[49]

Hood's army crossed the Tennessee River near Florence on December 25–26. A brief scare occurred when, in the midst of the crossing, a Federal gunboat was spotted five miles below the city. General Stewart dispatched the one remaining gun of Hoskin's Mississippi Battery and the two guns of Cowan's Mississippi Battery to take care of the matter. The three pieces set up along the bank, opened on the gunboat, and quickly drove it away.[50]

Hood, typically, attempted to minimize the disaster. He admitted the loss of fifty-four guns, but wrote: "We had fortunately still remaining a sufficient number of pieces of artillery for the equipment of the Army, since, it will be remembered, I had taken with me at the outset of the campaign a large reserve of artillery to use against gunboats."[51]

Postbattle rhetoric could hardly hide the fact that the western artillery, like the entire army, had been virtually destroyed at Nashville. Yankee quartermasters tallied sixty-four captured guns (forty-nine 12-pounder Napoleons, ten 12-pounder howitzers, two 10-pounder Parrotts, one 3-inch rifle, and two 6-pounders), seventy-five limbers, twenty caissons, and six wagons filled with artillery ammunition. Forty-five of the cannon were of Southern manufacture (mostly government-made Napoleons) and the remainder of U.S. make. At least seventeen of the guns were abandoned during the days following the battle.[52]

Before advancing into Tennessee, Hood counted 124 guns, but by December 21 only 59 remained.[53] The campaign had cost the Western long arm nearly half its ordnance, as compared to Braxton Bragg's 30 percent loss at Missionary Ridge. The depth of the disaster went beyond numbers, however. Many of the army's batteries—Douglas's Texas, Dent's Confederate, Stanford's Mississippi, Lumsden's Alabama, Tarrent's Alabama, the Eufaula (Alabama) Light Artillery, Selden's Alabama, the Louisiana Washington Artillery, and Fenner's Louisiana—were simply wiped out as fighting units. Gone, too, were some of the artillery's best officers: Colonel Robert F. Beckham dead, Captain John Rowan dead, Major Daniel Trueheart captured. Immediately following the battle, only seven field officers remained.

It seemed to be the western artillery's misfortune to have a series of army commanders who did not fully appreciate its vital role in combat. Albert Sidney Johnston considered the artillery only as an afterthought. Braxton Bragg was inflexibly locked into an approach that was obsolete by the time of the Civil War. Hood was essentially a romantic, who was impressed with the infantry charge, not the artillery barrage. Only one general seemed to appreciate the long arm: Joseph E. Johnston. It was soon to be reunited with its old friend.

Chapter 16

"What Will Become of Us?"

During the early days of January 1865, the debris of Hood's shattered army collected at Tupelo. Some of the batteries, their horses weakened to the point of dropping, barely made it. Only about 18,000 effective infantry and artillery remained.[1] Beauregard, commander of the Military Division of the west and Hood's superior, was hastening from Charleston to discover for himself the state of affairs. Although Hood had lost fully half of his artillery, he had informed Beauregard that there had been "no material loss since the battle of Franklin." When the latter arrived at Tupelo on January 14, he discovered the awful truth. He found a command that was "no longer an army." As for the artillery corps, it had been largely captured, abandoned, or destroyed.[2]

All concerned realized that the artillery, like the army as a whole, was but a hulk of its former organization. "I called at General Elzy's office to talk about reorganizing the artillery of this army," explained Captain Key on January 17. "So many guns were lost at Nashville and so great a number of horses were killed or starved on the retreat that all companies cannot be furnished, and as a result many batteries will have to be consolidated."[3] Captain Douglas questioned "what will become of us?" "As we have no guns now we may possibly get furloughs," he thought, but considered it more likely that "we will be supplied with guns before the spring campaign sets in."[4]

Unlike after the disaster at Missionary Ridge, however, no reserve supply of guns was available to draw upon. All the obsolete bronze pieces had already been melted down and recast into Napoleon guns, and production at government cannon foundries had been shut down now for some months. The answer to Captain Douglas's question was that the artillery corps was to be broken up for the most part and scattered across the western Confederacy. More than a half of the companies, those without guns and caissons, were ordered to Mobile to man the artillery, both field and heavy, in the fortifications there. Accompanying the column were Colonel Smith and Lieutenant Colonel Hoxton.[5]

Two battalions, Key's and Johnston's, pieced together enough ordnance to remain mobile and were ordered to accompany the remains of the infantry via Columbus, Mississippi, and Selma, Alabama, to Augusta to oppose Sherman. One slight shift in organization was made. General Beauregard requested of Hood that his son's South Carolina company be allowed to make the trip. René Beauregard's battery was thus exchanged with Rowan's, which was sent to Mobile.[6]

The batteries remained in Columbus for five or six days to rest the weary animals. The men and guns were then loaded aboard river steamers, and the horses went across country. "I received General Elzy's order, delivered early in the morning, to begin loading the pieces of artillery on the steamer 'Lily,' and in the evening we steamed out from the beautiful and gay town of Columbus," Key stated on January 25. The boat traveled about 125 miles daily, but docked each night to let the men sleep on the bank. At Demopolis, Alabama, forty of Goldthwaite's men were furloughed to see their relatives in Montgomery. Columbus, Georgia, was reached on February 4, where Key "gave a brief history of the three batteries and the many battles through which they had fought" to a greeting of ladies.[7]

The artillery reached Macon, Georgia, by rail on February 5. While at that place, Key visited with the army's former chief of artillery, Lieutenant Colonel Hallonquist, who had been piddling away his time there since the evacuation of Atlanta. Only with some regret did the captain learn that he would now join him. Beauregard issued an order replacing Key with Captain W. C. Jeffress as commander of the battalion. "The rest I needed and desired, but I could not for a long time consent to part from the remainder of the battalion," he said. It was some consolation that the men in his former battery were also ordered to remain at Macon to rest and recruit.[8]

The battalion remained more than a week at Macon to give the horses, which were coming overland, time to catch up. Some repairs were made, and the guns were remounted on the carriages. The column finally started to Augusta via Milledgeville, but there the guns were once again dismounted and sent on by rail because of the weakness of the horses.[9]

Meanwhile, the infantry of the army, some 10,000 troops, had been beginning to arrive at Charlotte, North Carolina, and

Newberry, South Carolina. Hood had by now been replaced and his successor, Joseph E. Johnston, was attempting to patch together a hodgepodge organization in an attempt to halt Sherman's relentless drive. "The troops arriving from the Army of Tennessee were still without artillery and wagons," explained Adjutant George Brent on February 3. "Three batteries were expected to arrive at Augusta in two or three days, but the other six, and the wagon trains, could not be expected to commence arriving before eight or ten days."[10]

Actually, Johnston already had more batteries than he could logistically support. His artillery was a heterogeneous mixture of companies from Charleston, Savannah, Wilmington, the Army of Northern Virginia, and Wheeler's horse artillery. A gunner in the Chatham Artillery later recalled that, by late March, Johnston was collecting his thirty light batteries at Hillsboro and consolidating the horses and ordnance to form ten good ones.

On March 4, Brent, at Augusta, advised Beauregard, at Charlotte, that "in this state of affairs it would be better to remove the artillery [of the Army of Tennessee]. All of the artillery companies left in Mississippi have gone to Mobile . . . except five companies sent to Demopolis. The order for its reorganization General Elzy informs me he did not receive and was not aware of its existence until I called his attention to it and gave him a copy."[11] Beauregard, on March 18, wired Chief of Artillery Elzy "that the light batteries not brought here [Raleigh] and not required for the defense of Augusta [should] be collected at Macon, where you will establish your headquarters and reorganize and equip your batteries." Later, the order was expanded to include "all of the artillery of the Army of Tennessee left in Alabama."[12]

The only batteries to make it as far as North Carolina were those of Johnston's battalion. They arrived at Salisbury on April 12, in time to discover that an estimated two thousand cavalry under Stoneman were approaching the town from the west. The battalion, which had no infantry support, was positioned across a small stream several miles from town. Johnston foolishly attempted to cover all three roads leading into Salisbury, and his guns were thus stretched four and a half miles.

Early the next morning, the enemy appeared in strength. The artillery opened fire across the whole length of the line, but the fight was lost almost before it began. By 9:00 A.M. Yankee troopers had swarmed over all three batteries and captured the guns, caissons, and half the men. One of the cannoneers felt it to be ironic that a battalion which had distinguished itself on so many of the battlefields of the west "fell in an obscure skirmish."[13]

On April 17 it was noted that "the artillery of the Army of Tennessee has not yet arrived [in North Carolina]." Nor would it. A few batteries, such as Goldthwaite's and Kolb's, made it as far as Augusta and then surrendered to Federal authorities.[14] Not one of the batteries that had gone north with Hood into Tennessee was with the remains of the army when it capitulated at Durham on April 26.

Perhaps that was the final symbol of the long arm's all too frequent nonrole in the Army of Tennessee. Although it was plagued by variables beyond its control—the rugged terrain of the western theater, poor ordnance, the lack of a militia base upon which to build—its true misfortune was the controllable variables that were mishandled: effective organization and an understanding of the changing role of the artillery. Thus, the western Confederate long arm, the "neglected branch of the army," as Melancthon Smith referred to it, passed from existence—to be remembered only by the field pieces that would one day dot the battlefield parks.

Appendix

Organizational Tables

Shiloh (April 6–7, 1862)

Army of the Mississippi*

Polk's Corps / Capt. Smith Bankhead
Clark's Division
    Russell's Brigade—Bankhead's Tenn. Battery, Capt. Smith
                Bankhead
    Stewart's Brigade—Stanford's Miss. Battery, Capt. Thomas J.
                Stanford
Cheatham's Division
    Johnson's Brigade—Polk's Tenn. Battery, Capt. Marshall T. Polk
    Stephens's Brigade—Smith's Miss. Battery, Capt. Melancthon
                Smith

Bragg's Corps / Major James Hallonquist
Ruggles's Division
    Anderson's Brigade—La. Washington Art'y (Fifth Co.), Capt. I. W.
                Hodgson
    Pond's Brigade—Ketchum's Ala. Battery, Capt. William H.
                Ketchum
Withers's Division
    Gladden's Brigade—Robertson's Fla. Battery, Capt. Felix
                Robertson
    Chalmers's Brigade—Gage's Ala. Battery, Capt. Charles P. Gage
    Jackson's Brigade—Ga.-Washington Art'y, Capt. I. P. Girardey

Hardee's Corps / Major Francis Shoup
    Hindman's Brigade—Warren (Miss.) Light Art'y, Capt. Charles
                Swett
                Pillow (Tenn.) Flying Art'y, Capt. William
                Miller

*Major Francis Shoup was the senior officer, but no army chief of artillery was assigned.

Note: Some returns list the Vaiden (Miss.) Light Art'y and Watson's (La.) Flying Art'y. It can be documented, however, that the former remained in the Corinth garrison, and the latter was at Grand Junction during the battle.

Cleburne's Brigade—Shoup's Ark. Battalion, Major Francis Shoup
> Trigg's Ark. Battery, Capt. John T. Trigg
> Helena (Ark.) Light Art'y, Capt. J. H.
> Calvert
> Hubbard's Ark. Battery, Capt. George T.
> Hubbard

Wood's Brigade—Jefferson (Miss.) Flying Art'y, Capt. William
> Harper

Reserve Corps

Trabue's Brigade—Byrne's Ky. Battery, Capt. Edward Byrne
> Cobb's Ky. Brigade, Capt. Robert Cobb

Bowen's Brigade—Pettus (Miss.) Flying Art'y, Capt. Alfred
> Hudson

Statham's Brigade—Rutledge's Tenn. Battery, Capt. Arthur M.
> Rutledge

Unattached

McClung's Tenn. Battery, Capt. H. L. W. McClung
Roberts's Ark. Battery, Capt. Franklin Roberts

Murfreesboro (Dec. 31, 1862–Jan. 2, 1863)

Army of Tennessee
Lt. Col. James H. Hallonquist

Polk's Corps / Capt. Felix Robertson*
Cheatham's Division—Maj. Melancthon Smith
Donelson's Brigade—Carnes's Tenn. Battery, Lt. L. G. Marshall
Stewart's Brigade—Stanford's Miss. Battery, Capt. Thomas J.
> Stanford
Maney's Brigade—Smith's Miss. Battery, Lt. William B. Turner
Smith's Brigade—Scott's Tenn. Battery, Capt. W. L. Scott
Withers's Division—Capt. J. R. B. Burtwell*
Deas's Brigade—Robertson's Fla. Battery, Capt. Felix H.
> Robertson
Chalmers's Brigade—Garrity's Ala. Battery, Capt. James Garrity
Walthall's Brigade—Barret's Mo. Battery, Capt. W. O. Barret
Anderson's Brigade—Waters's Ala. Battery, Capt. D. D. Waters

Hardee's Corps / Capt. Llewellyn Hoxton*
Breckinridge's Division—Maj. Rice E. Graves
Adams's Brigade—La. Washington Art'y (Fifth Co.), Lt. W. C. D.
> Vaught
Palmer's Brigade—Moses's Ga. Battery (G, 14th Ga. Light Art'y
> Battalion), Lt. R. W. Anderson
Preston's Brigade—Wright's Tenn. Battery, Capt. E. E. Wright

*Acting Chief

Hanson's Brigade—Cobb's Ky. Battery, Capt. Robert Cobb
Jackson's Brigade—Pritchard's Ga. Battery (Section)
        Lumsden's Ala. Battery, Lt. H. H. Cribbs

Cleburne's Division—Capt. Thomas R. Hotchkiss*
  Polk's Brigade—Helena (Ark.) Light Art'y, Lt. Thomas J. Key
  Liddell's Brigade—Warren (Miss.) Light Art'y, Lt. Harvey
        Shannon
  Johnson's Brigade—Jefferson (Miss.) Flying Art'y, Capt. Putman
        Darden
  Wood's Brigade—Semple's Ala. Battery, Capt. Henry Semple
McCown's Division—Maj. George M. Mathes
  Ector's Brigade—Douglas's Tex. Battery, Capt. James P. Douglas
  Rains's Brigade—Eufaula (Ala.) Light Art'y, Lt. W. A. McDuffie
  McNair's Brigade—Humphreys's Ark. Battery (First Arkansas
        Battery), Capt. J. T. Humphreys

Wheeler's Cavalry
  Wheeler's Brigade—Wiggins's Ark. Battery, Capt. J. H. Wiggins
  Wharton's Brigade—White's Tenn. Battery, Capt. B. F. White

Unattached
  Byrne's Ky. Battery, Capt. Edward Byrne

Chickamauga (September 19–20, 1863)

Army of Tennessee
Lt. Col. James H. Hallonquist

Polk's Wing
Cheatham's Division—Maj. Melancthon Smith
  Carnes's Tenn. Battery, Capt. W. W. Carnes
  Scogins's Ga. Battery, Capt. John Scogins
  Scott's Tenn. Battery, Lt. J. H. Marsh
  Smith's Miss. Battery, Lt. W. B. Turner
  Stanford's Miss. Battery, Capt. Thomas J. Stanford

Hill's Corps / Lt. Col. James Bondurant
  Cleburne's Division—Maj. Thomas Hotchkiss
  Helena (Ark.) Light Art'y, Lt. Thomas J. Key
  Douglas's Texas Battery, Capt. James P. Douglas
  Semple's Ala. Battery, Lt. Richard Goldthwaite
  Breckinridge's Division—Maj. Rice E. Graves
  Cobb's Ky. Battery, Capt. Robert Cobb
  Mebane's Tenn. Battery, Capt. John W. Mebane
  La. Washington Art'y (Fifth Co.), Capt. Charles H. Slocomb

Walker's Corps / (position vacant)
  Gist's Division

*Acting Chief

Ferguson's S. C. Battery, Lt. René T. Beauregard*
Martin's Ga. Battery, Capt. Evan P. Howell
Liddell's Division
Fowler's Ala. Battery, Capt. W. H. Fowler
Warren (Miss.) Light Art'y, Lt. Harvey Shannon

Longstreet's Wing

Buckner's Corps / Major Thomas Porter
  Stewart's Division—Maj. John W. Eldridge
  Everett's Ga. Battery (E, 9th Ga. Art'y Battalion), Lt. W. S.
    Everett
  1st Ark. Battery, Capt. John T. Humphreys
  Anderson's Ga. Battery (G, 14th Ga. Art'y Battalion), Lt. R. W.
    Anderson
  Eufaula (Ala.) Light Art'y, Capt. McDonald Oliver
  Preston's Division—Major A. Leydon
  Nottoway (Va.) Light Art'y, Capt. William C. Jeffress
  Peeple's Ga. Battery (D, 9th Ga. Art'y Battalion), Capt. T. M.
    Peeples
  Wolihin's Ga. Battery (C, 9th Ga. Art'y Battalion), Capt. W. A.
    Wolihin
  Hindman's Division—Maj. Alfred R. Courtney
  Garrity's Ala. Battery, Capt. James Garrity
  Robertson's Fla. Battery, Capt. S. H. Dent
  Waters's Ala. Battery, Lt. Charles W. Watkins
  Reserve Artillery—Maj. Samuel C. Williams
  Baxter's Tenn. Battery, Capt. Edmund D. Baxter
  Jefferson (Miss.) Flying Art'y, Capt. Putnam Darden
  Barbour (Ala.) Art'y, Capt. Robert F. Kolb
  Marion (Fla.) Light Art'y, Capt. Robert P. McCants

Hood's Corps
  Johnson's Division
  Bledsoe's Mo. Battery, Lt. R. L. Wood
  Culpepper's S. C. Battery (C, Palmetto Light Art'y), Capt. J. F.
    Culpepper
  Hood's Corps Artillery—Col. E. P. Alexander**

Reserve Artillery / Major Felix H. Robertson

Barret's Mo. Battery, Capt. W. Overton Barret
Havis's Ga. Battery, Capt. M. H. Havis
Lumsden's Ala. Battery, Capt. Charles L. Lumsden
Massenburg's Ga. Battery, Capt. T. L. Massenburg

Horse Artillery

Wheeler's Cavalry
  Wharton's Division
  White's Tenn. Battery, Capt. B. F. White

* At Home
**En route

Wiggins's Ark. Battery, Lt. J. P. Bryant

Forrest's Cavalry
  Armstrong's Division
    Huggins's Tenn. Battery, Capt. A. L. Huggins
    Morton's Tenn. Battery, Capt. John W. Morton
  Pegram's Division
    Huwald's Tenn. Battery, Capt. Gustave A. Huwald
    La. Battery (Section), Lt. Winslow Robinson

Chattanooga (December 10, 1863)

Army of Tennessee
Lt. Col. James H. Hallonquist

Hardee's Corps
Cheatham's Division—Maj. Melancthon Smith
  Fowler's Ala. Battery, Lt. John Phelan
  McCants's Fla. Battery, Capt. Robert P. McCants
  Turner's Miss. Battery, Capt. William B. Turner
Cleburne's Division—Capt. J. P. Douglas*
  Calvert's Ark. Battery, Lt. Thomas J. Key
  Semple's Ala. Battery, Lt. Richard W. Goldthwaite
  Swett's Miss. Battery, Lt. Harvey Shannon
Stevenson's Division—Capt. Robert Cobb*
  Carnes's Tenn. Battery, Capt. William W. Carnes
  Van den Corput's Ga. Battery, Lt. Meshack L. McWhorter
  Rowan's Ga. Battery, Capt. John W. Rowan
Walker's Division—Maj. Robert Martin
  Bledsoe's Mo. Battery, Capt. Hiram M. Bledsoe
  Ferguson's S. C. Battery, Capt. T. B. Ferguson
  Howell's Ga. Battery, Lt. Evan P. Howell

Breckinridge's Corps
Hindman's Division—Maj. Alfred R. Courtney
  Dent's Ala. Battery, Capt. S. H. Dent
  Douglas's Tex. Battery, Capt. James P. Douglas
  Garrity's Ala. Battery, Capt. James Garrity
Stewart's Division—Capt. Henry Semple*
  Fenner's La. Battery, Capt. Charles E. Fenner
  Oliver's Ala. Battery, Capt. McDonald Oliver
  Stanford's Miss. Battery, Capt. Thomas J. Stanford
Breckinridge's Division—Capt. Charles Slocomb*
  Mebane's Tenn. Battery, Capt. John W. Mebane
  Slocomb's La. Battery, Capt. C. H. Slocomb
  Cobb's Ky. Battery, Lt. Frank P. Gracey

*Acting Chief as indicated on return of Nov. 20, 1863

Reserve Artillery / Maj. Felix Robertson
Anderson's Ga. Battery, Capt. R. W. Anderson
Barret's Mo. Battery, Capt. W. Overton Barret
Havis's Ga. Battery, Lt. James R. Duncun
Lumsden's Ala. Battery, Lt. Harvey H. Cribbs

Horse Artillery
Wharton's Division
White's Tenn. Battery, Lt. Arthur Pue, Jr.
Martin's Division
Wiggins's Ark. Battery, Lt. A. A. Blake
Armstrong's Division
Huggins's Tenn. Battery, Capt. A. L. Huggins
Kelly's Division
Huwald's Tenn. Battery, Capt. Gustave A. Huwald

Dalton, Georgia (April 30, 1864)

Army of Tennessee
Brig. Gen. Francis A. Shoup

Hardee's Corps / Colonel Melancthon Smith
Hoxton's Battalion—Maj. Llewellyn Hoxton
   Phelan's Ala. Battery, Capt. John Phelan
   Marion (Fla.) Light Art'y, Lt. Thomas J. Perry
   Turner's Miss. Battery, Capt. William B. Turner
Hotchkiss's Battalion—Maj. Thomas R. Hotchkiss
   Helena (Ark.) Light Art'y, Capt. Thomas J. Key
   Semple's Ala. Battery, Lt. Richard W. Goldthwaite
   Warren (Miss.) Light Art'y, Lt. Harvey Shannon
Martin's Battalion—Maj. Robert Martin
   Bledsoe's Mo. Battery, Lt. C. W. Higgins
   Ferguson's S. C. Battery, Lt. René T. Beauregard
   Howell's Ga. Battery, Lt. W. G. Robson
Cobb's Battalion—Capt. Robert Cobb
   Cobb's Ky. Battery, Lt. R. W. Matthews
   Johnson (Tenn.) Light Art'y, Capt. J. W. Mebane
   La. Washington Art'y (Fifth Co.), Lt. W. C. D. Vaught

Hood's Corps / Colonel Robert F. Beckham
Courtney's Battalion—Maj. Alfred R. Courtney
   Garrity's Ala. Battery, Capt. James Garrity
   Confederate Battery, Capt. S. H. Dent
   Douglas's Tex. Battery, Lt. J. H. Bingham
Eldridge's Battalion—Maj. John W. Eldridge
   Eufaula (Ala.) Light Art'y, Capt. McDonald Oliver
   Fenner's La. Battery, Capt. Charles E. Fenner
   Stanford's Miss. Battery, Capt. T. J. Stanford
Johnston's Battalion—Maj. John W. Johnston
   Cherokee (Ga.) Art'y, Capt. Max Van den Corput

Stephens's (Ga.) Light Art'y, Capt. John B. Rowan
Marshall's Tenn. Battery, Capt. L. G. Marshall

Artillery Reserve / Lt. Col. James H. Hallonquist
Palmer's Battalion—Maj. Joseph Palmer
  Lumsden's Ala. Battery, Capt. Charles L. Lumsden
  Anderson's Ga. Battery, Capt. R. W. Anderson
  Havis's Ga. Battery, Capt. M. W. Havis
Waddell's Battalion—Maj. James P. Waddell
  Emery's Ala. Battery, Capt. W. D. Emery
  Bellamy's Ala. Battery, Lt. F. A. O'Neal
  Barret's Mo. Battery, Capt. W. Overton Barret
Williams's Battalion—Maj. Samuel C. Williams
  Barbour (Ala.) Light Art'y, Capt. Robert F. Kolb
  Jefferson (Miss.) Flying Art'y, Capt. Putnam Darden
  Nottoway (Va.) Light Art'y, Capt. William C. Jeffress

Horse Artillery / Lt. Col. Felix H. Robertson
  Huwald's Tenn. Battery, Lt. D. B. Ramsey
  White's Tenn. Battery, Capt. B. F. White
  Wiggins's Ark. Battery, Lt. J. P. Bryant
  Huggins's Tenn. Battery, Capt. A. L. Huggins
  Ferrell's Ga. Battery (Section), Lt. W. B. S. Davis

Atlanta (August 31, 1864)

Army of Tennessee
Colonel Robert F. Beckham

Hardee's Corps / Colonel Melancthon Smith
Hoxton's Battalion*
  Marion (Fla.) Light Art'y, Capt. Thomas J. Perry
  Phelan's Ala. Battery, Lt. Nathaniel Venable
  Turner's Miss. Battery, Capt. William B. Turner
Hotchkiss's Battalion—Capt. Thomas J. Key
  Helena (Ark.) Light Art'y, Lt. James G. Marshall
  Goldthwaite's Ala. Battery, Capt. Richard W. Goldthwaite
  Warren (Miss.) Light Art'y, Lt. Henry N. Steele
Martin's Battalion*
  Bledsoe's Mo. Battery, Capt. Hiram M. Bledsoe
  Ferguson's S. C. Battery, Lt. René T. Beauregard
  Howell's Ga. Battery, Capt. Evan P. Howell
Cobb's Battalion—Maj. Robert Cobb
  Gracey's Ky. Battery, Capt. Frank P. Gracey
  Mebane's Tenn. Battery, Lt. J. W. Phillips
  La. Washington Art'y (Fifth Co.), Capt. Cuthbert H. Slocomb
Palmer's Battalion*
  Lumsden's Ala. Battery, Capt. Charles L. Lumsden

**Commanding officer not indicated on original return.

Anderson's Ga. Battery, Capt. Ruel W. Anderson
Havis's Ga. Battery, Capt. Minor W. Havis

Lee's Corps / Lt. Col. James H. Hallonquist
Eldridge's Battalion*
Eufaula (Ala.) Light Art'y, Capt. William J. McKenzie
Fenner's La. Battery, Capt. Charles E. Fenner
Stanford's Miss. Battery, Lt. James S. McCall
Courtney's Battalion*
Dent's Ala. Battery, Capt. Staunton H. Dent
Douglas's Tex. Battery, Capt. James P. Douglas
Garrity's Ala. Battery, Lt. Phillip Bond
Johnston's Battalion—Capt. John B. Rowan
Cherokee (Ga.) Light Art'y, Lt. Meshack L. McWhorter
Stephens (Ga.) Light Art'y, Lt. William L. Ritter
Marshall's Tenn. Battery, Capt. Lucius G. Marshall
Williams's Battalion—Capt. Reuben F. Kolb
Barbour (Ala.) Light Art'y, Lt. Robert Cherry
Jefferson (Miss.) Light Art'y, Capt. Putnam Darden
Nottoway (Va.) Light Art'y, Lt. Samuel B. Wingo

Stewart's Corps / Lt. Col. Samuel C. Williams
Myrick's Battalion*
Cowan's Miss. Battery, Lt. George H. Tompkins
Pointe Coupee (La.) Art'y, Capt. Alcide Bouanchaud
Lookout (Tenn.) Art'y, Capt. Robert L. Barry
Storrs's Battalion*
Brookhaven (Miss.) Art'y, Capt. James A. Hoskins
Guibor's Mo. Battery, Capt. Henry Guibor
Ward's Ala. Battery, Lt. George W. Weaver
Preston's Battalion*
Gid. Nelson (Ala.) Art'y, Lt. Charles W. Lovelace
Tarrent's Ala. Battery, Capt. Edward Tarrent
Yates's Miss. Battery, Lt. W. J. Shelton

Horse Artillery
Wheeler's Corps*
Huwald's Tenn. Battery, Lt. D. Breck Ramsey
Ferrell's Ga. Battery, Lt. Nathan Davis
Huggins's Tenn. Battery, Capt. Almaria L. Huggins
White's Tenn. Battery, Capt. Benjamin F. White, Jr.
Wiggins's Ark. Battery, Lt. J. Wylie Calloway
Jackson's Division*
Croft's Ga. Battery, Capt. Edward Croft
King's Mo. Battery, Capt. Houston King
Waties's S. C. Battery, Lt. R. B. Waddell

*Commanding officer not indicated on original return.

Army of Tennessee
Major General Arnold Elzy

Lee's Corps / Lt. Col. Llewellyn Hoxton
Courtney's Battalion—Capt. James P. Douglas
  Dent's Ala. Battery, Capt. Staunton H. Dent
  Douglas's Tex. Battery, Lt. Ben Hardin
  Garrity's Ala. Battery, Lt. Henry F. Campbell
Eldridge's Battalion—Capt. Charles E. Fenner
  Eufaula (Ala.) Light Art'y, Capt. William J. McKenzie
  Stanford's Miss. Battery, Lt. James S. McCall
Johnston's Battalion—Maj. John W. Johnston
  Van den Corput's Ga. Battery, Lt. William S. Hoge
  Stephens (Ga.) Light Art'y, Lt. William L. Ritter

Stewart's Corps* / Lt. Col. Samuel C. Williams
Trueheart's Battalion
  Lumsden's Ala. Battery
  Selden's Ala. Battery
  Tarrent's Ala. Battery
Myrick's Battalion
  Bouanchaud's La. Battery
  Cowan's Miss. Battery
  Darden's Miss. Battery
Storr's Battalion
  Guibor's Mo. Battery
  Hoskins's Miss. Battery
  Kolb's Ala. Battery

Cheatham's Corps* / Col. Melancthon Smith
Hoxton's Battalion
  Perry's Fla. Battery
  Phelan's Ala. Battery
  Turner's Miss. Battery
Hotchkiss's Battalion
  Bledsoe's Mo. Battery
  Goldthwaite's Ala. Battery
  Key's Ark. Battery
Cobb's Battalion
  Ferguson's S. C. Battery
  Mebane's Tenn. Battery
  Slocomb's La. Battery

*Commanders not indicated on original return.

Note: Fenner's La. Battery and Marshall's Tenn. Battery, both of Lee's corps, were stationed at Murfreesboro and Columbia, respectively, during the battle.

Notes

Chapter 1

1. Thomas L. Connelly, *Army of the Heartland: The Army of Tennessee, 1861–1862* (Baton Rouge, 1967), 25; Robert H. White, ed., *Messages of the Governors of Tennessee, 1857–1869* (Nashville, 1959), V, 309; Memphis *Appeal*, May 11, 1861. The state adopted the organizational guidelines of the U.S. regular army. For the artillery, this meant that a company, or battery as it was sometimes called, consisted of from 94 to 155 officers and men and six field pieces. The cannon were attached to limbers and drawn by six horses hitched in pairs.

2. Civil War Centennial Commission, *Tennesseans in the Civil War* (Nashville, 1964), I, 118. All citations of this work are to volume I.

3. *The War of the Rebellion: A Compilation of the Official Records of the Union and Confederate Armies* (Washington, D.C., 1880–1901), Series 4, III, 900–903, Series 1, LII, pt. 2, 90 (hereafter cited as *O.R.;* unless otherwise indicated, all citations are to Series 1); Thomas A. Head, *Campaigns and Battles of the Sixteenth Regiment, Tennessee Volunteers* (McMinnville, Tenn., 1961), 236; Commission, *Tennesseans in the Civil War,* 136.

4. *O.R.,* Series 4, I, 417; Nashville *Union and American,* August 27, 1861.

5. Stanley F. Horn, ed., *Tennessee's War, 1861–1865* (Nashville, 1965), 19; Haynes to Pillow, June 11, 1861, Isham G. Harris Papers, Tennessee State Archives; John B. Lindsley, ed., *Military Annals of Tennessee, Confederate* (Nashville, 1886), 790, 805–6; *O.R.,* LII, pt. 2, 123, Series 4, I, 417.

6. Military Board Record Book, Vol. 63, Series 6, Record Group 21, Tennessee State Archives; Memphis *Appeal,* May 15 and June 30, 1861.

7. Dillard Jones, "Outfitting the Provisional Army of Tennessee: A Report on New Source Materials," *Tennessee Historical Quarterly,* XL (Fall 1981), 269.

8. Memphis *Appeal,* May 23, 1861; Military Board Record Book, Vol. 63, Series 6, Record Group 21, Tennessee State Archives.

9. *O.R.,* LII, pt. 2, 123; Francis T. Miller, ed., *The Photographic History of the Civil War* (New York, 1957), V, 65.

10. "Rutledge's Battery," *Confederate Veteran,* XXXVI (June 1928), 260.

11. Memphis *Appeal,* May 21, 1861; Broomfield L. Ridley, *Battles and Sketches of the Army of Tennessee* (Mexico, Mo., 1906), 473; Mark

M. Boatner, *Civil War Dictionary* (New York, 1961), 529, 798; A. L. Conger, *Fort Henry and Fort Donelson Campaigns* (Fort Leavenworth, Kans., 1923), 1398.

12. "List of Officers of the Corps of Artillery of Tennessee," Benjamin F. Cheatham Papers, Tennessee State Archives.

13. McCown would eventually attain the rank of major general and command a division in the Army of Tennessee; Jackson, a major general of cavalry; and Stewart, a lieutenant general and commander of a corps in the army.

14. Connelly, *Army of the Heartland*, 39–40; Commission, *Tennesseans in the Civil War*, 118–19.

15. Nashville *Union and American*, September 8 and October 4, 1861.

16. Polk to Benjamin, January 6, 1862, Leonidas Polk Papers, National Archives Record Group 109 (hereafter cited as NARG 109).

17. Connelly, *Army of the Heartland*, 33; Commission, *Tennesseans in the Civil War*, 118–19.

18. Memphis *Appeal*, February 27 and March 11, 1862.

19. Jennings C. Wise, *The Long Arm of Lee: The History of the Artillery Corps of the Army of Northern Virginia* (New York, 1959), 91–93; David G. McIntosh, "The Confederate Artillery: Its Organization and Development," *The Photographic History of the Civil War*, V, 58, 60.

20. Wise, *The Long Arm of Lee*, 93–94; J. B. Walton, "Sketches of the History of the Washington Artillery," *Southern Historical Society Papers*, XI (1883), 210–12.

21. Napier Bartlett, *Military Records of Louisiana* (Baton Rouge, 1964), 146–52; Miller, ed., *The Photographic History of the Civil War*, I, 95, V, 63; William C. Davis, ed., *The Image of War, 1861–1865* (New York, 1981), I, 150, 156, 303; William H. Owen, *In Camp and Battle with the Washington Artillery* (Boston, 1885), 403–5.

22. W. A. Pickering, "The Washington Artillery of Augusta, Ga.," *Confederate Veteran*, XVII (1909), 24–25; Allen D. Chandler, ed., *The Confederate Records of the State of Georgia* (Atlanta, 1910), III, 41, 43, 46.

23. Semple's Alabama Battery, Muster Roll, National Archives.

24. Stanford's Mississippi Battery, Muster Roll, National Archives.

25. Commission, *Tennesseans in the Civil War*, 120, 123, 140, 148; Willis Brewer, *Alabama: Her History, Resources, War Record, and Public Men from 1540–1872* (Montgomery, 1872), 696, 698; Pickering, "The Washington Artillery of Augusta, Ga.," 24; "Occupations of Members of the Fifth Company," Washington Artillery Papers, Louisiana Historical Association Collection, Tulane University.

26. Wirt A. Cate, ed., *Two Soldiers: The Campaign Diaries of Thomas J. Key, C.S.A., and Robert J. Campbell, U.S.A.* (Chapel Hill, 1938), 4; "Capt. Thomas L. Massenburg," *Confederate Veteran*, XII (December 1908), 630; "Robert Cobb, Maj. Gen. UCV," *Confederate Veteran*, IV (April 1894), 103; "History of Kolb's Battery," November 5, 1906, Kolb's Alabama Battery File, Alabama State Archives; "Maj. John William Johnston," *Confederate Veteran*, XIX (March 1911), 117; "Maj. James P. Douglas," *Confederate Veteran*, X (July 1902), 322.

27. Dunbar Rowland, *The Official and Statistical Register of the*

State of Mississippi (Nashville, 1908), 879; Head, *Campaigns and Battles of the Sixteenth Tennessee,* 263; Bartlett, *Military Records of Louisiana,* 27.

28. George Little and James R. Maxwell, *A History of Lumsden's Battery* (Tuscaloosa, 1905), 4–5; Ed Porter Thompson, *History of the Orphan Brigade* (Louisville, 1898), 857; W. H. Smith, "Melancthon Smith's Battery," *Confederate Veteran,* XII (November 1904), 532.

29. W. H. Brown, "History of Stanford's Mississippi Battery," typescript in Greenwood, Mississippi, Public Library.

30. James W. Silver, ed., *Mississippi in the Confederacy—Seen In Retrospect* (Baton Rouge, 1961), 104–5.

31. George A. Grammer Diary, August 20, 1861, Vicksburg National Military Park.

32. John E. Magee Diary, November 7, 1861, Duke University.

33. "Rutledge's Battery," 260.

34. Magee Diary, November 12, 1861, Duke; Mike Spradlin, ed., "The Diary of George W. Jones: A Partial History of Stanford's Mississippi Battery," *Camp Chase Gazette,* IX (April 1981), 7; Grammer Diary, October 31, 1861, Vicksburg NMP; Semple to wife, August 19, 1862, Henry C. Semple Papers, Alabama State Archives (hereafter cited as Semple Papers, ASA).

35. Magee Diary, December 1, 1861, Duke.

36. Semple to wife, August 19, 1862, Semple Papers, ASA.

37. Little and Maxwell, *A History of Lumsden's Battery,* 5.

38. Ibid., 5–6. Captains J. H. Calvert and Robert P. McCants are two examples of artillery officers in the Army of Tennessee who were forced to resign because of alcoholism.

39. "Sketch of Semple's Battery," Semple Papers, ASA; Magee Diary, November 8 and December 1, 1861, March 3, 1862, Duke; Stanford's Mississippi Battery, Military Service File, National Archives.

40. Rosalie Fitzpatrick Higgins Scrapbook, April 9, 1862, clipping, Semple Papers, ASA.

41. Harold L. Peterson, *Round Shot and Rammers* (New York, 1969), 119; L. Van Loan Naisawald, "Field Artillery in the War," *Civil War Times Illustrated* (June 1961), 24.

42. Brown, "History of Stanford's Mississippi Battery," Greenwood Public Library.

43. Richard L. Pugh to wife, April 11, 1862, Richard L. Pugh Letters, Louisiana State University.

44. Grammer Diary, August 30, 1861, Vicksburg NMP; *O.R.,* X, pt. 1, 411.

45. *O.R.,* LII, pt. 2, 127, Series 4, I, 63; Wise, *The Long Arm of Lee,* 38n.; Chandler, ed., *The Confederate Records of the State of Georgia,* III, 41.

46. "Compilation of Arkansas Batteries," Arkansas Historical Society; Ephraim McD. Anderson, *First Missouri Confederate Brigade* (Dayton, Ohio, 1972), 47; Joseph A. Wilson, "Bledsoe of Missouri," *Confederate Veteran,* VII (October 1899), 462; Cate, ed., *Two Soldiers,* 101.

47. Wise, *The Long Arm of Lee,* 78–79; Charles B. Dew, *Ironmaker to the Confederacy: Joseph R. Anderson and the Tredegar Iron Works* (New Haven and London, 1966), 12, 112; Memphis *Avalanche,* September 21,

1861; Tredegar Foundry Sales Book, Virginia State Library; Wright & Rice, Papers Relating to Citizens or Business Firms, National Archives Record Group 109 (hereafter cited as "Citizens File").

48. *O.R.*, IV, 385–87.

49. Quinby & Robinson, T. M. Brennan & Company, Noble Brothers & Company, A. B. Reading & Brother, "Citizens File"; William Preston Johnston, *The Life of Albert Sidney Johnston* (New York, 1878), 332.

50. Ed Porter Thompson, *History of the Orphan Brigade* (Louisville, 1898), 857; "List of Guns Furnished by Leeds & Company," April 29, 1863, Letters Sent, Ordnance Officer, Army of Tennessee, Chap. IV, Vol. 141, NARG 109; John Clark & Company, "Citizens File."

51. Emma Crutcher to William O. Crutcher, December 25, 1861, Phillip C. Crutcher Collection, Mississippi State Archives; Memphis *Avalanche*, September 21, 1861; Rome *Courier Tri-Weekly*, September 12, 1861; New Orleans *Picayune*, July 10, 1861.

52. William G. Stevenson, *Thirteen Months in the Rebel Army* (New York, 1959), 61; *O.R.*, IV, 468, VII, 388, 394.

53. Warren Ripley, *Artillery and Ammunition of the Civil War* (New York, 1970), 15, 22, 23, 366, 367.

54. Grady McWhiney and Perry D. Jamieson, *Attack and Die: Civil War Military Tactics and the Southern Heritage* (University, Ala., 1982), 59–60; Jac Weller, "The Field Artillery of the Civil War," *Military Collector and Historian,* V (June 1953), 33–34; Bruce Catton, *The Civil War* (New York, 1980), 158.

55. *O.R.*, III, 724, IV, 152; Bujac & Bennett, "Citizens File"; Douglas S. Freeman, ed., *A Calendar of Confederate Papers* (Richmond, 1908), 323. A recent examination of a surviving Noble Brothers field piece revealed that imprecise machinery had caused the bore to be off one inch, which caused the gun to shoot to the right of the true line of metal. Donald F. Long, "Ashe Ordnance Works Restores Original Noble Brothers Cannon," *The Muzzleloading Artilleryman,* Spring 1982, 38.

56. Bell I. Wiley, *The Life of Johnny Reb: The Common Soldier in the Confederacy* (New York, 1943), 299; Stevenson, *Thirteen Months in the Rebel Army,* 61; Charleston *Mercury,* April 2, 1862.

Chapter 2

1. *O.R.*, IV, 425; William C. Davis, *The Orphan Brigade: The Kentucky Confederates Who Couldn't Go Home* (Garden City, N.Y., 1980), 26, 27; Commission, *Tennesseans in the Civil War,* 136; Memphis *Appeal,* September 17, 1861.

2. Connelly, *Army of the Heartland,* 65, 74–75; Charles P. Roland, *Albert Sidney Johnston: Soldier of Three Republics* (Austin, Tex., 1964), 282.

3. *O.R.*, IV, 472, 484; Inventory of Buckner's Artillery, November 11, 1861, Robert Cobb, Military Service File, National Archives; Davis, *The Orphan Brigade,* 23, 38; Rowland, *Mississippi Statistical Register,* 866; Thomas L. Riddell, "Movements of the Goochland Light Artillery," *Southern Historical Society Papers,* XXIV (1896), 316.

4. *O.R.*, IV, 438, 526, VII, 750–51; Eldridge to Mackall, November

13, 1861, Letters and Telegrams Sent, Ordnance Officer, Nashville and Atlanta, December 1861–April 1862, Chap. IV, Vol. 8, NARG 109.

5. Jon L. Wakelyn, *Biographical Dictionary of the Confederacy* (Westport, Conn., 1977), 384; Boatner, *Civil War Dictionary,* 758; Francis A. Shoup, "How We Went to Shiloh," *Confederate Veteran,* II (May 1894), 138; Grammer Diary, August 30, 1861, Vicksburg NMP.

6. Lindsley, ed., *Military Annals of Tennessee,* 790; "List of Officers of the Corps of Artillery of Tennessee," Benjamin F. Cheatham Papers, Tennessee State Archives; Memphis *Appeal,* March 18, 1862.

7. *O.R.,* VII, 852–54.

8. E. P. Alexander, "Confederate Artillery Service," *Southern Historical Society Papers,* XI (1883), 99; Wise, *The Long Arm of Lee,* 413–14; Maury Klein, *Edward Porter Alexander* (Athens, Ga., 1971), 57–58.

9. Wise, *The Long Arm of Lee,* 141.

10. Johnston, *The Life of Albert Sidney Johnston,* 368, 371–75; William M. Polk, "General Polk at the Battle of Belmont," *Battles and Leaders of the Civil War* (New York, 1956), I, 354; Stevenson, *Thirteen Months in the Rebel Army,* 61; *O.R.,* III, 352, 359–60; Memphis *Appeal,* November 9, 10, 1861.

11. Commission, *Tennesseans in the Civil War,* 139; Connelly, *Army of the Heartland,* 97–98; Johnston, *The Life of Albert Sidney Johnston,* 402–9; R. M. Kelly, "Holding Kentucky for the Union," *Battles and Leaders,* I, 390; *O.R.,* VII, 105, 108, 110.

12. *O.R.,* VII, 849.

13. Johnston, *The Life of Albert Sidney Johnston,* 442, 443, 450, 479, 482.

14. Davis, *The Orphan Brigade,* 38–39; Lindsley, ed., *Military Annals of Tennessee,* 468; "Forrest's Chief of Artillery: Morton," *Confederate Veteran,* VIII (1900), 171.

15. Johnston, *The Life of Albert Sidney Johnston,* 441; Connelly, *Army of the Heartland,* 114, 116; *O.R.,* VII, 388–90; H. L. Bedford, "Fight between the Batteries and Gunboats at Fort Donelson," *Southern Historical Society Papers,* XIII (1885), 167, 170; R. R. Ross, "River Batteries at Fort Donelson," *Confederate Veteran,* IV (October 1896), 393.

16. *O.R.,* VII, 360; Lew Wallace, "The Capture of Fort Donelson," *Battles and Leaders,* I, 412.

17. Bedford, "Fight between the Batteries and Gunboats at Fort Donelson," 170–72; Ross, "River Batteries at Fort Donelson," 394–96; Connelly, *Army of the Heartland,* 120.

18. Riddell, "Movements of the Goochland Light Artillery," 319.

19. Stanley F. Horn, *The Army of Tennessee* (Norman, Okla., 1953), 93.

20. Davis, *The Orphan Brigade,* 68; Lindsley, ed., *Military Annals of Tennessee,* 859.

21. Johnston, *The Life of Albert Sidney Johnston,* 468, 478; Riddell, "Movements of the Goochland Light Artillery," 321–22.

22. Horn, *The Army of Tennessee,* 111; *O.R.,* VII, 425; Stevenson, *Thirteen Months in the Rebel Army,* 91.

1. Connelly, *Army of the Heartland,* 141; *O.R.,* VI, 919, X, pt. 1, 414. Watson's Louisiana Battery remained at Grand Junction, Tennessee, and did not participate in the upcoming battle. Edward C. Haydel to sister, April 6, 1862, Edward C. Haydel Letters, Louisiana State University.

2. Wiley Sword, *Shiloh: Bloody April* (New York, 1974), 70; Grammer Diary, March 12, 22, 23, 1862, Vicksburg NMP; *O.R.,* X, pt. 2, 327.

3. William Preston Johnston, "Albert Sidney Johnston at Shiloh," *Battles and Leaders,* I, 549; "Morning Report of Cobb's Battery, March 17, 1862," Robert Cobb, Military Service File, National Archives; *O.R.,* III, 904–5, X, pt. 2, 377. Baker's and Monsarrat's Tennessee batteries of Hardee's corps remained at Iuka with William H. Carroll's brigade.

4. Pickering, "The Washington Artillery of Augusta, Ga.," 24–25; James H. Colgin, ed., "The Life Story of Brig. Gen. Felix Robertson," *Texana,* VIII (Spring 1979), 154–55; Brewer, *Alabama,* 696, 698; *O.R.,* X, pt. 2, 307; Little and Maxwell, *A History of Lumsden's Battery,* 7.

5. *O.R.,* VI, 832, 847; Bartlett, *Military Records of Louisiana,* pt. 5, 152. The Orleans Guard Artillery remained at Grand Junction and did not participate in the upcoming battle. Edward C. Haydel to sister, April 6, 1862, Edward C. Haydel Letters, Louisiana State University.

6. *O.R.,* X, pt. 1, 398; Edward C. Bearss, "Shiloh Artillery Study," Project No. 17, Shiloh National Military Park.

7. Lindsley, ed., *Military Annals of Tennessee,* 810; *O.R.,* X, pt. 1, 398.

8. Connelly, *Army of the Heartland,* 150–51.

9. Alfred Roman, *The Military Operations of General Beauregard,* I (New York, 1884), 281.

10. Grady McWhiney, *Braxton Bragg and Confederate Defeat* (New York and London, 1969), 223–24.

11. Shoup, "How We Went to Shiloh," 137; *O.R.,* X, pt. 1, 413.

12. "Report of Ordnance and Ordnance Stores on Hand," Felix Robertson, Military Service File, National Archives; *O.R.,* X, pt. 2, 388.

13. Bearss, "Shiloh Artillery Study," Shiloh NMP: *O.R.,* X, pt. 2, 362.

14. Shoup, "How We Went to Shiloh," 140; *O.R.,* X, pt. 1, 411.

15. "The Battle of Shiloh—Report of L. D. Sandridge, Inspector General of the Louisiana Division," *Southern Historical Society Papers,* VIII (1880), 173.

16. Fairfax Downey, *The Sound of Guns: The Story of American Artillery from the Ancient and Honorable Company to the Atom Cannon and Guided Missile* (New York, 1955), 131; Thomas Jordon, "The Battle of Shiloh," *Southern Historical Society Papers,* XXXV (1907), 211.

17. Johnston, *The Life of Albert Sidney Johnston,* 555–56; L. Van Loan Naisawald, *Grape and Canister: The Story of the Field Artillery of the Army of the Potomac, 1861–1865* (New York, 1960), 150.

18. Magee Diary, April 3, 1862, Duke; *O.R.,* X, pt. 2, 383; Skates & Company, "Citizens File."

19. *O.R.,* X, pt. 1, 394, pt. 2, 388; Rowland, *Mississippi Statistical Register,* 852; Lindsley, ed., *Military Annals of Tennessee,* 810. A detachment of the Vaiden Light Artillery served a section of Stanford's Mississippi Battery during the battle.

20. Johnston, *The Life of Albert Sidney Johnston,* 559–60; Ed Porter

Thompson, *History of the First Kentucky Brigade* (Cincinnati, 1868), 87.

21. Spradlin, ed., "The Diary of George W. Jones," 7.

22. Roman, *The Military Operations of General Beauregard,* 285; *O.R.,* X, pt. 1, 574, 609; Grammer Diary, April 6, 1862, Vicksburg NMP.

23. Sword, *Shiloh: Bloody April,* 177; Shoup, "How We Want to Shiloh," 137.

24. Pugh to May, April 10, 1862, Richard L. Pugh Letters, Louisiana State University; *O.R.,* X, pt. 1, 550; M. F. Force, *From Fort Henry to Corinth* (New York, 1908), 124; L. D. G. to father and mother, April 8, 1862, Gage's Alabama Battery File, Alabama State Archives.

25. *O.R.,* X, pt. 1, 471, 513; Sword, *Shiloh: Bloody April,* 206; Nathaniel C. Hughes, *General William J. Hardee: Old Reliable* (Baton Rouge, La., 1965), 106–7. The site of this first artillery concentration is marked at the Shiloh park with several plaques.

26. Sword, *Shiloh: Bloody April,* 236, 238; Roman, *The Military Operations of General Beauregard,* 291.

27. Ed McDonald, Wayne Prader, and Mike Bianchi-Rossi, "Rifle Musket: American Firepower and Tactics, 1861–1865," *Conflict,* VII (1974), 14, 17; John K. Mahon, "Civil War Infantry Assault Tactics," *Military Analysis of the Civil War* (Millwood, N.Y., 1977), 263.

28. *O.R.,* X, pt. 1, 447, 445, 414; "List of Officers of the Corps of Artillery of Tennessee," Benjamin F. Cheatham Papers, Tennessee State Archives; Commission, *Tennesseans in the Civil War,* 144.

29. *O.R.,* X, pt. 1, 549, 565.

30. A. D. Kirwan, ed., *Johnny Green of the Orphan Brigade* (Lexington, 1956), 26; *O.R.,* X, pt. 1, 616–17, XXXII, pt. 3, 703; "Cobb's Battery *Not Captured* at Shiloh," *Confederate Veteran,* XIII (February 1905), 68. Cobb was forced to abandon two guns and all six caissons.

31. *O.R.,* X, pt. 1, 513; Pugh to May, April 8, 1862, Richard L. Pugh Letters, Louisiana State University.

32. Magee Diary, April 6, 1862, Duke; Spradlin, ed., "The Diary of George W. Jones," 7; *O.R.,* X, pt. 1, 610.

33. *O.R.,* X, pt. 1, 438, 479; Henry George, *History of the 3rd, 7th, 8th, and 12th Kentucky, C.S.A.* (Lyndon, Ky., 1911), 29.

34. McWhiney, *Braxton Bragg and Confederate Defeat,* 89. McWhiney and Jamieson conclude that Bragg missed the great lesson of Buena Vista, "which was the great advantage that defenders with sufficient mobile firepower enjoyed over the attackers." McWhiney and Jamieson, *Attack and Die,* 160.

35. McWhiney, *Braxton Bragg and Confederate Defeat,* 238–40.

36. *O.R.,* X, pt. 1, 472.

37. Ibid., 475.

38. Ibid., 479; Shoup, "How We Went to Shiloh," 139.

39. The number of guns participating in Ruggles's barrage has traditionally been placed at sixty-two. This is arrived at by taking his list of twelve batteries, one of which (Robertson's) had four guns and two of which (Ketchum's and Hubbard's) had only a two-gun section engaged, and assuming that the other companies possessed six guns each. Ruggles's memory lapsed, however, in reporting that a "Captain Trabue's battery" had been engaged. Actually, Byrne's battery belonged to Colonel Robert Trabue's brigade. Edward O. Cunningham ("Shiloh and the Western Campaign of 1862," Ph.D. dissertation, Louisiana State Uni-

versity, 1966, 397n.–398n.) theorizes that a section of Cobb's battery (also belonging to Trabue's brigade) wandered into line next to Byrne. Lieutenant Thrall of Hubbard's battery writes, however, that Byrne's company was the last in line. Also, Trigg's and Robert's companies were probably four-gun outfits, and Byrne's battery consisted of seven pieces because it had captured an extra 6-pounder in Kentucky. Bearss, "Shiloh Artillery Study," Shiloh NMP.

40. Sword, *Shiloh: Bloody April,* 292; *O.R.,* X, pt. 1, 477.

41. S. H. Dent to wife, April 9, 1862, Shiloh-Corinth Collection, Alabama State Archives.

42. *O.R.,* X, pt. 1, 478; James L. McDonough, *Shiloh: In Hell before Night* (Knoxville, 1977), 164; Shoup, "How We Went to Shiloh," 139.

43. Shoup, "How We Went to Shiloh," 139; *O.R.,* X, pt. 1, 472. The letters of Richard Pugh and the diaries of George Grammer, John Magee, and George Jones are all silent concerning Ruggles's unprecedented barrage.

44. Shoup, "How We Went to Shiloh," 139.

45. Roman, *The Military Operations of General Beauregard,* 299; *O.R.,* X, pt. 1, 550–51, 555; McWhiney and Jamieson, *Attack and Die,* 112.

46. Magee Diary, April 6, 1862, Duke.

47. Buell was able to ferry across all four of his batteries for the battle on the 7th.

48. *O.R.,* X, pt. 1, 170, 193, 518, 528; Richard B. Harwell, ed., *The Journal of a Confederate Nurse by Kate Jackson* (Baton Rouge, 1959), 10. Captain Ketchum was struck by a shell fragment but only slightly wounded. J. P. Barnes, "Incidents of the Great Battle," April 11, 1862, Ketchum's Alabama Battery, Alabama Battery Files, Alabama State Archives.

49. *O.R.,* X, pt. 1, 514–15.

50. Pugh to May, April 10, 1862, Richard L. Pugh Letters, Louisiana State University.

51. J. A. Chalaron, "Battle Echoes From Shiloh," *Southern Historical Society Papers,* XXI (1893), 219; *O.R.,* X, pt. 1, 515.

52. *O.R.,* X, pt. 1, 610–11.

53. Davis, *The Orphan Brigade,* 92–93.

54. *O.R.,* X, pt. 1, 436–37; Memphis *Appeal,* April 10, 1862.

55. Magee Diary, April 7, 1862, Duke; *O.R.,* X, pt. 1, 412, 437.

56. Thomas Jordon, "Notes of a Confederate Staff Officer at Shiloh," *Battles and Leaders,* I, 603; *O.R.,* X, pt. 1, 412, 611, 613.

57. Shoup, "How We Went to Shiloh," 140.

58. Ibid.

59. *O.R.,* X, pt. 2, 398, 399, 400; Thompson, *History of the Orphan Brigade,* 859.

60. *O.R.,* XXXII, pt. 3, 698–99, 702–5; Bearss, "Artillery Study," Shiloh NMP.

61. Bearss, "Artillery Study," Shiloh NMP; U. S. Grant, "The Battle of Shiloh," *Battles and Leaders,* I, 485; *O.R.,* X, pt. 1, 110, 274.

62. McWhiney and Jamieson, *Attack and Die,* 117.

63. Ibid.

1. Connelly, *Army of the Heartland*, 175–76; Horn, *The Army of Tennessee*, 147.

2. Commission, *Tennesseans in the Civil War*, 120, 127, 145, 149; Rowland, *Mississippi Statistical Register*, 852–69; Brewer, *Alabama*, 698, 702; *O.R.*, X, pt. 2, 548–51. See Appendix for detailed composition.

3. Lindsley, ed., *Military Annals of Tennessee*, 791, 795; Grammer Diary, May 8, 1862, Vicksburg NMP; Pugh to May, April 11, 1862, Richard L. Pugh Letters, Louisiana State University; Owen, *In Camp and Battle with the Washington Artillery*, 412–13.

4. Brown, "History of Stanford's Mississippi Battery," Greenwood Public Library.

5. *O.R.*, X, pt. 2, 642.

6. "Summary of Ordnance and Ordnance Stores on Hand, May 21, 1862, Grenada, Miss.," Box 31-G, Army of Mississippi Papers, Duke; *O.R.*, XVI, pt. 2, 741.

7. *O.R.*, XVI, pt. 2, 731.

8. Magee Diary, July 24, 25, 1862, Duke.

9. Ibid., July 30, 1862; Grammer Diary, August 9, 1862, Vicksburg NMP.

10. Grammer Diary, August 9, 1862, Vicksburg NMP; Magee Diary, July 23, 24, August 14, 1862, Duke.

11. Magee Diary, July 24, 25, August 9, 1862, Duke; Lindsley, ed., *Military Annals of Tennessee*, 811.

12. Magee Diary, August 16, 1862, Duke

13. Ibid., August 9, 1862; Semple to wife, August 9, 19, 1862, Semple Papers, ASA.

14. William R. Talley, "History of Havis' Georgia Battery," typescript, Kennesaw Mountain National Military Park.

15. McWhiney, *Braxton Bragg and Confederate Defeat*, 274–75; Semple to Hardee, November 28, 1862, Semple Papers, ASA; *O.R.*, X, pt. 2, 503.

16. Six of the guns captured at Richmond were issued to Lieutenant W. R. Marshall, who was charged with raising a new artillery company. His efforts were only partially successful. Commission, *Tennesseans in the Civil War*, 138.

17. Talley, "History of Havis' Georgia Battery," Kennesaw NMP; Grammer Diary, August 25, 1862, Vicksburg NMP.

18. Hughes, *General William J. Hardee*, 128; Connelly, *Army of the Heartland*, 263.

19. Head, *Campaigns and Battles of the Sixteenth Tennessee Volunteers*, 236–38; W. W. Carnes, "Artillery at the Battle of Perryville, Ky.," *Confederate Veteran*, XXXIII (1935), 8.

20. Kenneth A. Hafendorfer, *Perryville: Battle for Kentucky* (Owensburg, Ky., 1981), 191–92; Spradlin, ed., "The Diary of George W. Jones," 8.

21. Hafendorfer, *Perryville*, 217–34; Connelly, *Army of the Heartland*, 264.

22. *O.R.*, XVI, pt. 1, 1157; Smith, "Melancthon Smith's Battery," 532.

23. Connelly, *Army of the Heartland,* 265; Hafendorfer, *Perryville,* 251, 271.

24. *O.R.,* XVI, pt. 1, 345, 1133, 1041.

25. Connelly, *Army of the Heartland,* 265. A freak atmospheric condition prevented the sound of battle from reaching Buell's headquarters. Not until late afternoon was he notified that a battle had been raging on his left.

26. *O.R.,* XVI, pt. 1, 1108, LII, pt. 1, 53.

27. Ibid., XVI, pt. 1, 1157.

28. Joseph Wheeler, "Bragg's Invasion of Kentucky," *Battles and Leaders,* III, 16.

29. Ralph A. Wooster, "Confederate Success at Perryville," *Kentucky State Historical Register,* LIX (1961), 318–23.

30. Smith, "Melancthon Smith's Battery," 532; Little and Maxwell, *A History of Lumsden's Battery,* 13; Semple to Hardee, November 28, 1862, Semple Papers, ASA.

31. Semple to Buckner, n.d., Semple Papers, ASA.

Chapter 5

1. Connelly, *Autumn of Glory: The Army of Tennessee, 1862–1865* (Baton Rouge, 1971), 13–15, 19.

2. Grammer Diary, November 1–22, 1862, Vicksburg NMP; Little and Maxwell, *A History of Lumsden's Battery,* 13–14.

3. Semple to wife, December 9, 1862, Semple Papers, ASA.

4. Connelly, *Autumn of Glory,* 30–32.

5. *O.R.,* XXXII, pt. 3, 697, 700, 701; Lester N. Fitzhugh, ed., *Cannon Smoke: The Letters of Captain John J. Good: Good-Douglas Texas Battery, C.S.A.* (Hillsboro, Tex., 1971), vi–vii, 195; Brewer, *Alabama,* 700.

6. Connelly, *Autumn of Glory,* 30, 28.

7. *O.R.,* XX, pt. 1, 709, 814, 875, pt. 2, 465, 399–400.

8. *O.R.,* XX, pt. 2, 399; Semple to Buckner, November 28, 1862, Semple Papers, ASA.

9. *O.R.,* XVI. pt. 1, 1157, XX, pt. 1, 733, 758, 909, pt. 2, 235–41; "List of Batteries Receiving Leeds & Company Guns," April 29, 1863, Letters Sent, Ordnance Officer, Army of Tennessee, Chap. IV, Vol. 141, NARG 109; Rice E. Graves Report, January 25, 1863, John C. Breckinridge Papers, New York Historical Society (hereafter cited as Graves Report, NYHS).

10. Connelly, *Autumn of Glory,* 42; Semple to wife, December 19, 1862, Semple Papers, ASA.

11. *O.R.,* XX, pt. 2, 399–400.

12. Magee Diary, December 1, 3, 4, 1862, Duke.

13. Little and Maxwell, *A History of Lumsden's Battery,* 14.

14. *O.R.,* XX, pt. 1, 235–41, 838, pt. 2, 431–32, 500–501; Graves Report, NYHS. See Appendix for detailed composition of the artillery organization. At Murfreesboro, Bragg had one two-gun, seventeen four-gun, and six six-gun batteries.

15. Edwin C. Bearss, "Cavalry Operations in the Battle of Stones River," *Tennessee Historical Quarterly,* XIX (March 1960), 40–41; *O.R.,* XX, pt. 1, 453, 464, 965.

16. *O.R.*, XX, pt. 1, 782, 837; Graves Report, NYHS.

17. *O.R.*, XX, pt. 1, 782, 803, 837, 842, 909–10

18. Ibid., 268, 280, 705, 748, 925, 943. The army chief of artillery, Lieutenant Colonel James Hallonquist, had warned the battery commanders about bringing their caissons too close to the firing line. In a directive issued in late November, he wrote that "in case of an engagement . . . the caissons of batteries will not be brought up with the guns, but kept under cover in the rear, at a quarter of a mile or less distance. When ammunition chests of the pieces are about exhausted, the limbers of the caissons will be brought forward and their places supplied with those of the pieces." Lieutenant Colonel James H. Hallonquist, Circular, November 23, 1862, Bragg Papers, Letters Sent, Chap. II, Vol. 311, NARG 109.

19. Connelly, *Autumn of Glory*, 52; James L. McDonough, *Stones River: Bloody River in Tennessee* (Knoxville, 1980), 75, 78.

20. *O.R.* XX, pt. 1, 672.

21. Lindsley, ed., *Military Annals of Tennessee*, 818.

22. McDonough, *Stones River*, 85–87; Connelly, *Autumn of Glory*, 54; *O.R.*, XX, pt. 1, 235–36, 302, 320, 325.

23. Hughes, *General William J. Hardee*, 146.

24. *O.R.*, XX, pt. 1, 775, 937. See also troop position maps at Stone's River NMP Library.

25. *O.R.*, XX, pt. 1, 926, 956.

26. Ibid., 926, 956, 871; Grammer Diary, December 31, 1862, Vicksburg NMP.

27. *O.R.*, XX, pt. 1, 872, 966–67. White was operating with only three guns at this time because one had been captured several days earlier.

28. Ibid., 751, 768, 770.

29. G.C. Kniffen, "The Battle of Stone's River," *Battles and Leaders*, III, 628–29.

30. Magee Diary, December 31, 1862, Duke; *O.R.*, XX, pt. 1, 666, 842; Lindsley, ed., *Military Annals of Tennessee*, 816.

31. *O.R.*, XX, pt. 1, 803, 784, 805, 823.

32. Ibid., 880; Connelly, *Autumn of Glory*, 158.

33. *O.R.*, XX, pt. 1, 855.

34. Ibid., 455, 471, 476, 479, 521, 722, 732, 742, 756–57; McDonough, *Stones River*, 175.

35. Graves Report, NYHS; *O.R.*, XX, pt. 1, 668.

36. *O.R.*, XX, pt. 1, 759–60.

37. McDonough, *Stones River*, 179; Connelly, *Autumn of Glory*, 83; William C. Davis, *Breckinridge: Statesman, Soldier, Symbol* (Baton Rouge, 1974), 342, 351–52.

38. *O.R.*, XX, pt. 1, 785, 803, 823; Graves Report, NYHS.

39. Connelly, *Autumn of Glory*, 63; McDonough, *Stones River*, 185.

40. Graves Report, NYHS; *O.R.*, XX, pt. 1, 786.

41. *O.R.*, XX, pt. 1, 823.

42. Graves Report, NYHS.

43. Connelly, *Autumn of Glory*, 65; Davis, *Breckinridge*, 344; Edwin C. Bearss, "Stones River: The Artillery at 4:45 P.M., January 2, 1863," *Civil War Times Illustrated*, II (February 1964), 38–39.

44. *O.R.*, XX, pt. 1, 837–38; Little and Maxwell, *A History of*

Lumsden's Battery, 15; Davis, *Breckinridge,* 344. Robertson would later claim that Tarrent's two guns opened fire before the attack, which tipped the Federals off in advance. *O.R.,* XX, pt. 1, 760.

45. Davis, *Breckinridge,* 345.

46. Ibid., 787, 803, 824, 910–11; Paper by Robert C. Chambliss, Semple Papers, ASA.

47. *O.R.,* XX, pt. 1, 761, 803. Pritchard's two-gun Georgia battery was in a fixed fortification in Murfreesboro.

48. Ibid., 824.

49. Magee Diary, January 2, 1863, Duke.

50. *O.R.,* XX, pt. 1, 676–81, 233, 242.

51. McWhiney and Jamieson, *Attack and Die,* 118–19, 124.

52. *O.R.,* XX, pt. 1, 751, 804, 722.

53. McWhiney and Jamieson, *Attack and Die,* 118–19, 124.

Chapter 6

1. Lucia R. Douglas, ed., *Douglas' Texas Battery, C.S.A.* (Waco, Tex., 1966), 64.

2. Magee Diary, March 6, 1863, Duke.

3. Douglas to Sallie, April 21 and May 10, Douglas, ed., *Douglas' Texas Battery,* 65–66.

4. *O.R.,* XX, pt. 2, 493, XXIII, pt. 2, 649–50.

5. Connelly, *Autumn of Glory,* 109–10; *O.R.,* XXIII, pt. 2, 806.

6. "Artillery Strength, February 1 and March 1, 1863" and "Statement of Guns on Hand, April 30, 1863," Bragg Papers, Western Reserve Historical Society (hereafter cited as Western Reserve); Grammer Diary, January 12, 1863, Vicksburg NMP; Brewer, *Alabama,* 701; *O.R.,* XXIII, pt. 2, 967–68; Lindsley, ed., *Military Annals of Tennessee,* 819.

7. "Returns in Detail, Army of Tennessee, March 1863," Bragg Papers, Western Reserve; Connelly, *Autumn of Glory,* 115; "Inspection of Polk's Batteries by Felix H. Robertson, February 1, 1863," Inspection Reports and Related Records Received by the Inspection Branch of the Confederate Adjutant General's Office, NARG 109 (hereafter cited as AGIR).

8. *O.R.,* XXIII, pt. 2, 759, 843; Connelly, *Army of the Heartland,* 8.

9. E. T. Sykes, *Walthall's Brigade* (Columbus, Miss., 1905), 525.

10. Connelly, *Autumn of Glory,* 114–15; "Inspection of Polk's Artillery, February 1, 1863," AGIR.

11. "Return in Detail, Army of Tennessee Allowances for Baggage, March 1863," Bragg Papers, Western Reserve.

12. "Inspection of Polk's Artillery, February 1, 1863," AGIR.

13. *O.R.,* XX, pt. 1, 753, 768, 770, XXIII, pt. 2, 882; Semple to wife, March 15, 1863, Semple Papers, ASA.

14. *O.R.,* XXIII, pt. 2, 763; Oladowski to Gorgas, October 23, 1863, Letters Sent, Ordnance Officer, Army of Tennessee, Chap. IV, Vol. 141, NARG 109 (hereafter cited as ATOR).

15. Mallet to Oladowski, May 28, 1863, and Mallet to Gorgas, May 28, 1863, Central Ordnance Laboratory Letterbook, Chap. 4, Vol. 28, NARG 109.

16. "Inspection of Polk's Artillery, May 9, 1863," AGIR; Magee Diary, Duke; Invoices of Ordnance and Ordnance Stores, May 5, 1863, Robert Cobb, Military Service File, National Archives. According to the 1863 Confederate ordnance manual, a carriage for a 12-pounder howitzer should be made of white oak, painted an olive green color, and weigh 1,228 pounds. *The Confederate Ordnance Manual for the Use of Officers of the Confederate Army* (Dayton, Ohio, 1976), 38–39, 169, 343, 389.

17. Oladowski to Brent, January 15, 1863, and Oladowski to Gorgas, January 22, 1863, ATOR; Memphis *Appeal,* March 27, 1863; "Report of Ordnance and Ordnance Stores Passing through Atlanta, March 1863–June 1864," Chap. IV, Vol. 87, NARG 109.

18. Invoices of Ordnance and Ordnance Stores, Cobb's Battery, May 5 and 8, 1863, Robert Cobb, Military Service File, National Archives.

19. Oladowski to Humphreys, March 14, 1863, and Oladowski to Wright, August 13, 1863, ATOR.

20. "Statement of Ammunition on Hand, Army of Tennessee, April 30, 1863," Bragg Papers, Western Reserve.

21. "Inspection of Polk's Artillery, February 1 and May 9, 1863," AGIR.

22. Peterson, *Round Shot and Rammers,* 92; Oladowski to Wright, January 21, 1863, and Oladowski to Rains, October 11, 1863, ATOR; "Inspection of Polk's Artillery, May 9, 1863," AGIR.

23. *O.R.,* XX, pt. 1, 768, 771, XXIII, pt. 2, 763.

24. Hallonquist to Oladowski, January 26, 1863, James H. Hallonquist, Military Service File, National Archives; Oladowski to Wright, January 13, 1863, and Oladowski to Gorgas, March 9, 1863, ATOR.

25. James C. Hazlett, "The Napoleon Gun: Its Origin and Introduction into American Service," *The Military Collector and Historian,* XV (Spring 1963), 1–2; Ripley, *Artillery and Ammunition of the Civil War,* 26–27, 366.

26. Oladowski to Gorgas, March 9, 1863, ATOR; *O.R.,* XXIII, pt. 2, 967–69.

27. Dew, *Ironmaker to the Confederacy,* 184–85; G. W. Rains, *History of the Confederate Powder Works* (Augusta, 1882), 30; James C. Hazlett, "The Confederate Napoleon Gun," *The Military Collector and Historian,* XIV (Winter 1964), 108; Memphis *Appeal,* March 27, 1863; Arthur James L. Fremantle, *Three Months in the Southern States: April–June 1863* (New York, 1864), 176.

28. Charleston *Courier,* March 11, 1863; Oladowski to Gorgas, February 28, 1863, ATOR; *O.R.,* XXVII, pt. 4, 656–57, XXIII, pt. 2, 762–63; Macon *Telegram,* June 13, 1863; "List of Guns and Their Makers, Walker's Division, Army of Mississippi," 1863, Mississippi State Archives; Dew, *Ironmaker to the Confederacy,* 190; "Statement of Guns on Hand, April 30, 1863," Bragg Papers, Western Reserve.

29. "Statement of Guns on Hand, April 30, 1863," Bragg Papers, Western Reserve.

30. *O.R.,* XXIII, pt. 2, 843.

31. Oladowski to Wright, May 22, 1863, ATOR.

32. Oladowski to W. A. Taylor, June 1, 1863, and Oladowski to Wright, July 23, 1863, ATOR.

33. *O.R.,* XXIII, pt. 2, 967–69, XX, pt. 1, 778.

1. Richard M. McMurry, "'The Enemy at Richmond': Joseph E. Johnston and the Confederate Government," *Civil War History,* XXVII (March 1981), 19.

2. Connelly, *Autumn of Glory,* 27, 30–31. The army chief of ordnance, Colonel Hypolite Oladowski, was also a participant in the Pensacola-Mobile bloc. See Thomas R. Hay, ed., *Cleburne and His Command by Irving R. Buck* (Jackson, Tenn., 1959), 204.

3. *O.R.,* X, pt. 2, 503, XXXII, pt. 3, 706; James H. Hallonquist, Military Service File, National Archives; Bragg to Powell, March 25, 1862, Bragg Papers, Western Reserve; "1887 Annual Reunion of the Association of Graduates, U.S. Military Academy, West Point, New York," USMA, 78.

4. Hallonquist to Oladowski, January 26, 1863, "Report on Experiments Made at Estelle Springs, March 31, 1863," and Hallonquist to Oladowski, November 11, 1863, James H. Hallonquist, Military Service File, National Archives.

5. Colgin, ed., "The Life Story of Brig. Gen. Felix Robertson," 154–55; Boatner, *Civil War Dictionary,* 702–703; Ezra J. Warner, *Generals in Gray* (Baton Rouge, 1959), 260–61; *O.R.,* XXXII, pt. 3, 688; Robertson to L.P. Walker, February 23, 1861, and Special Orders No. 80, April 20, 1861, Felix Robertson, Military Service File, National Archives.

6. Talley, "History of Havis' Georgia Battery," 27–28, Kennesaw NMP; Little and Maxwell, *A History of Lumsden's Battery,* 32–33.

7. Davis, *Breckinridge,* 351–52; Connelly, *Autumn of Glory,* 83; Bragg to Adjutant General, February 24, 1863, Felix H. Robertson, Military Service File, National Archives.

8. Pickering, "The Washington Artillery of Augusta, Ga.," 25.

9. Alexander, "Confederate Artillery Service," 106.

10. Wise, *The Long Arm of Lee,* 723.

11. One of the finest battery commanders, Captain Thomas Stanford, was commissioned in May 1861. He was killed in May 1864, but had never been promoted. Captain Charles Lumsden, a graduate of the Virginia Military Institute, likewise never made field grade during his years of service. *Register of Former Cadets* (Lexington, Va., 1957), 28.

12. *O.R.,* XXIII, pt. 2, 724; Petition to the Honorable James A. Seddon, March 16, 1863, Melancthon Smith, Military Service File, National Archives; Bragg to Cooper, June 15, 1863, Bragg Papers, Letters Sent, Chap. II, Vol. 359, NARG 109.

13. Pickering, "The Washington Artillery of Augusta, Ga.," 25.

14. John W. Morton, *The Artillery of Nathan Bedford Forrest's Cavalry* (Kennesaw, Ga., 1962), 45–47; "Forrest's Chief of Artillery: Morton," *Confederate Veteran,* VIII (1900), 171; "Young Artillery Captains," *Confederate Veteran,* VI (1895), 175. Forrest later referred to Morton as that "little bit of kid with the big backbone." Bragg, likewise, often disregarded seniority in making recommendations for general officers. McWhiney, *Braxton Bragg and Confederate Defeat,* 343.

15. *O.R.,* XXXII, pt. 3, 688, 700; Commission, *Tennesseans in the Civil War,* 143; Stewart to Cooper, May 5, 1863, Series L, Vol. 43, No. 22,

RG 9, Mississippi State Archives; "Maj. John W. Eldridge," *Confederate Veteran,* XXI (July 1913), 352.

16. *O.R.,* XX, pt. 1, 776, 844, 849, XXXVIII, pt. 3, 688, 700.

17. Semple to Mackall, August 17, 1863, Semple Papers, ASA.

18. Endorsement of J. H. Hallonquist, August 21, 1863, and Cleburne to Hill, August 19, 1863, Semple Papers, ASA.

19. Bragg to Cooper, June 15, 1863, Letters Sent, Chap. II, Vol. 359, Bragg Papers, NARG 109; General Orders No. 119, July 22, 1863, Bragg Papers, Western Reserve.

Chapter 8

1. Bragg later admitted that the actual words exclaimed by Taylor were: "Captain, give them hell!"

2. McWhiney and Jamieson, *Attack and Die,* 36; McWhiney, *Braxton Bragg and Confederate Defeat,* 79, 83, 84.

3. McWhiney, *Braxton Bragg and Confederate Defeat,* 275; Connelly, *Army of the Heartland,* 273.

4. Connelly, *Autumn of Glory,* 26–28.

5. The term "battalion," though not formally adopted in Bragg's army until the spring of 1863, was commonly used by artillerymen prior to that time. See, for example, Magee Diary, August 16, 1862, Duke, and Grammer Diary, June 18, 1862, Vicksburg NMP.

6. Connelly, *Autumn of Glory,* 118, 125; *O.R.,* XX, pt. 2, 499.

7. *O.R.,* XXIII, pt. 2, 734–35; Maury Klein, *Edward Porter Alexander* (Athens, Ga., 1971), 57–58.

8. Alexander, "Confederate Artillery Service," 102; *O.R.,* XXIII, pt. 2, 744.

9. *O.R.,* XXIII, pt. 2, 774; General Orders No. 76, April 9, 1863, Hypolite Oladowski Papers, Duke.

10. *O.R.,* XX, pt. 1, 661; Commission, *Tennesseans in the Civil War,* 125.

11. "Report of Ordnance and Ordnance Stores, Horses, Mules, etc. Reserve Artillery, April 30, 1863," Felix H. Robertson, Military Service File, National Archives; *O.R.,* XX, pt. 2, 493, XXIII, pt. 2, 862.

12. Talley, "History of Havis' Georgia Battery," Kennesaw NMP.

13. McDonald, Praeder, and Bianchi-Rossi, "Rifle Musket," 15; McWhiney, *Braxton Bragg and Confederate Defeat,* 54, 93, 129–30, 136; Wise, *The Long Arm of Lee,* 162.

14. Commission, *Tennesseans in the Civil War,* 131, 157; Wiggins' Battery, Military Service File, National Archives; *O.R.,* XX, pt. 1, 65.

15. Morton, *The Artillery of Nathan Bedford Forrest's Cavalry,* 52–53, 57.

16. Ibid., 87–88; Commission, *Tennesseans in the Civil War,* 132.

Chapter 9

1. Connelly, *Autumn of Glory,* 156; James W. Bondurant, Military Service File, National Archives.

2. Magee Diary, July 2, 1863, Duke; Wiggins' Battery, Military Service File, National Archives; *O.R.*, XXIII, pt. 1, 534.

3. Douglas, ed., *Douglas' Texas Battery,* 69–70.

4. Oladowski to Mackall, July 14, 1863, ATOR.

5. *O.R.*, XXIII, pt. 2, 940–44.

6. Magee Diary, August 6, 1863, Duke; Grammer Diary, August 6, 1863, Vicksburg NMP.

7. *O.R.*, XXX, pt. 1, 233–36.

8. James R. Sullivan, *Chickamauga and Chattanooga Battlefields* (Washington, D.C., 1956), 11–12; *O.R.*, XXX, pt. 2, 420, 448–49, 450.

9. *O.R.*, XXX, pt. 2, 201, 244; Sullivan, *Chickamauga and Chattanooga Battlefields,* 12.

10. *O.R.*, XXX, pt. 4, 595.

11. Sullivan, *Chickamauga and Chattanooga Battlefields,* 12–13.

12. *O.R.*, XXX, pt. 2, 81, 159, 201, 244, 292, 307, 366, 420, 450.

13. Ibid., pt. 4, 632, pt. 2, 147.

14. Ibid., pt. 4, 621, 657, 658, 664, 665, pt. 2, 451.

15. Morton, *The Artillery of Nathan Bedford Forrest's Cavalry,* 117, 119.

16. Glenn Tucker, *Chickamauga: Bloody Battle in the West* (Dayton, Ohio, 1976), 128–37.

17. *O.R.*, XXX, pt. 2, 256, 270, 286.

18. Daniel H. Hill, "Chickamauga: The Great Battle in the West," *Battles and Leaders,* III, 650–51; *O.R.*, XXX, pt. 2, 93, 117.

19. *O.R.*, XXX, pt. 2, 412.

20. Lindsley, ed., *Military Annals of Tennessee,* 822–23; Tucker, *Chickamauga,* 144; Pickering, "The Washington Artillery of Augusta, Ga.," 25; *O.R.*, XXXII, pt. 2, 70; W. W. Carnes, "Chickamauga," *Southern Historical Society Papers,* XIV (1886), 399–400.

21. *O.R.*, XXX, pt. 2, 360, 450.

22. Ibid., 154, 174, 196; Douglas, ed., *Douglas' Texas Battery,* 72.

23. *O.R.*, XXX, pt. 2, 229–30; Davis, *The Orphan Brigade,* 188, 192.

24. *O.R.*, XXX, pt. 2, 230.

25. Ibid., 215–16.

26. Ibid., 174–75, 186, 196.

27. Ibid., 222; Tucker, *Chickamauga,* 246–47; *O.R.*, XXX, pt. 2, 256, 270, 287.

28. Tucker, *Chickamauga,* 263–64.

29. *O.R.*, XXX, pt. 2, 465–66, 499, 382, 400, 360.

30. Tucker, *Chickamauga,* 264.

31. Ibid., 275; *O.R.*, XXX, pt. 2, 459.

32. *O.R.*, XXX, pt. 2, 289, 360; James Longstreet, *From Manassas to Appomattox* (Bloomington, Ind., 1960), 451.

33. *O.R.*, XXX, pt. 2, 292; Talley, "History of Havis' Georgia Battery," Kennesaw NMP.

34. *O.R.*, XXX, pt. 1, 782, pt. 2, 358, 450.

35. "Gracey-Chickamauga-Whitaker," *Confederate Veteran,* VI (1895), 251; *O.R.*, XXX, pt. 2, 525; Tucker, *Chickamauga,* 343–44.

36. *O.R.*, XXX, pt. 2, 417.

37. Shelby Foote, *The Civil War—A Narrative: Fredericksburg to Meridian* (New York, 1963), 713.

38. *O.R.*, XXX, pt. 2, 360, 132.
39. McWhiney and Jamieson, *Attack and Die,* 121.
40. *O.R.*, XXX, pt. 2, 453.
41. Tucker, *Chickamauga,* 264; Longstreet, *From Manassas to Appomattox,* 451.
42. Lindsley, ed., *Military Annals of Tennessee,* 822–23; *O.R.*, XXX, pt. 2, 81, 159, 201, 244, 292, 307, 365, 366, 420, 450, 502. Data on casualties in Forrest's artillery are unavailable.
43. *O.R.*, XXX, pt. 2, 37, 81, 159, 201, 244, 292, 307, 366, 420, 450, pt. 1, 238–39.
44. Ibid., pt. 2, 81, 159, 201, 244, 292, 307, 366, 420, 450, 467, 501, pt. 1, 233; Naisawald, *Grape and Canister,* 443.
45. *O.R.*, XXX, pt. 2, 202, 244, 292, 307, 420, 450.
46. Ibid., pt. 1, 238–39, pt. 2, 41–42. The Northern and Southern lists of captures and losses vary significantly. Although the latter list is more detailed, it may not be as accurate because it apparently included all ordnance taken by the Yankees and in turn retaken by the Confederates. Thus, Bragg claimed the capture of fifty pieces, but Rosecrans acknowledged the loss of only thirty-nine. Too, Confederate ordnance officials may have listed only the material turned into the Atlanta Arsenal. For example, they counted only two captured Napoleon guns, but the Northerners acknowledged the loss of four. A close examination shows that Peeple's battery retained two light 12-pounders on the field in exchange for its two 24-pounder howitzers. The former were not included in Bragg's list of captures, though the latter were.

Chapter 10

1. Neal to "Dear Pa," n.d., A. J. Neal Letters, Emory University; Morton, *The Artillery of Nathan Bedford Forrest's Cavalry,* 127–28; Glenn Tucker, "The Battles for Chattanooga," *Civil War Times Illustrated,* August 1971, 5.
2. Klein, *E. P. Alexander,* 96–97; E. P. Alexander, *Military Memoirs of a Confederate* (Norwood, Mass., 1907), 449.
3. Alexander, *Military Memoirs,* 451; Klein, *E. P. Alexander,* 97.
4. Fairfax Downey, *Storming the Gateway: Chattanooga, 1863* (New York, 1960), 147–48.
5. Ibid.
6. Connelly, *Autumn of Glory,* 255, 257, 262; E. P. Alexander, "Longstreet at Knoxville," *Battles and Leaders,* III, 746.
7. Downey, *Storming the Gateway,* 148; Massenburg's Georgia Battery, Military Service File, National Archives; *O.R.*, XXXI, pt. 3, 626; Neal to "Dear Pa," October 12, 1863, A. J. Neal Letters, Emory.
8. Little and Maxwell, *A History of Lumsden's Battery,* 25–26; Talley, "History of Havis' Georgia Battery," Kennesaw NMP; Clyde C. Walton, ed., *Behind the Guns: The History of Battery I, 2nd Regiment, Illinois Light Artillery* (Carbondale, Ill., 1965), 70.
9. Anderson to Darden, October 19, 1863, J. T. Humphreys to Darden, October 19, 1863, Issues for Forage, October 14–18, 1863, and Semple to Chief of Artillery, Hill's corps, October 22, 1863, Semple Papers Papers, ASA.

10. Connelly, *Autumn of Glory,* 262.

11. Ibid., 250–52; Organization Circular, November 20, 1863, Bragg Papers, Western Reserve; Neal to "Dear Pa," November 20, 1863, A. J. Neal Letters, Emory.

12. William L. Ritter, "Sketch of the Third Battery of Maryland Artillery," *Southern Historical Society Papers,* XII (1883), 115; Oladowski to Stevenson, October 17, 1863, Oladowski to Gorgas, October 17, 1863, and Oladowski to Wright, October 28, 1863, ATOR.

13. Head, *Campaigns and Battles of the Sixteenth Tennessee Volunteers,* 245; Commission, *Tennesseans in the Civil War,* 137.

14. "Report of Artillery Strength, November 7, 1863" and "Report of the Artillery, October 31, 1863," Bragg Papers, Western Reserve. See Appendix for detailed composition of the organization.

15. Oladowski to Gorgas, November 5, 1863, Oladowski to W. D. Humphreys, November 12, 1863, Oladowski to Wright, November 19, 1863, and Oladowski to Cuyler, November 12, 1863, ATOR.

16. *O.R.,* XXXI, pt. 2, 659, 662, pt. 3, 634, 637, 645; Klein, *E. P. Alexander,* 98; Alexander, "Longstreet at Knoxville," 745–46; "Report of the Artillery, October 31, 1863," Bragg Papers, Western Reserve.

17. Connelly, *Autumn of Glory,* 270.

18. *O.R.,* XXXI, pt. 2, 685.

19. Ibid., 693–94, 717, 728; Tucker, "The Battles for Chattanooga," 31.

20. Connelly, *Autumn of Glory,* 273; Davis, *Breckinridge,* 386–87.

21. "Consolidated Report of Guns Engaged at Missionary Ridge, November 24–25, 1863," Bragg Papers, Western Reserve.

22. *O.R.,* XXXI, pt. 2, 740; Alexander, *Military Memoirs,* 475.

23. James C. Nisbet, *Four Years on the Firing Line* (Chattanooga, 1914), 249.

24. *O.R.,* XXXI, pt. 2, 513–15.

25. Ibid., 748.

26. W. W. Carnes, "At Missionary Ridge," *Confederate Veteran,* XX (May 1920), 185.

27. Glenn Tucker writes that the "artillery had not been idle during their two months on Missionary Ridge and had the ranges accurately calculated and tested." Tucker, "The Battles for Chattanooga," 39. The author has found no documentation to support this.

28. *O.R.,* XXXI, pt. 2, 748–49. Semple's battery was detached to guard the bridge over Chickamauga Creek.

29. Ibid., 750; Grammer Diary, November 25, 1863, Vicksburg NMP; Memphis *Appeal,* November 1, 1863; "Dr. Harvey Shannon," *Confederate Veteran,* XV (March 1907), 131–32.

30. *O.R.,* XXXI, pt. 2, 749; Hay, ed., *Cleburne and His Command,* 170.

31. Carnes, "At Missionary Ridge," 185; *O.R.,* XXXI, pt. 2, 753.

32. *O.R.,* XXXI, pt. 2, 79, 199, 230, 234, 278, 287, 288; Joseph S. Fullerton, "The Army of the Cumberland at Chattanooga," *Battles and Leaders,* III, 725–26.

33. *O.R.,* XXXI, pt. 2, 234, 238, 310, 313.

34. Fullerton, "The Army of the Cumberland at Chattanooga," 725–26.

35. Hughes, *General William J. Hardee,* 174; *O.R.,* XXXII, pt. 3, 699; Commission, *Tennesseans in the Civil War,* 151; Brewer, *Alabama,* 698.

36. Connelly, *Autumn of Glory,* 276; Sam R. Watkins, *Co. Aytch* (Jackson, Tenn., 1952), 125; Neal to "Dear Emma," November 25, 1863, A. J. Neal Letters, Emory.

37. Downey, *Storming the Gateway,* 189; Owen, *In Camp and Battle with the Washington Artillery,* 414; *O.R.,* XXXII, pt. 3, 704.

38. "Report of Guns Engaged, Ammunition Expended, etc. in Major F. H. Robertson's Command—1st Battalion Reserve Artillery, November 24–25, 1863," Bragg Papers, Western Reserve.

39. *O.R.,* XXXII, pt. 3, 704. See also Mebane plaque at the Chattanooga Military Park.

40. Memphis *Appeal,* December 2, 1863; Tucker, "The Battles for Chattanooga," 40; Thompson, *History of the Orphan Brigade,* 288; Fullerton, "The Army of the Cumberland at Chattanooga," 725; *O.R.,* XXXII, pt. 3, 703.

41. *O.R.,* XXXII, pt. 3, 701. See also Dawson plaque at the Chattanooga Military Park.

42. Nisbet, *Four Years on the Firing Line,* 253–54.

43. Ritter, "Sketch of the Third Battery of Maryland Artillery," 116–17.

44. Hay, ed., *Cleburne and His Command,* 181; P. O. Stephenson, "Reminiscences of the Last Campaign of the Army of Tennessee, from May 1864 to January 1865," *Southern Historical Society Papers,* XII (1884), 38–39; *O.R.,* XXXI, pt. 2, 758–60.

45. "Report of Casualties in the Engagements Before Chattanooga," Bragg Papers, Western Reserve.

46. "Consolidated Report of the Guns Engaged at Missionary Ridge, November 24–25, 1863," Bragg Papers, Western Reserve; *O.R.,* XXXI, pt. 1, 99–100, 553–54.

47. "Consolidated Report of the Guns Engaged at Missionary Ridge, November 24–25, 1863," Bragg Papers, Western Reserve; *O.R.,* XXXI, pt. 1, 99–100, 553–54.

Chapter 11

1. Cate, ed., *Two Soldiers,* 11–12; Little and Maxwell, *A History of Lumsden's Battery,* 30; Ritter, "Sketch of the Third Battery of Maryland Artillery," 117; Lindsley, ed., *Military Annals of Tennessee,* 824.

2. Hotchkiss Battalion, General Orders No. 3, January 24, 1864, Semple Papers, ASA.

3. Little and Maxwell, *A History of Lumsden's Battery,* 31; Grammer Diary, January 8, 1864, Vicksburg NMP.

4. Cate, ed., *Two Soldiers,* 11; Boatner, *Civil War Dictionary,* 758.

5. Cate, ed., *Two Soldiers,* 15; Grammer Diary, December 26, 1863, Vicksburg NMP.

6. Neal to "Dear Emma," March 25, 1864, A. J. Neal Letters, Emory.

7. *O.R.,* XXXI, pt. 3, 783.

8. Ibid., pt. 2, 657–64, pt. 3, 788, 860; Army of Tennessee, General Orders No. 18, December 16, 1863, Semple Papers, ASA; Commission,

Tennesseans in the Civil War, 151; Grammer Diary, December 10, 1863, Vicksburg NMP.

9. Connelly, *Autumn of Glory,* 289–90; Hardee to Ives, December 23, 1863, Bragg Papers, Western Reserve; *O.R.,* XXXI, pt. 3, 856–57, 860.

10. *O.R.,* XXXI, pt. 3, 826–28; Mebane Battery Requisition, December 31, 1863, Robert Cobb, Military Service File, National Archives.

11. "Statement of the Strength of the Army, December 20, 1863," Bragg Papers, Western Reserve; Howell's Georgia Battery, Muster Roll, December 31, 1863, National Archives.

12. Cate, ed., *Two Soldiers,* 31–32.

13. *O.R.,* XXXII, pt. 2, 510, 697; Joseph E. Johnston, "Opposing Sherman's Advance to Atlanta," *Battles and Leaders,* IV, 260.

14. Neal to "Dear Emma," March 8, 1864, A. J. Neal Letters, Emory; Grammer Diary, February 6 and April 6, 1864, Vicksburg NMP; Cate, ed., *Two Soldiers,* 68–69; Richard M. McMurry, *John Bell Hood and the War for Southern Independence* (Lexington, Ky., 1982), 100; W. B. Shepard to wife, March 31, 1864, Benjamin F. Cheatham Papers, Tennessee State Archives.

15. Howard M. Madaus and Robert D. Needham, *The Battle Flags of the Confederate Army of Tennessee* (Milwaukee, 1976), 63, 66–67, 102; Neal to "Dear Pa," March 26, 1864, A. J. Neal Letters, Emory.

16. Madaus and Needham, *The Battle Flags of the Confederate Army of Tennessee,* 94–96, 84.

17. Memphis *Appeal,* January 21, 1864; Grammer Diary, February 21, 1864, Vicksburg NMP; *O.R.,* XXXII, pt. 3, 670; "More About Re-Enlistments at Dalton," *Confederate Veteran,* X (September 1902), 399.

18. "History of Fenner's Battery, August 8, 1891," Thomas C. Porteous Papers, Louisiana State University; Brewer, *Alabama,* 698–99; *O.R.,* XXXII, pt. 3, 586.

19. *O.R.,* XXXII, pt. 3, 731; Ritter, "Sketch of the Third Battery of Maryland Artillery," 117; Cate, ed., *Two Soldiers,* 64.

20. Joseph E. Johnston, *Narrative of Military Operations* (Bloomington, 1959), 278–79; Lindsley, ed., *Military Annals of Tennessee,* 825; Ritter, "Sketch of the Third Battery of Maryland Artillery," 434, 436.

21. Ritter, "Sketch of the Third Battery of Maryland Artillery," 436–37.

22. *O.R.,* XXXII, pt. 2, 645, 697–98; Johnston, *Narrative of Military Operations,* 279.

23. Ritter, "Sketch of the Third Battery of Maryland Artillery," 434; *O.R.,* XXXII, pt. 3, 708; Lindsley, ed., *Military Annals of Tennessee,* 825.

24. *O.R.,* XXXII, pt. 3, 694; Macon *Telegraph,* January 30, 1864.

25. *O.R.,* XXXII, pt. 2, 697, 809; Johnston to Lawton, February 28, 1864, Joseph E. Johnston Papers, William and Mary.

26. *O.R.,* XXXII, pt. 3, 584, 794; McMurry, "'The Enemy at Richmond,'" 24.

27. *O.R.,* XXXII, pt. 2, 817; Cate, ed., *Two Soldiers,* 12–13.

28. *O.R.,* XXXII, pt. 3, 772–73; Wise, *The Long Arm of Lee,* 418, 711.

29. Charles M. Ramsdell, "General Robert E. Lee's Horse Supply, 1862–1865," *American Historical Review,* XXXV (1930), 773.

30. Wise, *The Long Arm of Lee,* 732–33.

31. *O.R.,* XXXII, pt. 3, 685–86, 696.

32. Ibid., 731.

33. Ibid., 772–73; McMurry, "'The Enemy at Richmond,'" 24.

34. Ralph W. Donnelly, "Confederate Copper," *Civil War History,* I (December 1955), 355–70; Hazlett, "The Confederate Napoleon Gun." Between January and June 1864, forty-one old guns were sent from Atlanta to Augusta for recasting. This amounted to more than 25,000 pounds of copper and 5,000 pounds of iron. "Record of Receipts and Deliveries at the Atlanta Armory, December 1863–June 1864," Vols. 17–18, NARG 109.

35. Rains to Oladowski, February 13, 1864, George W. Rains, Military Service File, National Archives.

36. Oladowski to Gorgas, February 5, 1864, and Oladowski to Rains, February 5, 1864, ATOR; Robertson to Oladowski, February 7, 1864, Felix H. Robertson, Military Service File, National Archives; W. C. Duxbury Report, April 25, 1864, Ordnance Department Correspondence, Vol. 111, Record Group 9, Mississippi State Archives (hereafter cited as Duxbury Report, MSA).

37. *O.R.,* XXXII, pt. 3, 685.

38. "Record and Receipts and Deliveries at the Atlanta Armory, December 1863–June 1864," Chap. IV, Vol. 18, NARG 109; Oladowski to Wright, February 8, 1864, ATOR; Duxbury Report, MSA.

39. Rains to Oladowski, February 13 and March 11, 1864, George W. Rains, Military Service File, National Archives.

40. *O.R.,* XXXII, pt. 3, 695, 699, 709.

41. Wright to Gorgas, February 12, 1864, Letters and Telegrams Sent, Atlanta Arsenal, Chap. IV, Vol. 16, NARG 109; Duxbury Report, MSA; Cate, ed., *Two Soldiers,* 68.

42. Ordnance Receipt, March 20, 1864, Cobb's Battalion, Robert Cobb, Military Service File, National Archives.

43. Duxbury Report, MSA.

44. *O.R.,* XXXII, pt. 2, 631, pt. 3, 695; Monthly Inspection of Courtney's Battalion, February 2, 1864, Ordnance Department Correspondence, Series L, Vol. 43, Record Group 9, Mississippi State Archives; Orders and Circulars, Augusta Arsenal, NARG 109.

45. Johnston to Bragg, March 30, 1864, Joseph E. Johnston Papers, William and Mary; *O.R.,* XXXII, pt. 3, 692, 695; Joseph Jones, "Roster of the Medical Officers of the Army of Tennessee," *Southern Historical Society Papers,* XXII (1894), 165–280.

46. Cate, ed., *Two Soldiers,* 31–32; Lindsley, ed., *Military Annals of Tennessee,* 824; *O.R.,* XXXII, pt. 3, 686, 688, 696.

47. *O.R.,* XXXII, pt. 3, 731, 801; Requisition for Forage, Robertson's Battalion, May 11, 1864, Felix H. Robertson, Military Service File, National Archives.

48. Neal to "Dear Emma," February 24, 1864, A. J. Neal Letters, Emory; Smith to A. G. Brown, May 5, 1864, Army of Tennessee Papers, 1862–1864, Duke.

49. Wise, *The Long Arm of Lee,* 566–70; Klein, *E. P. Alexander,* 71; Naisawald, *Grape and Canister,* 489–90; *O.R.,* XXXVIII, pt. 1, 121.

50. *O.R.,* XXXVIII, pt. 4, 721–22.

51. Ibid., pt. 1, 486, 825.

1. *O.R.,* XXXII, pt. 2, 697.

2. Ibid., pt. 3, 696; W. B. Shepard to wife, March 31, 1864, Benjamin F. Cheatham Papers, Tennessee State Archives.

3. Johnston to Bragg, March 30, 1864, Joseph E. Johnston Papers, William and Mary; *O.R.,* XXXII, pt. 3, 613.

4. Wise, *The Long Arm of Lee,* 733; J. W. Bondurant and Robert F. Beckham, Military Service Files, National Archives; Johnston to Bragg, March 30, 1864, Joseph E. Johnston Papers, William and Mary; *O.R.,* XXXII, pt. 3, 697, 706; *Biographical Register of the Officers and Graduates of the U.S. Military Academy from 1802 to 1867* (New York, 1879), 483.

5. *O.R.,* XXXII, pt. 3, 584–85; Klein, *E. P. Alexander,* 105–6.

6. *O.R.,* XXXII, pt. 3, 592, 636; McMurry, "'The Enemy at Richmond,'" 22. Lovell later served as a volunteer aide on Johnston's staff.

7. Wise, *The Long Arm of Lee,* 413, 418, 723–24; *O.R.,* XXXII, pt. 3, 686, 688.

8. *O.R.,* XXXII, pt. 3, 671.

9. Ibid., 714; J. W. Bondurant, Military Service File, National Archives.

10. Warner, *Generals in Gray,* 275–76; Boatner, *Civil War Dictionary,* 758; *O.R.,* XXXII, pt. 3, 671. Jennings Wise viewed Shoup's appointment over Carter as "only another evidence of the advantage held by West Pointers." Carter was a graduate of the Virginia Military Institute. Wise, *The Long Arm of Lee,* 734.

11. Cate, ed., *Two Soldiers,* 68, 73, 74, 75; *O.R.,* XXXII, pt. 3, 688, 742. In June, Johnston directed that Shoup supervise the construction of the Chattahoochee River fortifications. F. A. Shoup, "Dalton Campaign—Works at Chattahoochee River," *Confederate Veteran,* III (September 1895), 262–64.

12. Robertson to Bragg, March 14, 1864, Bragg Papers, Western Reserve.

13. *O.R.,* XXXII, pt. 3, 696; Joseph A. Wilson, "Bledsoe of Missouri," *Confederate Veteran,* VII (October 1899), 462–63.

14. E. B. Smith to Hotchkiss, January 21, 1864, Hotchkiss to Semple, February 1, 1864, Charges and Specifications Vs. Henry C. Semple, February 29, 1864, and General Orders No. 34, April 15, 1864, Semple Papers, ASA.

15. "Major John William Johnston," *Confederate Veteran,* XIX (March 1911), 117.

16. *O.R.,* XXXII, pt. 3, 696. See Appendix for detailed composition of the organization.

17. Cate, ed., *Two Soldiers,* 13, 89; Muster Roll, Semple's Alabama Battery, National Archives; "Inspection of the Artillery, September 20, 1864," AGIR.

18. Neal to "Dear Pa," March 14, 1864, A. J. Neal Letters, Emory.

19. *O.R.,* XXXII, pt. 3, 689–90, 697–98, 701–2, 705–6.

Chapter 13

1. Cate, ed., *Two Soldiers,* 78–79.

2. Melancthon Smith Journal of the Atlanta Campaign, May 17, 1864, Benjamin F. Cheatham Papers, Tennessee State Archives (hereafter cited as Smith Journal, TSA); *O.R.,* XXXVIII, pt. 4, 668, 688.

3. Sherman's chief of artillery, Brigadier General William F. Barry, reported that his artillery consisted of fifty batteries and 254 guns. This figure included the guns of the XVII Corps and serveral batteries that did not arrive until June. *O.R.,* XXXVIII, pt. 1, 120–21, 480–81, 487, 825, pt. 2, 472–73, 488, pt. 4, 491, 518, pt. 5, 762.

4. Ibid., pt. 3, 731–32, pt. 4, 676; Requisition for Forage, Robertson's Battalion, May 11, 1864, Felix H. Robertson, Military Service File, National Archives.

5. "History of Fenner's Battery," Thomas C. Porteous Papers, Louisiana State University.

6. *O.R.,* XXXVIII, pt. 1, 481; Memphis *Appeal,* May 11, 1864.

7. *O.R.,* XXXVIII, pt. 3, 873; Brewer, *Alabama,* 699; Richard M. McMurry, "Reseca: A Heap of Hard 'Fiten," *Civil War Times Illustrated,* XI (November 1970), 10.

8. *O.R.,* XXXVIII, pt. 3, 677, 873; Walter R. Rorer to Susan Willcox, March 31, 1864, James M. Willcox Papers, Duke.

9. McMurry, "Reseca: A Heap of Hard 'Fiten," 11.

10. Connelly, *Autumn of Glory,* 342; Kirwan, ed., *Johnny Green of the Orphan Brigade,* 128.

11. *O.R.,* XXXVIII, pt. 3, 796–97; "Sketch of Semple's Battery," Semple Papers, ASA; Lot D. Young, *Reminiscences of a Soldier of the Orphan Brigade* (Louisville, 1912), 83; Sykes, *Walthall's Brigade,* 568.

12. Ritter, "Sketch of the Third Battery of Maryland Artillery," 186–87.

13. Neal to "Dear Pa," May 15, 1864, A. J. Neal Letters, Emory.

14. *O.R.,* XXXVIII, pt. 3, 812–13; McMurry, "Reseca: A Heap of Hard 'Fiten," 46–47; John B. Hood, *Advance and Retreat: Personal Experiences in the United States and Confederate States Army* (Bloomington, Ind., 1959), 96.

15. *O.R.,* XXXVIII, pt. 3, 945, pt. 4, 720; Hay, ed., *Cleburne and His Command,* 212.

16. *O.R.,* XXXVIII, pt. 1, 65, 173, 185, 322, pt. 3, 817; Memphis *Appeal,* May 25 and June 8, 1864; "Sketch of Semple's Battery," Semple Papers, ASA; Rowland, *Mississippi Statistical Register,* 883; Lindsley, ed., *Military Annals of Tennessee,* 826.

17. *O.R.,* XXXVIII, pt. 3, 677, 873, XXXIX, pt. 2, 610; "Guibor's Missouri Battery in Georgia," Kennesaw *Gazette,* May 15, 1889, 2.

18. *O.R.,* XXXVIII, pt. 2, 752; Samuel French Diary, May 19, 1864, Samuel French Papers, Mississippi State Archives (hereafter cited as French Diary, MSA); John W. Powell, *Yankee Artilleryman: Through the Civil War with Eli Lilly's Indiana Battery* (Knoxville, 1975), 199; George S. Storrs, "The Artillery at Kennesaw," Kennesaw *Gazette,* June 15, 1889, 7.

19. Hood, *Advance and Retreat,* 104–6, 113–14.

20. Homer L. Kerr, ed., *Fighting with Ross' Texas Cavalry, CSA*

(Hillsboro, Tex., 1976), 144; Powell, ed., *Yankee Artilleryman,* 210–11.

21. Richard M. McMurry, "The Hell Hole: New Hope Church," *Civil War Times Illustrated,* February 1973, 35.

22. Ridley, *Battles and Sketches of the Army of Tennessee,* 304; "History of Fenner's Battery," Thomas C. Porteous Papers, Louisiana State University; Memphis *Appeal,* May 27, 1864; *O.R.,* XXXVIII, pt. 3, 761. The casualties in Stanford's, Fenner's and Oliver's batteries totaled eighteen, fifteen, and ten, respectively.

23. E. C. Dawes, "The Confederate Strength in the Atlanta Campaign," *Battles and Leaders,* IV, 281–82; *O.R.,* XXXVIII, pt. 3, 677, 873.

24. *O.R.,* XXXVIII, pt. 3, 677. See Appendix for detailed composition of the organization.

25. Ibid., pt. 4, 491, 518.

26. Hay, ed., *Cleburne and His Command,* 218–19.

27. *O.R.,* XXXVIII, pt. 3, 724–26; Memphis *Appeal,* June 2, 1864.

28. Smith Journal, May 27, 1864, TSA.

29. Memphis *Appeal,* June 7, 1864.

30. Thompson, *History of the Orphan Brigade,* 249–50.

31. Memphis *Appeal,* May 25 and June 8, 1864; *O.R.,* XXXVIII, pt. 3, 685, 873, 949.

32. "Guibor's Battery in Georgia," Kennesaw *Gazette,* May 15, 1889, 2; French Diary, June 18, 1864, MSA.

33. Storrs, "The Artillery at Kennesaw," 6–7.

34. Neal to "Dear Pa," June 20, 1864, A. J. Neal Letters, Emory.

35. Little and Maxwell, *A History of Lumsden's Battery,* 43.

36. Thompson, *History of the Orphan Brigade,* 271.

37. McWhiney and Jamieson, *Attack and Die,* 125.

38. Smith Journal, June 27, 1864, TSA.

39. *O.R.,* XXXVIII, pt. 3, 900, 968; Storrs, "The Artillery on Kennesaw," 7.

40. *O.R.,* XXXVIII, pt. 3, 878–79.

41. French Diary, July 2, 1864, MSA; Memphis *Appeal,* July 3, 1864.

42. Johnston, "Opposing Sherman's Advance to Atlanta," 274; *O.R.,* XXXVIII, pt. 5, 864–65.

43. Johnston, *Memoirs,* 351; *O.R.,* XXXVIII, pt. 1, 124, 173.

44. McWhiney and Jamieson, *Attack and Die,* 124.

Chapter 14

1. Cate, ed., *Two Soldiers,* 89; Sam B. Dunlap, "Experiences on the Hood Campaign," *Confederate Veteran,* XVI (April 1908), 187; Neal to "Dear Pa," July 20, 1864, A. J. Neal Letters, Emory; Douglas to Sallie, July 18, 1864, Douglas, ed., *Douglas' Texas Battery,* 114.

2. *O.R.,* XXXVIII, pt. 3, 679; Gustavus W. Smith, "The Georgia Militia about Atlanta," *Battles and Leaders,* IV, 332.

3. Allen P. Julian, "Atlanta's Defenses," *Civil War Times Illustrated,* III (December 1964), 23–24.

4. Wright to Mackall, March 3, 1864, Letters and Telegrams Sent, Atlanta Arsenal, Chap. IV, Vol. 16, NARG 109; *O.R.,* XXXVIII, pt. 3, 684; Johnston, "Opposing Sherman's Advance to Atlanta," 274.

5. *O.R.,* XXXI, pt. 3, 790, 821, XXXII, pt. 3, 629, 740; "Artillery Inspection, Army of Tennessee, August 10, 1864," AGIR.

6. Hood, *Advance and Retreat,* 166.

7. McWhiney and Jamieson, *Attack and Die,* 124–25.

8. *O.R.,* XXXVIII, pt. 3, 926, 967–69; Selden's Battery, Alabama Battery File, Alabama State Archives; McMurry, *John Bell Hood,* 143.

9. Cate, ed., *Two Soldiers,* 92.

10. Thompson, *History of the Orphan Brigade,* 261.

11. Cate, ed., *Two Soldiers,* 94–95.

12. Ibid., 96; *O.R.,* XXXVIII, pt. 3, 967.

13. Neal to "Dear Pa," July 23, 1864, A. J. Neal Letters, Emory.

14. Douglas to Sallie, July 23, 1864, Douglas, ed., *Douglas' Texas Battery,* 115–16.

15. *O.R.,* XXXVIII, pt. 3, 819–20.

16. Wilbur G. Kurtz, "The Fighting at Atlanta," *Civil War Times Illustrated,* III (December 1964), 14; Cox, *Atlanta,* 173.

17. *O.R.,* XXXVIII, pt. 1, 124, pt. 3, 967; Cate, ed., *Two Soldiers,* 101, 110; Douglas to Sallie, July 26, 1864, Douglas, ed., *Douglas' Texas Battery,* 118.

18. *O.R.,* XXXVIII, pt. 5, 637; McWhiney and Jamieson, *Attack and Die,* 116.

19. *O.R.,* XXXVIII, pt. 3, 674; McMurry, *John Bell Hood,* 138; Boatner, *Civil War Dictionary,* 703, 758.

20. Neal to "Dear Emma," August 7, 1864, A. J. Neal Letters, Emory. Lieutenant Neal was killed by a sharpshooter on August 10, 1864.

21. Curt Johnson and Mark McLaughlin, *Civil War Battles* (New York, 1981), 124.

22. Cate, ed., *Two Soldiers,* 117.

23. Ibid., 117–18.

24. Lindsley, ed., *Military Annals of Tennessee,* 828; *O.R.,* XXXVIII, pt. 3, 905.

25. *O.R.,* XXXVIII, pt. 1, 828, pt. 3, 904, 905; "Artillery Inspection, Army of Tennessee, August 18, 1864," AGIR.

26. "Artillery Inspection, Army of Tennessee," August 18, 1864," AGIR; *O.R.,* XXXVIII, pt. 1, 121. The Union artillery expended some 145,323 rounds during the campaign. *O.R.,* XXXVIII, pt. 1. 123.

27. "Artillery Inspection, Army of Tennessee, August 18, 1864," AGIR. On August 1, Captain Key wrote: "Because the Atlanta and Montgomery Railroad has been cut, depriving us, at least temporarily, of our sources of supplies, the artillery horses are becoming materially reduced from lack of their usual number of pounds of corn." Cate, ed., *Two Soldiers,* 106–7.

28. Joseph Erwin, "Swett's Battery at Jonesboro," *Confederate Veteran,* XII (1904), 112.

29. Cate, ed., *Two Soldiers,* 126–27; *O.R.,* XXXVIII, pt. 3, 685.

30. Smith Journal, TSA.

31. Hood, *Advance and Retreat,* 208; Cate, ed., *Two Soldiers,* 129; *O.R.,* XXXVIII, pt. 3, 684–85.

32. *O.R.,* XXXVIII, pt. 3, 684–85; Cate, ed., *Two Soldiers,* 133; "Report of the Reserve Artillery at Macon," n.d., Army of Tennessee Papers, Duke. The seventy wagons of the artillery reserve

were redistributed among the divisions. *O.R.,* XXXIX, pt. 3, 829.

33. Connelly, *Autumn of Glory,* 467.

34. *O.R.,* XXXII, pt. 3, 687, XXXVIII, pt. 3, 677, 683.

35. "Artillery Inspection, Army of Tennessee, August 18, 1864," AGIR; Brewer, *Alabama,* 700; Lindsley, ed., *Military Annals of Tennessee,* 826; Robert S. Bevier, *History of the First and Second Missouri Confederate Brigades, 1861–1865* (St. Louis, 1879), 191.

36. Frank E. Vandiver, "General Hood as Logistician," *Military Analysis of the Civil War* (Millwood, N.Y., 1977), 144–47.

37. "Artillery Inspection, Army of Tennessee, September 20, 1864," AGIR; September 15th Endorsement on W. C. Duxbury Report, MSA.

38. *O.R.,* XXXVIII, pt. 1, 124–25, pt. 3, 684–85.

39. "Artillery Inspection, Army of Tennessee, September 20, 1864," AGIR.

Chapter 15

1. Connelly, *Autumn of Glory,* 467, 470; Cate, ed., *Two Soldiers,* 137.

2. "Artillery Inspection, Army of Tennessee, September 20, 1864," AGIR; Cate, ed., *Two Soldiers,* 135; Lindsley, ed., *Military Annals of Tennessee,* 829.

3. Cate, ed., *Two Soldiers,* 133; Commission, *Tennesseans in the Civil War,* 124; Gustavus W. Smith, "The Georgia Militia during Sherman's March to the Sea," *Battles and Leaders,* IV, 667; "Artillery Inspection, Army of Tennessee, September 20, 1864," AGIR.

4. "Artillery Inspection, Army of Tennessee, September 20, 1864," AGIR; Wise, *The Long Arm of Lee,* 832.

5. *O.R.,* XLV, pt. 1, 683–84.

6. Wise, *The Long Arm of Lee,* 830–31; Warner, *Generals in Gray,* 82–83.

7. Richard J. Sommers, *Richmond Redeemed: The Siege at Petersburg* (Garden City, N.Y., 1981), 17.

8. Hood, *Advance and Retreat,* 166.

9. Thomas R. Hay, *Hood's Tennessee Campaign* (Dayton, Ohio, 1976), 46–47; *O.R.,* XXXIX, pt. 3, 805; Douglas to wife, October 9, 1864, Douglas, ed., *Douglas' Texas Battery,* 141; Ritter, "Sketch of the Third Battery of Maryland Artillery," 170.

10. Horn, *The Army of Tennessee,* 382.

11. Connelly, *Autumn of Glory,* 481.

12. *O.R.,* XXXIX, pt. 2, 888–89.

13. Morton, *The Artillery of Nathan Bedford Forrest's Cavalry,* 267.

14. *O.R.,* XLV, pt. 1, 1211, 1218, 1219, 1220, 1253.

15. Hay, *Hood's Tennessee Campaign,* 83–85; Dunlap, "Experiences on the Hood Campaign," 187.

16. Little and Maxwell, *A History of Lumsden's Battery,* 54.

17. Herman Hattaway, *General S. D. Lee* (Jackson, Miss., 1976), 133; Lindsley, ed., *Military Annals of Tennessee,* 830; Hood, *Advance and Retreat,* 291.

18. Dunlap, "Experiences on the Hood Campaign," 389.

19. See, for example, Horn, *The Army of Tennessee,* 398.

20. Hood, *Advance and Retreat,* 293.

21. Jacob D. Cox, *The March to the Sea* (New York, 1882), 83; Douglas, ed., *Douglas' Texas Battery,* 212; *O.R.,* XLV, pt. 1, 691, 743; Morton, *The Artillery of Nathan Bedford Forrest's Cavalry,* 275–76. Concerning Hood's supposed reason for not using artillery, even Stanley Horn admits that "there is a suspicion that this compunction was an afterthought." Horn, *The Army of Tennessee,* 398.

22. Hay, *Hood's Tennessee Campaign,* 134; Hay, ed., *Cleburne and His Command,* 58.

23. Connelly, *Autumn of Glory,* 503–4.

24. Hattaway, *General S. D. Lee,* 137.

25. *O.R.,* XLV, pt. 1, 683, 687, 1253, 1258; Douglas, ed., *Douglas' Texas Battery,* 150.

26. *O.R.,* XLV, pt. 1, 663, pt. 2, 651, 685.

27. Ibid., pt. 1, 1255; Lindsley, ed., *Military Annals of Tennessee,* 831.

28. Cate, ed., *Two Soldiers,* 159.

29. Ibid., 162.

30. Horn, *The Decisive Battle of Nashville,* 34; Connelly, *Autumn of Glory,* 507–8; *O.R.,* XLV, pt. 2, 641.

31. Cate, ed., *Two Soldiers,* 166.

32. Ibid., 167–168; Connelly, *Autumn of Glory,* 509.

33. Hattaway, *General S. D. Lee,* 140.

34. Cox, *The March to the Sea,* 111; Little and Maxwell, *A History of Lumsden's Battery,* 56. Young Lumsden survived the war only to be killed in a lumber manufacturing accident three years later. *Register of Former Cadets,* 28.

35. Horn, *The Decisive Battle of Nashville,* 145; *O.R.,* XLV, pt. 2, 194–95; Brewer, *Alabama,* 699, 704.

36. Marshall's battery was at Columbia and Fenner's at Murfreesboro. Two guns of the Washington Artillery had been captured at Murfreesboro on December 7. A section of Parrott guns from Stewart's corps was apparently still operating with Chalmers's cavalry. *O.R.,* XLV, pt. 1, 755, pt. 2, 691.

37. Connelly, *Autumn of Glory,* 511; Horn, *The Decisive Battle of Nashville,* 118–20.

38. Horn, *The Decisive Battle of Nashville,* 111, 118–19; Cox, *The March to the Sea,* 118.

39. *O.R.,* XLV, pt. 1, 68, 323, 688, 691–92.

40. Ibid., 498.

41. Ibid., 695; Ritter, "Sketch of the Third Battery of Maryland Artillery," 542–44.

42. Connelly, *Autumn of Glory,* 511.

43. Horn, *The Decisive Battle of Nashville,* 145.

44. *O.R.,* XLV, pt. 1, 692; Ed W. Smith, "Douglas' Texas Battery at the Battle of Nashville," *Confederate Veteran,* XII (November 1904), 531–32.

45. Ritter, "Sketch of the Third Battery of Maryland Artillery," 543; *O.R.,* XLV, pt. 1.

46. *O.R.,* XLV, pt. 1, 692, 707; Charles E. Fenner to S. D. Lee, June 28, 1904, Eufaula Light Artillery File, Alabama State Archives.

47. Fenner to Lee, June 28, 1904; *O.R.,* XLV, pt. 1, 692; Connelly, *Autumn of Glory,* 511.

48. Lindsley, ed., *Military Annals of Tennessee,* 831.

49. *O.R.*, XLV, pt. 1, 692.

50. T. G. Dabney, "Gen. A. P. Stewart on Strong Topics," *Confederate Veteran,* XVII (January 1909), 31–32.

51. Hood, *Advance and Retreat,* 303–04.

52. *O.R.*, XLV, pt. 1, 48–49.

53. Ibid., 682.

Chapter 16

1. Horn, *The Army of Tennessee,* 422; Cate, ed., *Two Soldiers,* 174.

2. Connelly, *Autumn of Glory,* 513; Horn, *The Army of Tennessee,* 422.

3. Cate, ed., *Two Soldiers,* 180.

4. Douglas, ed., *Douglas' Texas Battery,* 152.

5. *O.R.*, XLIX, pt. 1, 1047. Batteries ordered to Mobile included Dent, Douglas, Garrity, Eufaula, Fenner, Rowan, Lumsden, Tarrent, Cowan, Perry, Phelan, Turner, Mebane, and Slocomb.

6. Ritter, "Sketch of the Third Battery of Maryland Artillery," 172.

7. Cate, ed., *Two Soldiers,* 183, 185, 186, 187.

8. Ibid., 196, 197.

9. Ibid., 187–88; Lindsley, ed., *Military Annals of Tennessee,* 836.

10. *O.R.*, XLII, pt. 2, 1084–85.

11. Ibid., XLVII, pt. 2, 1323.

12. Ibid., 1436, 1441, 1445, XLIX, pt. 2, 1146.

13. Lindsley, ed., *Military Annals of Tennessee,* 838–40.

14. *O.R.*, XLVII, pt. 3, 808; Brewer, *Alabama,* 703, 704.

Bibliographical Essay

A basic source for this study was the *Official Records of the Union and Confederate Armies* (Washington, D.C., 1880–1902). Although the ORs are indispensable for understanding the artillery's role in some battles, they do not include any Confederate battery After Action Reports for Perryville and Chattanooga or the Atlanta and Tennessee campaigns.

The single most important collection of personal papers dealing with the western long arm is the Henry C. Semple Papers, Alabama State Archives. Numerous unpublished documents relating to this subject are also in the Braxton Bragg Papers, William P. Palmer Collection, Western Reserve Historical Society.

The Inspection Records and Related Reports Received by the Inspector's Branch of the Confederate Adjutant General's Office, National Archives Record Group 109, and W. C. Duxbury Report, April 25, 1864, Ordnance Department Correspondence, Vol. 111, Record Group 9, Mississippi State Archives, are excellent sources concerning the state of the artillery at various times during the period 1863–64.

Copies of the correspondence of army Chief of Ordnance Hypolite Oladowski are in Letters Sent, Ordnance Officer, Army of Tennessee, Chap. IV, Vol. 141, National Archives Record Group 109. Many of these letters detail the armament modernization effort undertaken in 1863. The Hypolite Oladowski Papers, Duke University, unfortunately contain only a few fragmentary documents.

The "List of Officers of the Corps of Artillery of Tennessee," Benjamin F. Cheatham Papers, Tennessee State Library and Archives, outlines the educational and military backgrounds of that state's battery commanders.

For some unknown reason, the rather lengthy Rice Graves After Action Report of the Battle of Murfreesboro did not find its way into the ORs. Fortunately, it is extant in the John C. Breckinridge Papers, New York Historical Society.

The diaries of one officer and three enlisted men are known to survive and, though none spans the entire war, they provide valuable insight into life in the western artillery. Included are Wirt A. Cate, ed., *Two Soldiers: The Campaign Diaries of Thomas J. Key, C.S.A., and Robert J. Campbell, U.S.A.* (Chapel Hill, N.C., 1938); John Euclid Magee Diary, Duke University; George A. Grammer Diary, Vicksburg National Military Park; Mike Spradlin, ed., "The Diary of George W. Jones; A Partial History of Stanford's Mississippi Battery," *Camp Chase Gazette*, XI (April 1981), 6–11. No study of the Army of Tennessee's artillery is complete without extensive use of the Key and Magee diaries.

In addition, the human angle is revealed in the invaluable letters of artillerymen Andrew J. Neal, Emory University; Richard L. Pugh, Louisiana State University; and James Douglas, in Lucia R. Douglas, ed., *Douglas' Texas Battery, C.S.A.* (Waco, Tex., 1966).

Crucial biographical information concerning the army's artillery officer corps is contained in the Military Service Files, National Archives, and "1887 Annual Reunion of the Association of Graduates, U.S. Military Academy, West Point, New York," a pamphlet on file at the academy. James H. Colgin, ed., "The Life Story of Brig. Gen. Felix Robertson," *Texana*, VIII (Spring 1979), 154–82, is surprisingly silent on the numerous controversies that surround his career. Two standard works, Ezra J. Warner, *Generals in Gray* (Baton Rouge, 1959), and Mark M. Boatner, *Civil War Dictionary* (New York, 1961), offer biographical data on artillery officers who held the rank of general.

Confederate Veteran offers brief sketches of a number of artillery commanders. These include "Capt. Thomas L. Massenburg," XII (December 1908), 630–31; "Forrest's Chief of Artillery: Morton," VIII (April 1900), 171; "Maj. John William Johnston," XIX (March 1911), 116–17; "Robert Cobb, Maj. Gen. UCV," IV (April 1894), 103; Joseph A. Wilson, "Bledsoe of Missouri," VII (October 1899), 462–63; "Young Artillery Captains," VI (June 1895), 175; "Major James P. Douglas," X (July 1902), 322; "Dr. Harvey Shannon," XV (March 1907), 131–32; and "Major John W. Eldridge," XXI (July 1913), 352.

Several artillery field officers wrote helpful works concerning specific actions. The most significant of these is Melancthon Smith, "Journal of the Atlanta Campaign," Benjamin F. Cheatham Papers, Tennessee State Library and Archives. Postwar reminiscences include Francis A. Shoup, "How We Went to Shiloh," *Confederate Veteran*, II (May 1894), 137–40, and George S. Storrs, "The Artillery at Kennesaw," Kennesaw *Gazette*, June 17, 1889, 6–7.

A number of articles written by western artillerymen are indispensable in filling the gaps that exist in the ORs. In *Confederate Veteran*, these include W. W. Carnes, "The Artillery at Perryville," XXXIII (1925), 8–9, and "At Missionary Ridge," XX (May 1920), 185; W. H. Smith, "Melancthon Smith's Battery," XII (November 1904), 532; Ed W. Smith, "Douglas' Battery in the Battle of Nashville," XII (November 1904), 531–32; "Rutledge's Battery," XXXVI (July 1928), 259–60; James G. Holmes, "The Artillery at Bentonville," III (April 1895), 103; Joseph Erwin, "Swett's Battery at Jonesboro," XII (March 1904), 112; Sam B. Dunlap, "Experiences on the Hood Campaign," XVI (April 1908), 187; T. G. Dabney, "General A. P. Stewart on Strong Topics," XVII (January 1909), 281–83; and "Gracey-Chickamauga-Whitaker," VI (1895), 251. Among the articles in the *Southern Historical Society Papers* are Thomas L. Riddell, "Movements of the Goochland Artillery," XXIV (1896), 316–23, and J. A. Chalaron, "Battle Echoes From Shiloh," XXI (1893), 215–24. Also significant is "Guibor's Missouri Battery," Kennesaw *Gazette*, May 15, 1889, 2–3.

Composite battery sketches are presented in Dunbar Rowland, *The Official and Statistical Register of Mississippi* (Nashville, 1908); John B. Lindsley, ed., *The Military Annals of Tennessee, Confederate* (Nashville, 1886); Civil War Centennial Commission, *Tennesseans in the Civil War,* I (Nashville, 1964); Willis Brewer, *Alabama: Her History,*

Resources, War Record, and Public Men from 1540–1872 (Montgomery,
1872).

Unit histories are extremely rare. The most complete is George Little
and James R. Maxwell, *A History of Lumsden's Battery* (Tuskaloosa,
Ala., 1905). William L. Ritter wrote a series of articles on an outfit that
became Rowan's Georgia Battery in "Sketch of the Third Battery of
Maryland Artillery," *Southern Historical Society Papers,* XII (1883),
113–18, 186–93, 433–42, 537–44, XII (1884), 170–72. Background on
the western horse artillery, and specifically Morton's Tennessee Battery, is contained in John W. Morton, *The Artillery of Nathan Bedford
Forrest's Cavalry* (Kennesaw, Ga., 1962).

Both published sources on the Louisiana Washington Artillery are,
on the whole, disappointing as they relate to the Fifth Company:
William M. Owen, *In Camp and Battle with the Washington Artillery*
(Boston, 1885), and J. B. Walton, "Sketches of the History of the Washington Artillery," *Southern Historical Society Papers,* XI (1883),
210–17. The order book, manuscripts, and reminiscences in the Washington Artillery Papers, Louisiana Historical Association Collection,
Tulane University, fill in some gaps, but much of the material relating
to the Fifth Company concerns the 1865 duty tour in Mobile.

William R. Talley's "A History of Havis' Georgia Battery," typescript
at Kennesaw National Military Park, and W. R. Brown's "A History of
Stanford's Mississippi Battery," typescript at the Greenwood, Mississippi, Public Library, offer surprisingly little crucial material considering their length. On the other hand, W. A. Pickering's "The
Washington Artillery of Augusta, Ga.," *Confederate Veteran,* XVII
(1909), 24–26, is brief but significant. "History of Fenner's Battery,
August 8, 1891," Thomas C. Porteous Papers, Louisiana State University, offers only minor assistance.

The National Archives contains files and muster rolls for a number of
batteries. The amount of information available varies from company to
company, but not infrequently nuggets can be discovered. The same is
true of the Alabama Battery Files, Alabama State Archives.

Jennings C. Wise, *The Long Arm of Lee: The History of the Artillery
Corps of the Army of Northern Virginia* (New York, 1959), offers the
opportunity to compare the experiences of the Army of Tennessee's
artillery with that of its sister army. Unfortunately, Colonel Wise chose
not to treat the life of the common artilleryman or the interactions
among the officer corps and he rarely veered from the ORs.

Edwin C. Bearss, "Shiloh Artillery Study," Project No. 17, Shiloh
National Military Park, and "Stones River: The Artillery at 4:45 P.M.,
Jan. 2, 1863," *Civil War Times Illustrated,* II (February 1964), 38–39,
though marred by several errors, are basically sound studies that detail
the armament composition of various batteries.

Among the works dealing with the Civil War artillery, Warren
Ripley's *Artillery and Ammunition of the Civil War* (New York, 1970),
and James C. Hazlett, "The Confederate Napoleon Gun," *Military Collector and Historian,* XVI (Winter 1964), 104–10, are invaluable.

Finally, Thomas L. Connelly's comprehensive command-level study
of the Army of Tennessee in *Army of the Heartland: The Army of Ten-*

nessee, 1861–1862 (Baton Rouge, 1967) and *Autumn of Glory: The Army of Tennessee, 1862–1865* (Baton Rouge, 1971) is indispensable for understanding the complicated facets of the army's history.

The most concise study of the tactical use of artillery both prior to and during the war is presented in several chapters in Grady McWhiney and Perry D. Jamieson, *Attack and Die: Civil War Military Tactics and the Southern Heritage* (University, Ala., 1982).

Index

Alabama artillery companies:
Bellamy, 124, 128, 154; Emery,
124, 129; Eufaula Light Artillery
(McTyre, Oliver, McKenzie), 55,
58, 60, 72, 99, 103, 116, 128, 179,
180, 181, 220n, 224n; Fowler
(Phelan), 71, 92, 96, 98, 129, 150,
153, 224n; Gage, 9, 16, 28, 33, 40,
45; Ketchum (Garrity), 9, 28, 37,
40, 76, 110, 114, 129, 150, 162,
178, 203n, 224n; Kolb, 93, 97, 115,
170, 185; Lumsden, 10, 12, 28, 45,
52, 57, 58, 62, 64, 66, 88, 92, 103,
129, 148, 152, 154, 176, 181, 223n,
224n; Selden, 143, 157, 181;
Semple (Goldthwaite), 8, 11, 12,
48–68 passim, 97, 98, 118, 121,
129, 143, 144, 146, 149, 158, 185;
Tarrent, 148, 176, 181, 224n;
Ward, 143, 146, 154; Waters, 9, 45,
61, 74, 76, 114, 121
Alexander, E. P., 102; provides
leadership in Lee's army, 21;
opinion of Army of Tennessee,
106; at Chattanooga, 59–60;
requested as Johnston's chief of
artillery, 135
Alexander's Battalion, 93, 99,
105–06, 110
Ammunition: fixed, 12; allowance,
32, 47; expenditures, 103, 118;
board for study of, 73; poor
quality, 72, 103; supply, 74, 154;
average rounds per gun, 109, 122,
163, 166
Arkansas artillery companies:
Helena Light Artillery (Calvert,
Key), 14, 51, 52, 53, 63, 98, 113,
121, 125, 129, 149, 160, 164, 167;
Hubbard, 36, 38, 203n;
Humphreys (1st Arkansas,
Rivers), 55, 60, 74, 76, 96, 107,
121, 157; Roberts (Wiggins), 38,

57, 89, 91, 204n; Trigg, 14, 33, 38,
204n
Armament: defective, 16, 74;
composition, 75, 76, 94, 109, 128,
149, 167; modernization, 75–76,
109, 127–28
Artillery Corps, Army of Tennessee:
lack of militia base, 7–8; drills,
12–14, 56–57, 92, 123; recruiting
difficulties, 7, 71, 124, 167, 174;
battery accessions, 19–20, 28, 45,
48, 108, 123–24, 143, 146, 148;
battery transfers, 45, 121, 165,
167, 224n; camp life, 11–12, 121;
strength of, 28, 71, 92, 94, 109,
121, 130, 142, 156, 165, 174;
transportation, 72, 129–30. *See
also* Officer Corps, Organization
Artillery Corps, Army of Northern
Virginia: militia base, 7–8;
reinforcements from, 93–94, 106;
compared to western artillery, 75,
82, 90, 126, 131, 160, 168–69
Artillery Corps, Army of the
Cumberland: strength, 57, 93;
effectiveness at Murfreesboro, 66,
69; immobilized at Chattanooga,
107; ordnance losses, 68, 213n;
armament modernized, 77;
compared to Southern artillery,
132
Artillery fire: crossfire, 153;
enfilade, 37, 62, 113, 154; frontal,
62; indirect, 111–12; declining
effectiveness of, 152, 155, 159
Artillery Reserve: established, 88;
enlarged, 49, 131; restructured,
160; ordered to Macon, 165
Artillery tactics: Mexican War, 85;
obsolete, 32, 44; massing, 37–39,
51, 63, 86, 100; offensive, 32, 44,
68–69, 102, 157, 159, 160;
defensive, 111, 160

Baruch Awards
1927–1982

1927 Carpenter, Jesse Thomas, "The South as a Conscious Minority 1789–1861." New York University, Washington Square, New York, 1930.

1929 Whitfield, Theodore M., "Slavery Agitation in Virginia, 1829–1832." Out of Print.

1931 Flanders, Ralph Betts, "Plantation Slavery in Georgia." Out of Print.

1933 Thompson, Samuel, "Confederate Purchasing Agents Abroad." Out of Print.

1935 Wiley, Bell Irvin, "Southern Negroes 1861–1865." Yale University Press, New Haven, Connecticut, 1938.

1937 Hill, Louise Biles, "Joseph E. Brown and the Confederacy." Out of Print.

1940 Haydon, F. Stansbury, "Aeronautics of the Union and Confederate Armies." Out of Print.

1942 Stormont, John, "The Economic Stake of the North in the Preservation of the Union in 1861." Not Published.

1945 Schultz, Harold Sessel, "Nationalism and Sectionalism in South Carolina 1852–1860." Duke University Press, Durham, North Carolina, 1950.

1948 Tankersly, Allen P., "John Brown Gordon, Soldier and Statesman." Privately Printed.

1951 Todd, Richard C., "Confederate Finance." University of Georgia Press, Athens, Georgia, 1953.

1954 Morrow, Ralph E., "Northern Methodism and Reconstruction." Michigan State University Press, 1956. Cunningham, Horace, "Doctors in Gray." Louisiana State University Press, Baton Rouge, Louisiana, 1958.

1957 Hall, Martin H., "The Army of New Mexico." "Sibley's Campaign of 1862." University of Texas Press, Austin, Texas, 1960.

1960 Robertson, James I., Jr., "Jackson's Stonewall: A History of the Stonewall Brigade." Louisiana State University Press, Baton Rouge, Louisiana, 1963.

1969 Wells, Tom Henderson, "The Confederate Navy: A Study in Organization." University of Alabama Press, University, Alabama, 1971.

1970 Delaney, Conrad, "John McIntosh Kell, of the Raider *Alabama*." University of Alabama Press, University, Alabama, 1972.

1972 Dougan, Michael B., "Confederate Arkansas—The People and Politics of a Frontier State." University of Alabama Press, University, Alabama, 1976.

1974 Wiggins, Sarah Woolfolk, "The Scalawag in Alabama Politics, 1865–1881." University of Alabama Press, University, Alabama, 1976.

1976 Nelson, Larry Earl, "Bullets, Ballots, and Rhetoric." University of Alabama Press, University, Alabama, 1980.

1978 Franks, Kenny A., "Stand Watie and the Agony of the Cherokee Nation." Memphis State University Press, Memphis, Tennessee, 1979.

1980 Buenger, Walter L., "Stilling the Voice of Reason: The Union and Secession in Texas, 1854–1861." University of Texas Press, Austin, Texas, 1984.

1982 McMurry, Richard M., "John Bell Hood and the War for Southern Independence." University Press of Kentucky, Lexington, Kentucky, 1982.